The Politics of Literary Prestige

The Politics of Literary Prestige

Prizes and Spanish American Literature

Sarah E.L. Bowskill

BLOOMSBURY ACADEMIC
NEW YORK · LONDON · OXFORD · NEW DELHI · SYDNEY

BLOOMSBURY ACADEMIC
Bloomsbury Publishing Inc
1385 Broadway, New York, NY 10018, USA
50 Bedford Square, London, WC1B 3DP, UK
29 Earlsfort Terrace, Dublin 2, Ireland

BLOOMSBURY, BLOOMSBURY ACADEMIC and the Diana logo are trademarks of
Bloomsbury Publishing Plc

First published in the United States of America 2022
Paperback edition published 2023

Copyright © Sarah E.L. Bowskill, 2022

For legal purposes the Acknowledgements on p. vii constitute an extension of this copyright page.

Cover design: Eleanor Rose
Cover image © Alamy

All rights reserved. No part of this publication may be reproduced or transmitted in any form or by any means, electronic or mechanical, including photocopying, recording, or any information storage or retrieval system, without prior permission in writing from the publishers.

Bloomsbury Publishing Inc does not have any control over, or responsibility for, any third-party websites referred to or in this book. All internet addresses given in this book were correct at the time of going to press. The author and publisher regret any inconvenience caused if addresses have changed or sites have ceased to exist, but can accept no responsibility for any such changes.

A catalog record of this book is available from the Library of Congress

ISBN: HB: 978-1-5013-5077-1
PB: 978-1-5013-7603-0
ePDF: 978-1-5013-5079-5
eBook: 978-1-5013-5078-8

Typeset by Deanta Global Publishing Services, Chennai, India

To find out more about our authors and books visit www.bloomsbury.com and sign up for our newsletters.

CONTENTS

List of tables vi
Acknowledgements vii

Introduction: Literary prestige, politics, the prize network and the roles of the author in society 1

1 Literary prizes, controversy and the state in Spanish America 25

2 Peninsular publishers, Spanish American authors and prizes for literature in Spanish 51

3 Spanish American authors on the world stage 71

4 Roberto Bolaño, Carmen Boullosa and Fernando Iwasaki find their voice in the prizes game 93

5 The Premio Biblioteca Breve and the forgotten women of the Boom 111

6 Women winning prizes: A no win situation? 125

7 Prizes for literatures in indigenous languages 155

8 The never-ending network? 177

References 183
Index of Prizes 207
General Index 209

TABLES

6.1 Showing Percentages of Women Winners of Major International Literary Prizes 129
6.2 Showing Percentages of Women Winners of Literary Prizes in the Spanish-speaking World for Literature in Spanish 130
6.3 Showing Percentages of Women Winners of Awards which Recognize a Lifetime of Work as Opposed to a Single, Named Text 132
6.4 Showing Percentages of Women Winners of State-sponsored, National-level Literary Prizes in Spanish American Countries 133
6.5 Showing all Prizes Awarded under the Auspices of the Instituto Nacional de Bellas Artes (INBA), Mexico 135
6.6 Showing Percentages of Women Winners of Privately Run Literary Prizes in the Spanish-speaking World for Literature in Spanish 137
6.7 Showing Numbers and Percentages of Women on the Juries of a Selection of Literary Prizes 140

ACKNOWLEDGEMENTS

This project has been in development for some time, so I owe many a debt of gratitude. I would like to begin by thanking Queen's University Belfast for supporting my work with essential periods of institutional funded research leave. I also received financial support, through the Core Disciplinary Research Group in Modern Languages, for research trips to the Biblioteca de Catalunya in Barcelona and the newspaper archive of the Centro Nacional de Literatura (CNL) in Mexico City. These visits, and the assistance I received from staff in these archives, were fundamental to the successful completion of this book.

I am very fortunate to have wonderful colleagues, who I count as friends, in Spanish and Portuguese at Queen's University Belfast. I would like to take this opportunity to thank my fellow Latin Americanists, Ricki O'Rawe, Fiona Clark and Tori Holmes. Thanks to Isabel Torres for being an excellent mentor and for her willingness to go for coffee! Geraldine Lawless has also proved herself very willing to go for coffee and was kind enough to read and give feedback on some very early drafts. I am delighted that we have been able to renew our friendship since she came to Queens. I am grateful to those I worked with on the Committee of the Society for Latin American Studies during the period of writing this book including Jens Hentschke, David Wood, Caroline Williams, John Fisher and Eamon McCarthy.

When this book was little more than an idea in my mind, I enjoyed the tremendous support and encouragement of Patience Schell, Hilary Owen, Catherine Davies, Par Kumaraswami, Kirsty Hooper, Niamh Thornton and Nuala Finnegan.

The first tangible result of this project came in the form of an article published in 2012 in *Hispanic Review*. I received thorough and thoughtful feedback on that piece from the editor and anonymous reviewers as I did on the proposal and drafts of this monograph. I would, therefore, like to thank all of the reviewers and the University of Pennsylvania Press for permission to reuse arguments that appeared in Bowskill, S.E.L. (2012), 'Politics and Literary Prizes: A Case Study of Spanish America and the Premio Cervantes', *Hispanic Review* 80 (2): 289–311.

Since approaching Bloomsbury I have had the pleasure of working with outstanding editors Katherine De Chant and Amy Martin who have helped in so many ways to make this project better. Any remaining shortcomings are entirely down to the author.

On a personal note, I would like to thank Mike and Darren at Exsto and Heather Weir for taking my mind off work when I needed it the most. I have always benefitted enormously from the unconditional love and support of my family and friends, so my final, heartfelt thanks go to Mum, Dad, Edward, Andy, Sarah and Claire. I couldn't have done it without you, and I wouldn't have wanted to either!

Introduction

Literary prestige, politics, the prize network and the roles of the author in society

In June 2021 the website escritores.org, a resource for authors writing in Spanish, listed over 150 literary prizes open to entries in that month alone. These figures are not exceptional. Prizes for Spanish American literature are ubiquitous and proliferating. This ever-expanding network of prizes exists because soft power seeks to attract and co-opt through culture.[1] Thus, politics and literary prestige are inextricably linked. Prizes are used by states, institutions, publishers and, increasingly, other private enterprises as an aid to sustain their power and authority as they seek to harness authors' reputations to achieve their goals and as endorsement for the values they represent.[2] In return, they offer, to differing degrees, financial rewards, a public platform and publicity. At stake in these exchanges are the politics of literary prestige and the role of the author in society.

This book provides the first comprehensive study of prizes for Spanish American literature. Uncovering the history of prizes for Spanish American literature allows us to understand why they have proliferated, how the different prizes relate to one another, and the political significance of the various awards. The result is an appreciation of the extent to which literary prestige in Spanish America, and for Spanish American literature, is politicized as well as an awareness of the roles Spanish American authors perform in different contexts. The book concludes with a reflection on the future of literary prizes and the alternatives currently available for authors who do not wish to participate in the prize network. Literary prizes are

---

[1] This understanding of soft power is derived from Nye (2004).
[2] Throughout this book, nation refers to the imagined community and state to the administrative apparatus and governing bureaucracy which uses the nation to sustain itself.

shown to be one of the main instruments which create value in the literary field, sustain political agenda and define the roles available to authors in society. Sociological and book history approaches to literature are combined with textual analysis to fully understand the politics of prestige that underpin literary prizes for Spanish American literature. In this way, the book addresses the enduring issue of the relationship between literature and politics which has occupied thinking since Plato's *The Republic*.

The chapters cover the emergence of prizes from state-sponsored national prizes for literature and prizes, including the Casa de las Américas prizes, the Premio Rómulo Gallegos, the Premio Cervantes and the Nobel Prize for Literature, which aimed to broker regional ties and international relations beyond Spanish America. It examines the more concealed politics of literary prestige behind publisher-run prizes that originated in Spain including the Premio Biblioteca Breve, the Premio Herralde and the Premio Alfaguara. The book explores how Spanish American authors have responded, through their fiction, and re-examines the history of the Boom and the Premio Biblioteca Breve to reveal the full extent to which literary prestige in Spanish America is gendered. Furthermore, it assesses the impact of awards that are restricted on the basis of the gender or ethnic identity of the author in terms of the extent to which they create new opportunities and contribute to canon formation. A picture emerges of the political agenda that have sought prestige through association with Spanish American literature and its authors. The prizes reflect, seek to legitimize and bolster political positions including nationalism, totalitarianism, communism, liberal democracy, internationalism, globalization, free-market capitalism and identity politics. Neoliberal values, epitomized in public–private partnerships, are also increasingly in evidence in the prize network as they are in the political sphere.

Prizes enable new positions within the literary field as new participants enter and literature evolves. Prizes also reflect political change. As new politics emerge, prize criteria are amended and new prizes are created to underpin new regimes with literary prestige. States, institutions, publishers and other companies establish new prizes as they seek to acquire prestige in the literary field or to use literary prestige to enhance their status in the related fields of politics or the economy. In accepting these new prizes authors accept the legitimacy and authority of the awarding bodies. The two parties become aligned as part of a pact. The terms of the pact vary depending on the nature of the prize, the awarding body and the time period. Spanish American state-sponsored national prizes, discussed in Chapter 1, see the authors align themselves with the state and its nation-building agenda. If the regime changes, as happened under the Pinochet dictatorship in Chile, or changes are made to the way the prize is run, as in the case of the Premio Rómulo Gallegos in Venezuela, scandal may ensue. In the case of the Premio Cervantes, offered by the Spanish state to all authors writing in Spanish, and the Nobel Prize for Literature, studied in Chapter 3, Spanish American authors have entered a pact with institutions defending democracy. New prizes for authors writing in indigenous languages, the focus of Chapter 7, or women authors, considered in Chapter 6, are based on identity politics. In the case of publisher- and other privately run prizes, the focus of Chapter 2, the pact was originally tied to a post-Second-World-War internationalism, in opposition to the isolationism of the Franco era. Increasingly the pact is with the priorities of globalization and the free market in which Spanish American authors are the latest commodity to bring economic and symbolic profits to the former colonial centres.

Even as Spanish American authors enter into these pacts, they retain agency with some ability to negotiate their relationship with the awarding body and the way in which the award will be understood. Prize ceremonies for national prizes, the Premio Cervantes and the Nobel Prize for Literature create a space and a privileged platform from which authors are invited to speak. In so doing, they fulfil the roles of author-statesperson and public intellectual for the nation or spokesperson for international audiences. The difference being that a spokesperson is called upon to talk about specific issues whereas a public intellectual has greater freedom to set the agenda. Winners of publisher-run prizes are required to give interviews and participate in events to market their work. Today, prizes run by the major publishing houses for literature in Spanish position the author as a celebrity within a global Hispanic culture and transnational economy. The nature of the platform offered is fundamentally different depending on the prize and its politics. Book tours and audience question and answer sessions or readings at literary festivals take the place of substantial speeches in front of royalty and politicians. The author is increasingly brought to the people. In the context of publisher-run prizes, celebrity visibility replaces the voice of the public intellectual speaking to power. The growing participation of previously marginalized groups in the privately run prize network, therefore, may not be the cause for celebration it may seem. Prizes which restrict entries on the grounds of gender or ethnicity position the authors as spokespeople in relation to these issues and so their roles are again circumscribed.

Prizes, prestige and politics

Literary prizes bestow prestige on an author and their work. They are also evidence of, and an attempt to assert, the authority of the awarding body to bestow such an honour. Prestige is a form of symbolic capital. Pierre Bourdieu identified different forms of capital among them symbolic, political and economic. These are the main forms of capital within the prize network. Symbolic capital is 'a capital of honour and prestige' which 'takes the form of prestige and renown' (Bourdieu 2012, 179). 'Social agents' who make up the literary field, and include individuals and institutions, compete with one another to create value and secure prestige (Bourdieu 1993, 29–30). Academies, journals, magazines, critics and publishers, as well as authors, are all part of the literary field (Bourdieu 1993, 32). Literary prestige is one of the 'specific profits [...] which are at stake in the [literary] field' (Bourdieu 1993, 30). In other words, status within the literary field relies on the accumulation of prestige. Prizes are a means for authors to achieve this goal. Today, prizes are one of the principal mechanisms by which the literary field is constituted and organized, but they also play a role in the field of politics.

Politics, understood as either pertaining to governments or the distribution of power or both, is at the heart of every literary prize. At stake when it comes to the politics of literary prestige is who will become renowned, who gets to decide and on what grounds these decisions are made. Bourdieu considered literary prizes to be unsuitable for the acquisition of prestige because they perform 'a function analogous to that of fashion "collections"' (1993, 100). In other words, prizes recognize trends rather than lasting value. To some extent, Bourdieu is correct, as indicated by the common complaint that many winners of the Nobel Prize for Literature are quickly forgotten. However, the very transience of the prizewinners' renown is noteworthy because it signals that prizes are responding to a specific political (and literary) moment and are intended to be immediately useful to the awarding body. The longevity of the individual winner's renown is less important than that of the award itself. A prize that endures is one whose agenda continues to be relevant.

James English proposes that the proliferation of literary prizes is the result of them being 'the single best instrument for negotiating transactions between cultural and economic, cultural and social, or cultural and political capital – which is to say that they are our most effective institutional agents of capital intraconversion' (2005, 10). The success of these processes of intraconversion relies on acts of 'make-believe' and 'collective misrecognition' which are needed to fool ourselves into ignoring the way in which the symbolic economy is tied to the realms of politics and economics (Bourdieu 2012, 173, 176). Elsewhere, Bourdieu similarly writes that in the circulation of capital 'deliberate misrecognition' is vital as it enables the author to maintain the properly disinterested position (1993, 96–7). Significantly, in the Spanish American case, the disavowal of political capital may be less important than in the Anglophone and Francophone contexts addressed by English and Bourdieu. The difference between these contexts can be explained with reference to different understandings of the role of Spanish American authors nationally as states(wo)men and public intellectuals and internationally as spokespeople. The propensity in all contexts to overlook the political aspects of transactions where the state is not directly involved represents a particularly powerful collective fantasy which this book seeks to dispel. The proliferation of prizes speaks to their effectiveness as agents of capital intraconversion and to a widespread willingness to participate in the collective act of make-believe that divorces politics from literary prestige. Most importantly, however, the proliferation of prizes is the result of the multiplication of political positions seeking legitimacy through association with literary prestige.

Faced with a tendency to see the literary sphere in its ideal form as being separate from politics, this book demonstrates that, when it comes to literary prizes for Spanish American literature, politics is ever present. The importance of insisting on the politics of culture has been recognized elsewhere by Frederick Buell who has observed '"Culture" is not a term above politics' (1994, 36). Culture, Buell observes, was instrumental in the 'rise of the modern world system, and the flowering of the nation-state as the world's dominant social form' (1994, 127). Culture has also been 'an important strategic component in the construction of global relationships' (Buell 1994, 37). Having consolidated a 'geopolitical order' in which culture was 'territorialized attached to territory', Buell posits that we are increasingly seeing the deconstruction of these ties between culture and territory in the context of globalization (1994, 127). The evolution of literary prizes for Spanish American literature tracks this trajectory even as the links between culture, politics and power persist.

State-sponsored prizes for Spanish American literature have been instrumental in nation-building and the development of international ties within the region and the Spanish-speaking world. Privately funded prizes, and especially publisher-run awards, have tended to be viewed as commercial and apolitical. François Delprat sums up this view when he writes: 'En somme la notion de Prix, serait entendu comme appartenant au monde de la marchandise' (In short, the notion of Prize, would be understood as belonging to the world of the commodity) (2005, 227).[3] The politics of publisher-run awards fostering a deterritorialized literature in Spanish have been all the more effective precisely because such awards have been able to conceal the way they keep symbolic and economic profits outside the region, most often in Europe, even as they consecrate Spanish American authors.

A politicized literary field, however, may not be as negative as we have been led to believe. Bourdieu posits the ideal position for the author as one of the greatest possible independence from the state because this is the position from which the most literary prestige can be accrued (1993, 38–9). Yet he acknowledges that this pure state is impossible because the field 'whatever its degree of independence [. . .] continues to be affected by the laws of the field which encompasses it, those of economic and political profit' (Bourdieu 1993, 39). The literary field is always already part of the political field. The true problem then is buying into the myth or, in other words, allowing the disavowal of the economy of the field to go unchallenged. Failure to question

---

[3] All translations in this book are by the author unless otherwise stated.

the politics of the economy of prestige means unequal power relations prevail and the role of the author in society is increasingly circumscribed. The findings should give pause to those who proclaim that the market now rules overlooking the politics of that very claim. As the Nobel Prize-winning economist Paul Krugman said, 'everything is political' (2003).

The prize network

The prizes, like the political positions they help to sustain, coexist creating a prize network. The prize network for Spanish American literature, which connects and overlaps with other networks with different remits, has expanded significantly. James English has referred to the 'daunting ubiquity' and 'unrelenting proliferation of prizes' describing 'the cultural universe' as being 'supersaturated with prizes' (2005, 17). With so many prizes on offer, we may think that the achievement of winning a literary prize is diminished or that all prizes are diminished as a result of becoming common currency. This abundance, however, does not devalue all prizes. One explanation for this is because, 'as the world draws more tightly together into a single system, it multiplies its circulation of differences' (Buell 1994, 137). The literary field is likewise increasingly interconnected as a system not only by common languages but now through publisher mergers, more agile distribution chains and enhanced technologies. As differences multiply as a result of this coalescence, so do prizes as the prize network expands to account for new positions.

My point of reference to understand prizes as networked is Ulises A. Mejias's (2013) study of digital social networks. For Mejias a network 'is a system of linked elements or nodes' (2013: ebook Chapter 1). Networks 'give shape to social systems' and they are 'plural, fluid and overlapping' (2013: ebook Chapter 1). Understanding prizes as networked reflects that they are part of a system of connected awards in that their existence and who they reward impact on one another. This conceptualization also alerts us to the fact that prizes give shape to the literary field connecting stakeholders, principally awarding institutions and authors, but also creating links to other prizes, reviewers and critics as well as booksellers. The prize network is also fluid and overlapping because it, like a computer network, is made up of smaller networks which can enable or deny further access. In the context of information technology, a near-me area network (NAN) operates among devices in close proximity, a local area network (LAN) has limited range, for example within one building, but a NAN can connect to a LAN which can be connected to a metropolitan area network (MAN) which covers, as the name implies, multiple buildings in a city. Wide area networks (WAN) are less restricted by geography, the prime example being the internet which is a worldwide WAN. Information in a network gets passed back and forth, but it does not circulate without restriction. Your password may give you access to one network but not necessarily any other. In the same way, accessing the literary field and prestige in the form of prizes does not necessarily lead to winning other prizes.

Networks of prizes open to authors of one nationality connect to the network of prizes open to all Spanish American authors and those for authors writing in Spanish which connects to the network of prizes for authors of any nationality writing in any language. Prizes in the network also connect to one another on the basis of genre, an author's age, gender, ethnicity, language and so on. The result is that a single prize can be part of multiple, overlapping networks. The position of a prize in the network can also be altered as happens, for example, when the prize criteria are changed.

In proposing the existence of a prize network, I seek to undo the assertion that sub-national, national and international literary fields and mechanisms for bestowing prestige are disconnected. Where we may once have thought about the world in terms of the discrete categories of the nation, or of the 'First' and 'Third' worlds, overlooking global connections that have existed for centuries, today there can be little doubt that politics, culture and economics at all levels are connected. The challenge then is to understand the relationships, hierarchies and power struggles within the world system, because, as Buell has noted, this 'single system has come to be perceived as more and more complex, increasingly centreless, and featuring a multiplication of interacting parts that are increasingly fragmented and unstable' (1994, 10). The overarching prize network has likewise come to be characterized in this way mirroring global politics. In the face of this new global order, 'nation-states' are obliged to 'reformulate their cultural identities for a more complexly interconnected era' (Buell 1994, 10–11). Prizes are one way for states and institutions to achieve such reformulations as reflected, for example, in the emergence of prizes for women and authors writing in indigenous languages. Of course, there are edges to any system or network even as the network operates to co-opt and colonize newly emerged positions. The limited off-the-network or, perhaps more accurately, edge-of-network positions will be discussed in the book's final chapter.

Understanding literary prizes as a network that gives shape to the wider literary field helps us to overcome a binary that has become ingrained in literary studies. An opposition has been created between 'world' and 'universal' literature which, per David Damrosch's (2003, 4) definition, circulates beyond its culture of origin and especially in the major centres of what Pascale Casanova (2004) has termed the 'world republic of letters' and national literatures which circulate and are valued in more limited contexts separated from world literature. The terminology 'world literature', 'universal literature' and 'the world republic of letters' creates a semblance of opening up literary prestige beyond European contexts when in fact Europe is retained as the centre of value creation and consecration. As Ignacio López-

Calvo writes, '[w]orld literature' was intended to replace 'the old-fashioned Eurocentric conception of the literary-world system as a canon of European masterpieces within their own national territories' (2018, 16). However, the term 'world literature' quickly became problematic in a Spanish American context as it came to be seen as 'una modalidad reciente del colonialismo intelectual metropolitano' (a recent modality of metropolitan intellectual colonialism) (Bencomo 2006, 24). This dichotomy between national and world literature and the power relations it seeks to conceal needs to be re-evaluated. Thinking about the politics of prestige in the prize network gives us a way to begin to do so.

The usefulness of the concept of the network for challenging the Eurocentrism of the concept of world literature has been amply demonstrated. Even as studies of world literature tend to emphasize a division between national and international literature, metaphors of the network (or 'red' in Spanish), system or constellation have provided a way for Latin Americanists to conceptualize an alternative understanding. In *Remapping World Literature*, which provides an excellent range of studies on the matter of world literature in relation to Latin America, many of the essays draw on the concept of the network or related metaphors. Gesine Müller, Jorge J. Locane and Benjamin Loy refer to world literature as a 'system' (2018, 2). Müller also refers to 'literary circulation nodes' when describing the path taken by the works of Gabriel García Márquez on their way to becoming canonical (2018, 158). Ignacio Sánchez Prado refers to world literature as a 'red' (network) (2018, 61). Daniel Link also prefers to understand world literature as a network 'con sus nodos brillando intermitentemente' (with intermittently shining nodes) to avoid presenting it inaccurately as excessively unified and coherent (2018, 82). The concept of the prize network I seek to develop here is rooted in this same desire to overcome a sense of division in this case between prizes offered within restricted national contexts versus, for example, the Nobel Prize for Literature. Until now the concept of the prize network has not been deployed to understand how literary prizes are connected or to challenge existing hierarchical views of the relationships between awards based in Europe or which are less obviously tied to the state than many Spanish American prizes. Recognizing connections and the existence of feedback loops alerts us to the way in which some authors go back and forth winning different prizes over the course of their careers carrying with them their previous achievements in ways which affect the meanings and significance attached to subsequent awards.

The network metaphor is also found in the context of film studies where Quintín refers to the film festival circuit as 'an organic network, a significant system. A galaxy' (2009, 40). The film festival galaxy is centred on the sun that is Cannes, with film festivals such as Venice, Berlin and Rotterdam seen as 'lesser stars that likewise possess their own orbiting planets' (Quintín 2009, 44). Here, however, the emphasis tends towards separate orbits of influence rather than the intricate connections I propose within the prize network.

Prizes are networked but occupy different positions in the literary field which reflect their different politics. The functioning of the range of literary prizes is similar to that described by Marijke De Valck with reference to film festivals. She writes:

> Despite the proliferation of festivals, the network/system has not collapsed. The reason for this is that there is a strict task division between festivals; a small number of major festivals have leading positions as marketplace and media events and the remaining majority may perform a variety of tasks ranging from launching young talent [. . .] to supporting identity groups such as women [. . .] or ethnic communities. (2006, 45)

However, De Valck overlooks the politics of the different festivals within the network, which will be foregrounded in this study of literary prizes. She also envisages festivals as being in hierarchical relationships with one another, and these relationships are taken for granted as inherent to the network. Thus, she writes: 'This hierarchical task division, on the one hand, protects the cultural value of prizes and competition programmes. It allows (some) filmmakers, on the other hand, to go through (series of) lower-level discoveries and encouragements before reaching global inauguration by winning an award at one of the major festivals' (2006, 45). Such hierarchies are not a given and instead reflect, and are the result of, the politics of prestige in the network.

The most prestigious prizes are not de facto more prestigious but have acquired prestige in the literary field as a result of the successful alignment between politics and literary prestige. If literary prestige is attached, as in Bourdieu's conceptualization, to those authors who show the greatest independence from politics, then state-sponsored prizes lose their aura. If, on the other hand, literary prestige, as in nineteenth-century Spanish America, is attached to those author-statesmen who used their literature to serve their country, then state-sponsored prizes would be for them the pinnacle of achievement. The nodes in the network only have the temporary appearance of being hierarchical because of the success of different prizes in aligning political values and literary prestige or in obscuring such alliances. Prizes are thus a means for the awarding bodies to vie for prestige, to forge allegiances based on shared values and to bid for political legitimation.

Understanding prizes as being networked decentralizes prestige and foregrounds the mutability of all positions. The Nobel Prize, often thought of as being at the centre of world literature, came to be 'a peace prize in literary disguise' (Feldman 2000, 56). It epitomized the most widely and long-held political belief of the twentieth century, namely the importance of world peace. Over time, and as a result of the global conflicts of the last century, this political stance was increasingly universalized and came to be associated with literary prestige. The result is that this prize is widely seen as the most prestigious even as it is also often perceived as politically motivated. The crisis that surrounded the Nobel in recent years was not the result of questionable aesthetic choices, of which some would argue there have been plenty, but because it lost its political legitimacy. Prizes should, therefore, be understood as networked as opposed to being thought of as being in a hierarchical pyramid relationship to one another or as being divided according to a centre-periphery model.

The result of hierarchical thinking is that we do not connect or appropriately value all prizes. An imaginary author might go from winning the Premio Estatal de Literatura Joven 'Nellie Campobello' prize awarded by the state of Chihuahua in Mexico for a short story written by 18- to 29-year-olds, to winning the Premio Herralde awarded by the publisher Anagrama, to winning the Premio Sor Juana for women authors writing in Spanish, to winning the Premio Bellas Artes Narrativa Colima (Institute of Fine Art award for Narrative) for published work awarded by a national, state-sponsored institution in Mexico, to winning the Nobel Prize for Literature. She may then go back to Chihuahua to receive a new state prize named in her honour. In this trajectory she occupies many positions in the literary field and may position herself differently in relation to the politics of each award and how each institution seeks to use her as an author. She may go from speaking about water shortages in the state of Chihuahua to talking about her process of writing, to hesitating when asked about her role as a woman author reluctant to be pigeonholed in this way, to talking about a forthcoming Mexican election, to talking about Spanish American relationships with the wider world in the context of vaccine diplomacy and unequal access to healthcare before returning to Chihuahua to talk about her pride in the new institute named after her and her hopes for the future of culture in Chihuahua. One award does not lead to the next in any straightforward or predictable way, and she may win the Nobel Prize without ever, for example, winning the Premio Herralde. Regardless, she carries with her the legacy of each award and has a degree of choice in opting in or out of these awards and in what she says or does not say on each occasion.

The significance of presenting prizes as a network, therefore, is to avoid implying that authors climb a kind of ladder progressing from prizes that are less prestigious to those that are more prestigious or from those at a local or national level to those that are international or from those with more restricted entry criteria to those that draw from a larger pool of potential winners. This may often be the case since male prizewinning authors in particular who become embedded in the network have increasing freedom to move between the different types of awards. The first prize, whichever it may be, endows an author with a certain amount of symbolic capital and positions them in the prize network and gives them status within the literary field. Their symbolic capital can then be drawn on by an awarding institution seeking legitimacy from literary prestige. The receipt of a second prize acts as confirmation of the author's prestige making them potentially more valuable to other awarding bodies and so on. An author who has won a prize goes around with the aura of the prize attached to them. For this reason, newspaper articles often list the accolades a writer has received to date. Prizes, like the role of judging prizes, thus tend towards being concentrated in the hands of a few authors in a kind of snowball effect. The more prizes an author wins the more their symbolic capital, the more valuable they become to awarding institutions and the more selective they may become in which awards they accept or enter. In this scenario an author also becomes increasingly able to negotiate from their privileged position.

Some authors move through the prize network more easily than others as will be discussed in Chapters 5, 6 and 7. Women authors and those writing in indigenous languages face an uphill struggle because they have historically occupied positions of less social prestige which translated into less literary prestige and combined to make them appear less valuable as partners in the prize pact. When it came to state-sponsored prizes seeking to position authors as public intellectuals, this role, as well as that of author itself, was more readily available to male, non-indigenous authors, and so they were more likely to win prizes. As spokespeople, some Spanish American authors, usually those with past experience as author-statesmen and public intellectuals, have found success as authors in the context of a globalized literature in Spanish and on the world stage. As visible celebrities, women and indigenous authors may also fare a little better but only at a wider cost. Their licence to speak may be restricted as they are called upon only as representatives of their gender or ethnicity. The role of celebrity author might also appeal to authors seeking an independent, apparently depoliticized form of literary prestige. Again, this comes at a cost to them and to society as this role leaves them with a very limited sphere of influence cut off from power.

Prizes and the roles of the author in society

Authors, once they have established themselves in the literary field, are increasingly able to select the points in the prize network with which they wish to engage. In other words, they have greater freedom to choose which pacts they wish to enter into and with whom. Authors can refuse prizes or, perhaps more commonly today, boycott them as has happened under dictatorships in Spanish America and as is happening now in relation to the Premio Rómulo Gallegos, both discussed in Chapter 1. Authors can also opt not to submit their work to publisher-run prizes or to make choices between different publishers' awards. Equally, they may opt only to submit to publisher-run prizes so as to appear to be independent of state-funding and politics. In the latter case, the author could be said to adopt a 'globally oriented' position (López-Calvo

2018, 18). This does not mean, however, that this stance is politically neutral particularly when the result of such a stance is that profit and the authority to consecrate Spanish American literature lies outside Spanish America.

By making the politics of literary prestige visible, we enhance not only our understanding of the relationship between power and prestige but also our understanding of the changing and multiple roles of the author in society. Just as different prizes reflect different political agenda, so too do different awards require the winner to take on a different role or function. These roles, like prizes, are not mutually exclusive and can overlap. As Sarah Brouillette (2007) has argued with reference to J. M. Coetzee, how we interpret texts is influenced by the presentation of the author figure. Understandings can differ at national and international levels. For this reason, it is possible for Spanish American authors to enter into pacts at different points in the prize network, to position themselves accordingly, and be understood differently by different audiences.

The evolution of literary prizes for Spanish American literature has seen authors go from states(wo)men and public intellectuals publicly intervening in debates over current affairs to spokespeople on the world stage, to increasingly voiceless but visible celebrities aligned with a Eurocentric publishing industry and a global literature in Spanish. Bourdieu proposed that the greater an author's independence from the state, the greater their prestige (1993, 39). The most prestigious authors inclined, and were able to, detach themselves from 'the powers that be' (1993, 41). The withdrawal of patronage was seen as a welcome step as it led, ideally, to greater independence for the author. In reality, it has more often led to a greater reliance on the market. This split between being indebted to politics versus being free to prioritize aesthetics was mapped by Pascale Casanova onto the international stage where she argued that the most successful authors are those who distance themselves from 'national literary space' and associate themselves with universal literature and international literary space (2014, xii). This dichotomy has already been brought into question. The boundaries between national and world literature do not hold. We must also, therefore, challenge the idea that an author can only be either reliant on the state or totally independent of it when the truth for most Spanish American authors is somewhere in between these two poles and, as Ignacio Sánchez Prado has pointed out, those authors who go on to be consecrated beyond Spanish America are those who previously benefitted from state support (*Pierre Bourdieu* 2018, 205). The fact that these authors later claim to reject such politicized forms of prestige shows the extent to which they are willing to bow to the illusion of world literature which so benefits existing hierarchies and perpetuates the misguided notion that it is possible to separate literary prestige from politics.

In a postscript to the *Rules of Art*, Bourdieu subsequently recognized that the polarization of the literary field that he had described was 'threatening to disappear, since the logic of commercial production tends more and more to assert itself over avant-garde production (notably in the case of literature through the constraints of the book market)' (1996, 345). He continued: 'the boundary has never been so blurred between the experimental work and the *bestseller*' (1996, 347). As the boundaries within the literary field and between autonomous and heteronomous poles become less distinct, so too does the author come to occupy multiple, interchangeable roles.

It is likely that the Spanish American literary field was never, in any meaningful way, polarized with art versus commerce or the politically engaged artist versus the independent one. The challenge of applying imported models to Latin America is widely recognized. Pamela Smorkaloff (1997, 144–5) reports that the epilogue of the Cuban edition of Robert Escarpit's *Sociología de la literatura*, published in 1970, already noted the limitations of the French models of literary sociology for understanding the Cuban context. One of the reasons for its inadequacy was because the situation in colonized Cuba was different from that of colonial France (Smorkaloff 1997, 145). Of course, this observation is true for all Spanish American countries. Spanish American authors did not go from enjoying the patronage of royalty and nobility to being independent and free to pursue art for art's sake. They went, in most cases, from being members of the creole elite, excluded from the highest ranks of the colonial viceroyalties, to founding statesmen ready to put their pens into the service of new nations in need of an identity that would set them apart from Spain and their neighbours with whom they shared a common language.

In the twentieth century, nation-building continued to be tied to culture and state-sponsored national prizes were established by all Spanish American states.[4] The award ceremonies brought authors together with presidents and government officials. The importance of such ceremonies is underscored by the insistence of the Nobel Committee that the winner attends in person and gives a speech and by the scandal, discussed in Chapter 1, when this honour was refused to an author in Paraguay. The ability of the author to speak to power at these events is paramount in affirming their role as public intellectuals. As Alejandra Lajous elaborates with reference to the Mexican Premio Nacional de Literatura (National Prize for Literature),

> dado el valor simbólico-político de la ceremonia misma, ésta crea la ocasión y proporciona el foro adecuado para que el Estado, a través del secretario de Educación Pública [y aún el presidente], señale a la élite cultural del país lo que espera de ella; da ocasión a que se defina el papel que el Estado asigna al intelectual. Por otro lado, los premiados se encuentran en la circunstancia ideal – una vez reconocida su autoridad

---

[4] See Chapter 6, Table 4 for a list of these awards and the dates they were created.

moral – para hacer un reclamo, una petición, o simplemente reafirmar su solidaridad con el Estado (quoted in Díaz Arciniega 1993, 155–6).

Given the political-symbolic value of the ceremony itself, this creates the occasion and provides the appropriate forum for the State, in the person of the Minister for Public Education (and even the President) to signal to the cultural elite of the country what is expected of them; it gives the opportunity for defining the role that the state assigns to the intellectual. On the other hand, the prize-winners find themselves in the ideal circumstance, once their moral authority has been recognized – to air a grievance or to petition or simply to reaffirm their solidarity with the State.

Ignacio Chávez, winner of the Mexican National Prize in 1961, perfectly understood the significance of his speech when he said: 'espero que me sea permitido aprovechar esta ocasión excepcional para hacer una llamada a la conciencia de la nación. El hombre que habla es nada, pero la tribuna que hoy se le presta es alta' (I hope that I will be allowed to take advantage of this exceptional occasion to make a call to the conscience of the nation. The man speaking is nothing, but the platform that he is given today is great) (quoted in Díaz Arciniega 1993, 155).

In Chapter 3 we will see how Spanish American authors, who had been states(wo)men and public intellectuals for their respective nations, are called upon by the institutions behind the Nobel Prize for Literature and the Premio Cervantes awarded by the Spanish Ministry for Culture as 'cultural representatives' in the sense described by Graham Huggan (2001, 65). The Spanish American authors thus become spokespeople interpreting their countries for foreign audiences. This is the role assigned to them in the context of these awards. They are invited to speak but with a narrower remit. Nevertheless, these occasions give them the opportunity to negotiate and call for new, less Eurocentric, more equal relationships.

Accepting an award implies a pact with the state or organization bestowing it, but it does not mean that the author bows down to political power. Ignacio Chávez, like the Spanish American authors discussed in Chapter 3, understood the prize ceremony as an opportunity to 'make a call to the conscience of the nation' or, as I will term it, a chance to talk back. In a democratic context, the value of a dissenting author may be even greater than that of a known supporter. Such was the case, discussed in Chapter 1, with the Rómulo Gallegos prize awarded to Mario Vargas Llosa in 1964. Recognizing Vargas Llosa, then a supporter of the Castro regime in Cuba, enabled the recently established democratic Venezuelan government to boast of its political tolerance in accepting opposing views. When it comes to prizes under dictatorships, also discussed in Chapter 1, dissent is not tolerated. As states now seek to project themselves as inclusive, state-sponsored prizes for authors, many of whom combined this role with that of activists, writing in indigenous languages feed into identity politics. At the same time independent groups, such as the one that founded the Premio Sor Juana Inés de la Cruz, seek to use prizes to petition for equal rights within the literary field and beyond. The prizewinning author is positioned as a spokesperson for this group as is often apparent when it comes to the subject of journalist's questions even though authors may wish to resist being pigeonholed according to their gender or ethnicity.

The experience of the author as the recipient of publisher-run prizes differs from that when they win state-sponsored prizes which points to the different conception of the role of the author in society at stake in these awards. For publisher-run prizes, as will be seen in Chapter 2, the author is prized above all for their visibility and ability to saturate the cultural landscape with news of their award. Henseler provides an excellent example based on the experience of peninsular author Espido Freire who won the Planeta Prize:

> she participated in book presentations throughout Spain that took several weeks and covered cities such as Madrid, La Coruña, Bilbao, Zaragoza, Barcelona, Santander, Valencia, Seville, Málaga, Vitoria and Bilbao. In these cities, she gave press conferences and signed books in commercial centers such as the department store El Corte Inglés. She also travelled to Mexico, Venezuela, Colombia and Argentina, where she took part in book presentations, receptions at embassies, book-signing events, and up to sixteen interviews a day. The campaign was carefully planned by the publishing house and covered all terrain: from television to print and radio advertising, and from specialized to general information sources. (2003, 138)

Yet politics still come into play. Authors whose published political views are aligned with the values of the publishers and their owners are more likely to win prizes. This coincidence is particularly evident where there is a confluence of newspaper and literary publishing in large media groups such as PRISA. This scenario connected the Spanish newspaper *El País* and the Premio Alfaguara (Pablo Sánchez 2008) and is also evident in the relationship between the Argentine newspaper and the Premio Clarín and Clarín Alfaguara. In these situations, the role of representative and spokesperson is still very much available to the Spanish American authors, but this is not the role assigned to them by the prize and its organizers. For this reason, they may find it easier to sidestep questions about politics as winners of such awards.

The view of the Spanish American author as statesman and public intellectual, as discussed by Doris Sommer (1991) and Ángel Rama (1996 first published 1984), originates in the nineteenth century. A transformation in the roles available to Spanish American authors came about over the course of the twentieth century as a result of the Boom in Spanish American literature. From the late 1950s, the men who are today household names principally Julio Cortázar, Carlos Fuentes, Gabriel García Márquez and Mario Vargas Llosa, became the first generation of Spanish American authors able to make a living as professional writers independently, if they wished, from the state and with a presence on the world stage. This change was thanks in no small part to the money and prestige gained from literary prizes such as the Premio Biblioteca Breve discussed in Chapter 2. As new options opened up, the Boom authors were caught between and often sought to occupy contradictory positions. In the words of Nicola Miller: 'First, many of the "boom" writers, echoed by some Western literary critics, began to emphasize the distinctive contribution of intellectuals as 'keepers of the national consciousness' (1999, 2). On the other hand, 'the cosmopolitan novelists of the literary "boom" publicly lamented the Spanish American "tradition of the president-poet" which obliged them to become politically active to the detriment of their creative potential' (Miller 1999, 2). The heirs to the Boom novelists, the Spanish American authors of the late twentieth and early twenty-first centuries, increasingly align themselves with the latter category buying into the fallacy that world literature and its awards are free from politics. In reality, they replace state patronage with 'commercial patronage' (Franco 2002, 261). In doing so, however, the literary prestige of the cosmopolitan novelist and publisher-run prizes is far from politically neutral. The politics have just been better concealed, authors have simply replaced one master for another and the role of author-statesperson and public intellectual for that of visible celebrity combined, if they wish, with those of representative and spokesperson.

The position of the author has tended to be seen as a binary choice. It is possible to be both public intellectual for the nation, international spokesperson and deterritorialized global celebrity by accepting different prizes. That said, an author's credibility as public intellectual may be damaged by excessive association with celebrity. Conversely, a tendency to be outspoken might preclude the kind of visibility that is attractive to the global market. To some extent these roles need to be seen as interchangeable positions that can be assumed more or less simultaneously and are dependent on the perspective and position of the reader-audience. At the same time, authors pursuing the myth of a purely literary prestige are increasingly rejecting overtly politicized forms of prestige and states are increasingly reluctant to give authors the power to speak against them hence the appeal of public–private partnerships for national prizes which allow the state to withdraw from its role as much as the authors are withdrawing from theirs.

On the one hand, we may welcome the range of roles now open to Spanish American authors as a result of the range of different prizes on offer. However, authors may be seduced by the illusion of independence which is associated, for now and in the current literary centres, with greater prestige but do not consider the cost to them and society. Publisher-run prizes which position the author as celebrity are most prone to cause scandal which amounts to little more than accusations of cronyism and highly subjective squabbling over who is more or less deserving from an aesthetic point of view. These circumscribed debates of limited consequence are the result of the way in which authors in the context of these prizes allow themselves to be co-opted by the free market restricting their sphere of influence and their relevance. The pact they make no longer calls on them to speak about politics because this would make the transaction of literary prestige and politics too visible in contexts where literary prestige is associated with apparent independence. The authors comply. Given platforms, such as book tours and interviews where soundbites reign supreme as opposed to speeches, they are at once more visible, less vocal and less and less effective in the public sphere. They are co-opted as the ideal poster boys and girls for regimes that have successfully limited space for dissent. Authors may welcome this illusion of independence, especially where it helps in the ultimate goal that Sánchez Prado attributes to Mexican authors participating in world literature, and which may apply to all Spanish American authors, which is 'to avoid being pegged as merchants of authenticity' or 'native informants' (*Strategic Occidentalism* 2018, 20). If authors consciously accept these politics and their resulting marginalization from power so be it. Or they can follow the examples of the few who are exploring alternatives to the prize network whose successes and limitations are discussed in Chapter 8. That is their choice. But it is a political one and one which may not be to their advantage and may be to society's detriment. In the words of García Márquez, states need authors 'because we give them prestige they lack; they fear us because our sentiments and views can damage them. In the history of power in Latin America there are only military dictatorships or intellectuals' (quoted in Miller 1999, 43). If the role of the author as public intellectual is being eroded, we may not like the consequences. As critics it is our duty to insist on and expose the politics of literary prestige when it comes to all prizes for all authors regardless of nationality so that the power of such awards is not underestimated.

The critical context

This book fills a significant gap in existing studies about literary prizes and Spanish American literature. The need for a comprehensive study of these awards has been identified by Jorge J. Locane who notes that, despite literary prizes being an established part of the literary landscape, 'una taxonomía precisa está pendiente' (a precise taxonomy is pending) (2017, 100). Studying the Chilean Premio Nacional de Literatura (National Prize for Literature), Pablo Faúndez Morán similarly commented on this critical lacuna: 'Llamativamente, a pesar de que la mayoría de los países latinoamericanos, e incluso España, cuentan con Premios Nacionales de Literatura entregados en distintas modalidades y con distintas periodicidades, la extensa revisión bibliográfica realizada para este estudio no dio con publicaciones académicas dedicadas a este tipo de galardones' (Strikingly, despite the fact that the majority of Latin American countries, and even Spain, have national prizes for literature awarded in various categories and over different time periods, the extensive bibliographical search done for this study uncovered no academic publications dedicated to this type of award) (2016, 9). This study fills this critical gap and goes beyond national prizes to include other types of prize that are a feature of the contemporary Spanish American literary landscape. By focusing on the full range of prizes open to Spanish American authors and examining prizes from the perspectives of different stakeholders, this book provides a comprehensive overview and understanding of the prize network, its interconnections and, above all, its politics.

The frame of reference for this book is Spanish America and prizes for Spanish American literature. The basis for this grouping is the common experience in the region of nation-building following independence and the shared language which arose from the experience of colonization. It is in this language that much, but not all, literature from Spanish America is written. The importance of the Spanish language for creating a connection through literature between Spain and her former colonies means that when we think about prizes for Spanish American literature, we must also consider those prizes awarded from Spain and the significance of prizes in intercontinental relations which feature prominently in Chapters 2 and 3.

Studies of literary prizes in Spanish America are limited, but where they exist, they largely focus on a single prize. Anadeli Bencomo's (2007) article is something of an exception. It focuses largely, but not exclusively, on the Premio Herralde to argue that commercial prizes are replacing state prizes. This change is seen as signifying a move from national to transnational global markets. I propose that we are not seeing a move from one to the other. Rather, these prizes coexist in the prize network, but there is a growing and concerning tendency for Spanish American authors to prefer publisher-run prizes because they perceive them as free from politics and therefore more prestigious. Bencomo (2006) goes into more detail about the Premio Rómulo Gallegos. I draw on and update her findings in my analysis of that award in Chapter 1. In Chapter 1 I also draw on François Delprat's (2005) comparison of the Premio Rómulo Gallegos and the Premio Casa de las Américas. Chapter 2 draws on Locane (2017) to understand the influence of the Premio Herralde on Latin American literature. Chapter 3 builds on my own previously published article on Spanish American authors and the Premio Cervantes (Bowskill 2012). The subject of women authors and literary prizes has been studied by Nuala Finnegan (2007) in relation to Ángeles Mastretta winning the Premio Rómulo Gallegos. Chapter 6 considers the extent to which the problems Mastretta faced are widespread and the effectiveness of prizes for women authors in providing a gateway for women to enter the wider prize network.

In the Mexican context Víctor Díaz Arciniega (1991) has studied the Premios Nacionales (National Prizes). Sánchez Prado provides a useful overview of Mexican prizes (*Pierre Bourdieu* 2018, 196–7), and Claudia G. Sorais Castañeda (unpublished study referenced in Hind 2019) presents some fascinating statistics in relation to the Aguascalientes poetry prize. The latter are used and located in a broader context in Chapter 6.

In the Chilean context, Faúndez Morán (2016) provides an excellent study of the Premio Nacional (National Prize) from its inception until 2014 going into detail about the circumstances and reception surrounding each award. In addition to this thesis the other classic study of the Chilean National Prize is *El club de la pelea: los Premios Nacionales de Literatura* by Andrés Gómez Bravo. These studies inform my discussion of the Premio Nacional under Pinochet in Chapter 1.

As Faúndez Morán (2016, 9) notes, other studies of the Chilean national prize are largely biographies and anthologized samples of the work of the winners. These publications are part of a wider trend in Spanish America which, while important in processes of canon formation and in making visible the prize's trajectory so as to enhance its literary prestige, do not seek to understand the politics of the prizes or locate them in a broader context. Examples of this type of publication include *25 años Premio Nacional de Literatura Efraín Huerta* by Sara Uribe (2007) and 'Premio Nacional de Literatura "Miguel Ángel Asturias": semblanzas de los galardonados 1988-2012' by Nancy Maldonado de Maraya (2013). In Panama entries to the 'Leyendas Nacionales' category, discussed in Chapter 1, have been reprinted multiple times (González Ruiz 1953). The speeches of the winners of the Premio Rómulo Gallegos have also been anthologized by Boris Caballero Escorcia (2011) affirming the importance of acceptance speeches as discussed in Chapter 3.

Important work has been done in the Spanish context which, where relevant, informs the discussion of publisher-run prizes in Chapter 2. Burkhard Pohl's study of the relationship between Spanish publishers and Latin American authors in the 1990s is particularly insightful. Again, almost all studies focus on a single prize. Samuel Amell's 'Los premios literarios y la novela de la postguera' (1985) is an exception. Fernando González-Ariza (2004) and Carlos de Arce (1972) have written about the Premio Planeta. Margarita Lezcano (1992) published a study of the Premio Nadal in the 1970s, and González Ariza notes two other early articles about the Nadal by Eduardo Godoy Gallardo (1970) and W. J. Grupp (1956). Several essays on peninsular prizes feature in the collection *Entre el ocio y el negocio: Industria editorial y literatura en la España de los 90* (López de Abiada et al. 2001). Nicola Witt in this volume analyses the narrative category of the Premio Nacional de Literatura (National Prize for Literature), the Premio de la Crítica (Critics' Award), the Premio Nadal and the Premio Planeta. José Belmonte Serrano reflects why prizes exist, recalls some notable scandals and identifies different phases of the Premio Planeta. Also in this volume, José Manuel López de Abiada analyses the novel by Manuel Vázquez Montalbán about the Premio Planeta. Additional bibliography relating to peninsular prizes can be found in these sources. In Spain anthologies commemorating major anniversaries of prizes are also common.

Perhaps the most studied prize in relation to Spanish American literature is the Premio Biblioteca Breve established by Carlos Barral of Barcelona-based publishing house Seix Barral and the prize often credited with creating or at least consolidating the Boom. In preparing this manuscript I have enjoyed re-reading Alejandro Herrero-Olaizola's *The Censorship Files. Latin American Writers and Franco's Spain* and Mario Santana's *Foreigners in the Homeland. The Spanish American New Novel in Spain, 1962-1974* both of which are rich in archival material about Spanish American literature under Franco. Studies of the Boom are also clearly important in this respect and too numerous to mention, but Ángel Rama's *El boom en perspectiva* remains a touchstone and Philip Swanson's account (2005) an excellent overview.

The seminal work on literary prizes, to which this book is very much indebted, remains *The Economy of Prestige. Prizes, Awards, and the Circulation of Cultural Value* (2005) by James English. English recognizes that politics are always in play when it comes to literary prizes and the creation of cultural value. Cultural value does not 'emerge in a political vacuum, the participants uncolored by and indifferent to prevailing hierarchies of class, race, gender, or nation; its production is always politicized' (2005, 27). Yet politics is not as much at the forefront of English's study of the Anglophone context as it is here reflecting differences between the English and Spanish-speaking literary fields. In the final section of *The Economy of Prestige* English considers the 'global economy of cultural prestige' and identifies the importance of the legacies of colonialism in evidence in literary prizes for African literature which are also relevant to the present study. These legacies are also in play in many prizes for Spanish American literature based outside the region. This book seeks to more fully account for the particularities of the Spanish American context where state-sponsored national prizes are a persistent and important feature of a literary field that is more obviously inflected with politics. As will be seen in Chapter 2, however, while politics may be obscured in contexts where privately run awards dominate they are ever present.

Studies of literary prizes in Anglophone and Francophone contexts are more common, although again there is a tendency to focus on a single prize. Sylvie Ducas (2013) provides an overview of literary prizes in France. Diana Holmes (2016) analyses the French Prix Goncourt and its penchant for recognizing 'middlebrow' fiction. The work of these authors as well as Claire Squires (2006, 2007 and with Gortshacher et al. 2006) has been useful in helping me to think through the important differences as well as similarities between the French, Anglophone and Spanish American contexts. Richard Todd's *Consuming Fictions: The Booker Prize and Fiction in Britain Today* (1996), Graham Huggan's *The Post-Colonial Exotic: Marketing the Margins* (2001) and Sarah Brouillette's *Postcolonial Writers in the Global Literary Marketplace* (2007), all excellent books, have helped me to understand the politics of prizes in the context of postcolonial relations even as I recognize the different postcolonial experiences of Spanish America and the contexts these critics describe. This reading was supplemented by article-length studies of prizes relating to Anglophone literatures in Africa by L. Attree (2013), Doseline Kiguru (2016) and D Pucherová (2011). Nathalie Heinich's (1999) fascinating study of authors' experiences of winning the Goncourt Prize helped me to realize the importance of considering the perspectives of different stakeholders. Prizes first caught my attention as mechanisms of canon formation while writing my own doctoral thesis and subsequent monograph on the twentieth-century Mexican canon in which I discuss the politics behind the creation and first instance of the Mexican Premio Nacional de Literatura (National Prize for Literature) (Bowskill 2011). Edward Mack's (2010) study of the Japanese Akutagawa and Naoki Prizes was an important, and very readable, reminder of how prizes relate to the wider process of circulation and canon formation.

Unsurprisingly, as probably the world's best-known award for literature, the Nobel Prize has caught the critical imagination. Burton Feldman (2000) provides an excellent overview of all of the Nobel prizes. Richard Wires (2008) and Renee Winegarten (1994) analyse the prize for literature specifically. Kjell Espmark, member of the Swedish Academy, provides an insider's perspective (1986). Julia Lovell (2006) looks at the politics surrounding China's bid to have a Chinese laureate and the eventual award to Mo Yan. Rebecca Braun (2011) looks at the prize from a European perspective and has also studied literary prizes in Germany (2014). These texts inform my discussion of the Spanish American winners of the Nobel Prize for Literature in Chapter 3 even as I depart from the tendency to discuss the politics surrounding the choice of laureate to consider the political significance the authors try to negotiate for the award through their acceptance speeches.

In the early stages of this project, I was fortunate enough to enjoy several productive conversations about prizes and the institutional apparatus surrounding literature with Par Kumaraswami, Kirsty Hooper and Niamh Thornton. The work of Par Kumaraswami and Antoni Kapcia (2012) in Cuba, as well as the extensive body of work by Ignacio Sánchez Prado, including, but not limited to, *Strategic Occidentalism* (2018), *Pierre Bourdieu in Hispanic Literature and Culture* (2018) and *Mexican Literature in Theory* (2018), in the Mexican context has long been a source of inspiration for how to approach the study of the sociology of literature in Spanish America. Readings about the Spanish American context have been complemented by the work of Sarah Brouillette (2007, 2019).

This book continues my interest in the relationship between literature and nation-building. My studies of nation-building began in a master's class taken by Patience Schell whose research at the time focused on education and nation-building in Mexico. The rich literature on nation-building, particularly when it comes to nation-building through literature, underpins this study and includes the seminal works *Foundational Fictions* by Doris Sommer (1991), *The Lettered City* by Ángel Rama (first published 1984. English translation 1996) and Beatriz González Stephan's *Fundaciones* (2002). This reading has been complemented by the equally significant work on the need to think beyond national borders and to locate Spanish American literature within broader contexts. This work includes the aforementioned work on world literature by Gisèle Sapiro (2016) and the contributors to the collection of essays in *Remapping World Literature* (Müller et al. 2018) as well as works by, for example, Jon Beasley Murray (2003) and Philip Swanson (2012, 2020).

It would have been possible to write this book focusing solely on one national context. To do so would have provided interesting insights into the workings of national institutions and debates on the way in which prizes have been used to further national agenda such as that of decentralizing culture in Mexico. Nevertheless, by focusing on Spanish American literature and its reception at home and abroad, this book recognizes the ways in which cultural production circulates, acquires meaning and value within and beyond national boundaries. In so doing, it follows a critical tradition in which concepts such as hybridization (Canclini 2005, first published 1995), transculturation (Rama 2012, first published 1982) and contact zones (Mary Louise Pratt 1991) point to the permeability of borders within contexts of unequal power relations.

The structure of this book

The overarching principles behind the structure of this book can be thought of in different ways mirroring the intersecting nature of the prize network. Together, the chapters present the perspectives of, and politics in play for, different stakeholders including states, publishers, authors, judges and critics in the prize network. Another defining feature of the book is its use of a wide range of sources which enable us to capture the perspectives of these groups. The chapters also track the different political positions which have invoked the prestige of literary prizes including nation-building, totalitarianism, communism, liberal democracy, internationalism, free-market capitalism, neoliberalism and identity politics. Each chapter foregrounds one perspective, one type of source and one political position, but there is considerable overlap throughout so as to avoid giving one-sided accounts.

The book is notionally divided into three sections. The first section, comprising Chapters 1 and 2, examines the perspectives and motivations of states and publishers in establishing literary prizes. Chapter 1 studies the creation of state-sponsored national and international prizes for literature, their role in nation-building and as the focus for dissent at moments of national crisis and transition. The main case studies are drawn from Panama and Venezuela with reference to Chile, Paraguay and Cuba. Chapter 2 focuses on prizes run by publishers with origins in Spain which have been increasingly dominated by Spanish American authors. The chapter studies the Premio Biblioteca Breve, which was awarded from 1958 to 1972 and was then revived in 1999, as well as the Premio Planeta, the Premio Herralde and the Premio Alfaguara. It demonstrates how these prizes are politically inflected even though they are most associated with the commercialization of literature. Consideration is also given to prizes from within Spanish America which have sought, less successfully, to occupy similar positions in the literary field including the Premio Emecé, the Premio Losada de Novela and the Premio Internacional de Narrativa Siglo XXI-UNAM (International Prize for Narrative), jointly sponsored by the Mexican National Autonomous University and the publisher Siglo XXI. Chapter 1 draws on the texts of the laws which created the various state-sponsored national and international prizes. Chapter 2 draws on material from Carlos Barral's personal archive to understand the politics behind the Premio Bilbioteca Breve. It uses comments made by Alfaguara employees reported in press coverage to reveal their view of the prize and presentations of the prizes shown on the YouTube channels of Alfaguara and Anagrama to show how the author's visibility is maximized by these awards.

The second section, comprising Chapters 3 and 4, looks at how authors respond to winning prizes. Chapter 3 examines the speeches given by Spanish American winners of the Nobel Prize for Literature and the Premio Cervantes awarded by the Spanish state. These prizes position the author as spokesperson and defender of democracy. The prize ceremonies for these awards provide authors with a unique platform from which to talk back and try to negotiate their position in relation to world literature and the position of Spanish America in relation to the rest of the world. Chapter 4 analyses three texts by Spanish American authors who found their voice in the prize network by writing about literary prizes in their fiction. The texts studied are Fernando Iwasaki's *España, aparta de mi estos premios* (2009), the short story 'Sensini' (1997) by Roberto Bolaño and *El complot de los románticos* (2009) by Carmen Boullosa.

The final section, comprising Chapters 5, 6 and 7, looks at the winners and losers or, to put it differently, the politics of inclusion and exclusion that prizes enable. It considers the experiences of those who have been largely excluded from the prize network and the effectiveness of prizes that have emerged in the context of identity politics that seek to address the historic marginalization of women authors and authors writing in indigenous languages. Chapter 5 studies the work of Mexican Ana Mairena and Cuban Nivaria Tejera both of whom, like their better-known counterparts, the male Boom authors, were connected to the Premio Biblioteca Breve and Seix Barral but who did not benefit from the same reception. These, the chapter argues, are the wrongly forgotten women of the Boom. Chapter 6 provides compelling statistical evidence to reveal the extent to which Spanish American women authors have been excluded from the prize network. Alongside these facts and figures is a discussion of the role of the Premio Sor Juana in seeking to recognize Spanish American literature by women. Chapter 7 studies the history of the Mexican Premio Nezahualcóyotl locating it within the wider context of policies aimed at changing the relationship between indigenous communities and the state in Mexico and beyond. The four novels that have won the prize to date are analysed to show how the prize is contributing to the creation of a new canon of literature in indigenous languages which represents a departure from past trends and addresses common themes and issues. These chapters foreground the voice of the critic and the critical reception of prizes and prizewinning texts in press coverage. They combine this approach with textual and statistical analysis.

The book concludes by considering the latest developments in the prize network noting the emergence of neoliberal prizes involving partnerships between the state and private enterprise and the alternatives to the prize network that are being explored by some authors. Together, the chapters in this book are an invitation to think about how literary prizes might come to underpin a better politics and to reflect on the desired role of the author in contemporary society.

1

Literary prizes, controversy and the state in Spanish America

Today almost every country in Spanish America has at least one annual, state-sponsored national prize for literature.[1] These awards began to emerge across Spanish America in the early twentieth century. The legal documents which created national prizes for literature demonstrate the same nation-building impetus that underpinned many post-independence state-led projects. Some Spanish American countries, most notably Cuba and Venezuela, also established prizes that were open to all Spanish American authors or to authors writing in Spanish regardless of nationality. These prizes aimed to secure the nation's status within the international community and set a wider political agenda for the region. This chapter uses the legal texts, an essay by a prize judge and press coverage of controversies surrounding literary prizes in Spanish America to understand how state-sponsored prizes are tools of nation-building which have often become battlegrounds reflecting wider political debate at times of crisis, transition and regime change.

Particular attention will be paid to the evolution of the national prize for literature in Panama and the crisis surrounding the Premio Nacional de Literatura (National Prize for Literature) in Chile during the Pinochet regime. To demonstrate the ways literary prizes are also used to broker international relations the chapter looks at the significance of the Cuban Premio Casa de las Américas awards followed by a study of the Premio Rómulo Gallegos focusing on the crises that have plagued the award since President Hugo Chávez took office in Venezuela. Together, the case studies

---

[1] A list of these prizes and the date each was established can be found in Chapter 6, Table 3.

give a clear sense of the literary and political stakes involved when it comes to state-sponsored awards.

Inspired by European romanticism, post-independence states across Spanish America associated nationhood with the possession of a national literature. Thus, in the nineteenth century, author-statesmen put their pens to the task of consolidating the imagined community of the nation.[2] These men held high political office and produced novels which were widely read in schools and aimed to inspire love for the nation. The nation-building significance of these texts was such that Doris Sommer (1991) has called them 'foundational fictions'. Histories of literature were another way that the new nations assumed tangible form (González-Stephan 2002, 214). National prizes for literature added to this tradition of nation-building through literature as the former colonies continued to assert their new identities and sought to establish themselves as places of culture and civilization. One of the earliest awards was established in Argentina. In August 1913 the proposal to create national prizes for science and literature was debated in the Cámara de Senadores (Senate) in Argentina. The role of literature in securing national pride and international status is underscored in the remarks made by one senator speaking in support of the new awards who referred to the fact that while Argentina was economically competitive with countries that were older and more populous, the country lagged behind intellectually (*Diario de Sesiones* 1913, 1095–8). The prizes, he argued, were needed if Argentina were to assume its rightful position in the world order. These sentiments were to be echoed throughout Spanish America as the century progressed.

As the twentieth century progressed Spanish American countries faced new challenges as revolutions and military coups created upheavals which destabilized still relatively new nations. When it came to addressing the challenges of recovering following periods of turmoil and change, many Spanish American governments once again looked to literature to bolster their legitimacy as well as their claim to be nation states. It was in these moments, when nations had recently experienced a transition or crisis, that state-sponsored national prizes for literature often emerged.

The awards established, organized and funded by the state typically evoke the link between literature and nation in their name. Most are called simply the Premio Nacional de Literatura (National Prize for Literature) followed by the name of the country. Some, including Nicaragua's Premio Rubén Darío (est. 1942) and Ecuador's Premio Eugenio Espejo (est. 1975) as well as Panama's Premio Ricardo Miró (est. 1942) discussed in this chapter, are named after statesmen who were also authors. The prizes thus present these men as role models ensuring that literary prestige and the role of the author-statesman are still most readily associated with male authors.

---

[2]The term 'imagined community' is taken from Anderson (1991, 6–7).

The regulations typically stipulate that only nationals or long-term residents are eligible for the prizes thus the winner's success is implicitly attributed to their place of birth or residence. The awarding of medals in addition to prize money invites comparison with military or sportspeople representing their country. National and literary prestige are visibly connected at much-photographed prize ceremonies where presidents or ministers present the medals to the laureate.

The links between literature and the state become even more tangible when the national prizes are for unpublished works which are subsequently published in editions subsidized by, and bearing the insignia of, the state. The press, the same instrument that Benedict Anderson reports enabled the 'creole pioneers' to imagine the new nations of Spanish America, announce the awards and provide ample coverage of prize ceremonies.[3] The readers of newspapers outnumber those of histories of literature, or even of literature itself, and so the prizes guarantee a steady stream of articles reminding citizens to take pride in their nation as embodied in its literature. The prizes, perhaps even more effectively than literary histories, harnessed literary prestige for the purposes of nation-building.

The new national prizes enabled Spanish American states to showcase national literary achievements on a regular basis to the mutual benefit of authors and the state. In calling upon authors to serve the state by giving a speech in front of assembled dignitaries, national prizes position authors as public intellectuals, defined here as those who intervene in public debate. In accepting state-sponsored awards authors enter into a pact whereby they accept recognition and financial support in exchange for at least tacit support of the state's political agenda. However, Spanish American authors can refuse prizes and the implied pact with the state. They have done so in the past and continue to do so today in Venezuela as will be seen later in this chapter.

Pacts between authors and states wishing to showcase their democratic credentials have been the most successful. Liberal and democratic regimes in particular derive symbolic rewards from presenting themselves as benevolent benefactors rewarding literary merit regardless of the author's political beliefs. In so doing, they demonstrate values of tolerance and inclusivity as well as the strength to withstand criticism. Authors in turn welcome such awards because they offer a less overtly politicized form of literary prestige which today is seen as desirable while still giving them the opportunity to take on the role of public intellectual speaking to power.

Scandal arises when the pact between authors and the state is broken as often happens during political crises. This link between literary prestige,

---

[3] On the role of newspapers in nation-building in Spanish America, see Anderson (1991), chapter 4 which is entitled 'Creole Pioneers'.

politics, understood here and throughout this chapter as the kind of power wielded by politicians and institutions of the state, and state-sponsored national prizes in Spanish America leads to markedly different discourses in comparison to privately funded awards in the Anglophone world. James English has studied the scandals surrounding the British Booker Prize and the American Pulitzer. In these cases, scandal results from 'the judges' dubious aesthetic dispositions, as betrayed by their meagre credentials, their risible lack of habitus, or their glaring errors of judgement' (English 2005, 190). Judges also provoked scandal if they were seen to be influenced by personal relationships (English 2005, 193–4). Refusing a prize has been another cause of scandal, but such an action is increasingly seen as anachronistic (English 2005, 221). English suggests that 'the question of what strategies and tactics fall acceptably within the rules of the prize game, or where the artist can legitimately stand vis-à-vis the prize', comes 'down to the question of where the artist stands in relation to society' (2005, 243). State-run Spanish American prizes are different because of the different rules of the prize game that pertain there and, ultimately, due to the very different way such awards seek to position the author in relation to society. The role of author-statesman and public intellectual that is so ingrained into the Spanish American context means that controversies around national prizes revolve around politics far more than aesthetics or personal differences.

State-sponsored national prizes for literature

In 1942, the Ayuntamiento Provincial de Panamá (Provincial Town Hall of Panama City) created the Premio Anual de Literatura Ricardo Miró (Ricardo Miró Annual Prize for Literature) for unpublished works. The legal text appeared in the *Gaceta Oficial* on 16 April 1942).[4] The prize was named after Ricardo Miró (1883–1940) who the legal text identified as the greatest Panamanian poet to date. Miró's poem 'Patria' (Fatherland) (1909), in which he expressed his longing for his homeland, was written while he was serving as consul in Barcelona making him ideally placed to embody the values of literary nation-building that the prize sought to instil in future generations.

The prize consisted of publication and first, second and third prizewinners received a gold, silver or bronze medal and 500, 250 or 125 balboas, respectively. The legal text which created the award proclaimed that literature could contribute to nation-building and fostering national identity.

---

[4]To the best of my knowledge, there are no existing studies of the prize itself. Fong (2004) analyses the short stories that have won the prize. Guardián (1994) and González Ruiz (1953) edited anthologies of prizewinning texts.

Article 1 stated, '[q]ue la cultura es uno de los ingredientes más eficaces en la cristalización de una nacionalidad' (that culture is one of the most effective ingredients for crystallizing a nationality). Consequently, Article 2 stated, 'las instituciones públicas tienen el deber de estimular las actividades intelectuales en cuanto son medio de expresión de las aspiraciones ideales de la nación' (public institutions have a duty to stimulate intellectual activities in so much as they are the means of expressing the ideal aspirations of the nation). The prize fulfilled the authorities' obligations and authors now had a responsibility to use their skills in the service of national ideals.

The Premio Anual Ricardo Miró was unusual in the history of Spanish American national prizes for literature because, although it was Panama's foremost award of its kind, it was created by local and not national government. However, the Panamanian prize was typical in the way it sought to use literary prestige to bolster national pride. Moreover, although it originated in the capital city, the national government was involved from the start as the jury was selected by the provincial governor, the mayor of Panama City, the director of the National Library, the rector of the National University and an official from the Ministry of Education. In 1946, when the provincial town halls disappeared, the prize, now renamed the Premio Literario Ricardo Miró (Ricardo Miró Prize for Literature), came fully under the jurisdiction of the Ministry of Education. The new law (Ley 27 1946) for the renamed prize continued to associate literature with the national good. Article 1 proclaimed that 'la cultura es el más alto exponente de la elevación intelectual de un pueblo' (culture is the greatest symbol of the intellectual elevation of a people). Article 2 reaffirmed the duty of state institutions to promote 'las actividades intelectuales de la Nación' (the intellectual activities of the Nation). The law also stipulated that the jury would henceforth take charge of the competition 'adaptándolo a las necesidades culturales de la Nación' (adapting it to the cultural needs of the Nation). The jury was thus given some discretion but, in 1949, when they exercised these powers, the prize became the focal point for debates about the definition of literature, which texts were worthy of specifically literary prestige, and which would best contribute to the consolidation of modern Panama.

One juror, Baltazar Isaza Calderón, who, until the previous year, had been dean of the faculty of philosophy, literature and education at the recently created University of Panama, wrote about his experiences of the 1949 controversy in an essay entitled 'Sobre el concurso literario Ricardo Miró' (About the Ricardo Miró Literary Contest) (1957). The first part is dated 28 July 1949 and responds to criticisms in the press about the proposal to remove sociology as a category for submissions. The decision was made on the grounds that sociology was a scientific discipline unrelated to literature (Isaza 1957, 109). Such texts were not sufficiently unique to Panama and therefore not useful to the nation-building goals of the prize. The definition of 'literature' was at stake, but this was no obscure scholarly debate. Failure to properly support literature, now understood as predominantly fictional writing, was presented as a risk to the nation and its international standing as Panama, Isaza wrote, 'anda a la zaga de otros del continente en materia de desarrollo artístico' (is behind other Spanish American countries in terms of artistic development) (1957, 109). The perceived threat was all the more real because the prize had shown the potential to develop a national literature which would become a source of national pride. The judges, in Isaza's view, had acted to safeguard it by excluding sociological texts. Those speaking against the decision were effectively cast as unpatriotic.

In the second part of the essay, dated 30 July 1949, Isaza addressed another change to the prize categories which had proven to be even more controversial than the exclusion of sociological texts. The organizing committee had proposed a new category called 'Leyendas Nacionales' (National Legends). 'National Legends' was the term used to refer to texts which had roots in oral traditions of indigenous populations. In retrospect this was a very successful initiative. The texts submitted in this category over the years were subsequently gathered together and published by Sergio González Ruiz in 1953 in an edition that has been frequently reprinted. Isaza's defence of the decision to recognize National Legends as literature was based on an understanding of literature and the prize as tools of nation-building. Isaza said that the 'inexplorado filón de la tradición que atesoran nuestros grupos indígenas' (unexplored vein of tradition that our indigenous groups hold dear)' is likely to hold 'una riqueza solo a medias sospechada' (a richness of which we are only partly aware) (1957, 111). His comments reveal that the National Legends category was intended to gather indigenous literary heritage as part of a rich cultural tradition to which modern Panama could lay claim.

One objection to the National Legends category was that it represented a retrograde step not appropriate for a forward-looking nation. According to this racist view, the country's indigenous past had no place in modern Panama which should be the proper focus of prizewinning texts. Isaza believed, however, that the legends provided a bedrock of originality on which to build the nation. Culture, he wrote, was a great leveller, but it also 'tiende fatalmente a uniformar' (fatally tends to make everything the same) (1957, 112). National legends were a safeguard against this cultural homogenization because 'delata lo que tenemos de esencialmente propio y constituye la auténtica reserva de esa alma antigua que no quiere morir' (they reveal what we have that is essentially ours and constitute the authentic reserve of this ancient soul that does not want to die) (1957, 112). Isaza's concern with finding something uniquely Panamanian echoes earlier concerns of nineteenth-century Spanish American intellectuals who, faced with the problem of having a common language with their former colonizers and their newly independent neighbouring countries, looked to foster national literature as a means of differentiating themselves. By recognizing the legends that were unique to Panama, the Premio Literario Ricardo Miró would be similarly useful in enhancing a sense of national identity.

In further service to the nation, Isaza argued, the National Legends category would help to integrate those peripheral communities, which were seen as the main source of these legends, into the nation and raise awareness of Panama's unique past among urban populations who were at risk of losing their sense of identity. The committee was concerned by the 'creciente desprendimiento que el cosmopolitismo y el progreso técnico implican' (growing detachment, caused by cosmopolitanism and technical progress) among urban populations (Isaza 1957, 113). The traditions of the remote villages would be preserved as an anchor to modern Panama but, Isaza left no doubt, rural communities should be taught basic hygiene and be introduced to 'los adelantos técnicos modernos' (modern technical advances) (1957, 113). In a familiar story of attitudes to indigenous populations in Spanish America in the mid-twentieth century, the prize sought to build the nation based on the appropriation of the indigenous past and the assimilation of indigenous people into modernity. The specific connection seen here between indigenous legends and national literary prestige, however, was far from the norm. More typical was the awarding of the first Premio Nacional de Literatura (National Prize for Literature) in Mexico in 1935 to the *indigenista* novel *El indio* by Gregorio López y Fuentes.[5] However, the manner in which the Panamanian state used literary prestige in the form of prizes for nation-building was typical and occurred throughout Spanish America in the twentieth century.

In 1968 a coup installed a military junta in Panama. Shortly thereafter, the law governing national prizes was amended in ways which speak to a desire to exercise greater control over the award and reflect the challenges of developing a national literature. This law was published in the *Gaceta Oficial* on 19 October 1970. The proposed changes were said to be needed to enhance the 'beneficios para la cultura nacional' (benefits for national culture) (Decreto 332 1970). Henceforth, the prize would be divided into the following categories: novel, short story, poetry, theatre and essay.

The importance of quality was now emphasized in the legal text. The winning text would be the work the juries chose as 'la mejor' (the best) of those presented in each category. The assumption that the choice of the best work is an objective rather than a subjective judgement is implicit in all prizes, but here it became explicit. The law further sought to guarantee the quality of the winning texts by making only a single award in each category. The prize would now consist of 2,000 balboas, a gold medal and a parchment. A document on the website of the present-day Instituto Nacional de Cultura

---

[5]For a discussion of this award and the surrounding politics, see Bowskill (2011), chapter 1.

(National Institute for Culture) shows that the full range of awards was seldom made in the early decades of the prize.[6] The poetry award had been the most successful as the three medals were regularly awarded in this category. Very often the silver or bronze medal went unallocated especially in the essay and novel competitions in the first decade of the prize. The inability to produce works worthy of recognition was seen as reflecting poorly on the nation although recognizing lesser works also posed a threat. For this reason, the law was changed.

Clearly anticipating the concerns of the junta, in an essay dated 1956 and entitled 'La Entrega de Premios Del Concurso Ricardo Miró' (The awarding of the prizes of the Ricardo Miró contest), Isaza had already considered the challenges Panama faced in developing a national literature of sufficient quality and quantity. In line with the actual trajectory of the prize, he wrote that poetry was often the first genre to develop but other genres 'llevan una marcha más lenta, requieren mayor madurez y enriquecimiento espiritual' (take longer and required greater maturity and spiritual enrichment) (Isaza 1957, 121). He was, nevertheless, optimistic that the novels that had been recognized to date showed promise, and he believed that authors would continue to improve provided that the competition continued and was not diluted, as was being threatened at the time of writing, by the possibility of the prize being opened up to the arts more broadly (Isaza 1957, 123). Panamanian literature, it seemed, needed time and the valuable support of the prize to become a true source of national pride.

Even so, Isaza was not blind to the perceived risk that the prize could damage, rather than enhance, the nation's status if not enough entries of a sufficient quality were received or if the prizes were seen to go to lesser works. In this vein, Isaza concluded his 1956 essay reflecting on the dilemma faced by the judges. The prize was established with nation-building in mind and so, he warned, the selection process must be rigorous: 'el Concurso Miró ha sido instituido con la finalidad patriótica de estimular el desenvolvimiento de las letras nacionales, esa finalidad ha de cumplirla a través de un proceso de selección cada vez más exigente' (the Miró contest was established with the patriotic aim of stimulating the development of national literature, this goal must be accomplished by means of an increasingly demanding selection process) (Isaza 1957, 125). The jury must not be too lenient simply to foster the nascent literary tradition by applying 'un criterio de benevolencia' (a benevolent criteria) (Isaza 1957, 125). Such a practice would only lead to an inferior literary

---

[6]See the document 'Premio Literario Ricardo Miró 1942–2008' produced by the Instituto Nacional de Cultura (http://bdigital.binal.ac.pa/bdp/descarga.php?f=artpma/ConcursoMiro.pdf). In some cases, it seems that the official record is incomplete, but there are nevertheless numerous instances where the result is recorded as 'desierto', that is, a conscious decision was made not to make an award.

tradition 'que no resistiría una mediana comparación con las que crecen en otros pueblos del continente' (which would not stand up to even an average comparison with that [tradition] which is growing in other countries of the continent) (Isaza 1957, 125). The honour of the country was at stake and to betray it with poor judgement would not satisfy 'nuestro orgullo ni colmar los anhelos de nuestro patriotismo' (our pride nor fulfil the yearnings of our patriotism) (Isaza 1957, 125). Interlinked as literature and nation-building were, the prize held out the promise of enhancing Panama's status on the international stage and creating a literary tradition which would be a source of pride. Yet the situation was precarious, and the fate of both literature and the nation was in the hands of the judges.

The military junta ended in 1990, but similar concerns persist in Panama today. In 2002 the name of the prize changed to the Concurso Nacional de Literatura Ricardo Miró (Ricardo Miró National Literary Contest) reinforcing the link between literature and nation-building. In 2003 prizes were not awarded in two categories. In 2014, echoing earlier concerns about quality, the jury decided that none of the works submitted were worthy candidates and declined to name a winner. Debates over what should be done played out in the national press (Caballero 2003; Lewis 2014). The preferred solution in 2014 was to criticize the jury for being ill qualified to judge. As previously noted, such criticism is unusual in Spanish America when it comes to state-sponsored awards but was effective in this case because it saved both authors and the state from embarrassment. There may be new governments and new names for the prize, but old concerns remain when it comes to using literary prestige for nation-building.

The Chilean Premio Nacional de Literatura, like the Premio Annual Ricardo Miró, was established in 1942. The Chilean prize was created following a campaign by the Sociedad de Escritores (Writers' Society) seeking to provide financial support for struggling authors.[7] In 1972 Salvador Allende's government passed a generous new law providing a lifetime pension for the winner in addition to the prize money. This law (Ley 17595 8 January 1972) was very much in keeping with the original aims of the prize to provide financial support for authors whose work contributed to national pride but for whom writing fiction did not provide a viable income. At this time, however, the prize also went from an annual to a biannual award following complaints from right-wing politicians that it was always a struggle to find recipients as Chile did not have so many worthy writers (Faúndez Morán 2016, 216). The anxiety seen in Panama that the nation's reputation would be damaged if lesser authors were given

---

[7]Chapter 1 of Faúndez Morán (2016) provides an in-depth history of the circumstances which led to the creation of the prize.

such a prestigious award is evident again here even though by this point Chile had two Nobel laureates in literature.

The Pinochet dictatorship which succeeded Allende saw the rapid introduction of a series of amendments to the laws governing all of the national prizes. Changes to the Premio Nacional de Literatura were designed to ensure that the government had a tighter control over the outcomes of the prize and that it aligned with their new vision for the nation. Despite, or perhaps because of, the efforts of the regime, controversy was common as the prize, like all state-sponsored prizes, created a space for dialogue between the state and authors. In this period, the national prize for literature became a rallying point for dissenting voices to challenge the authority and legitimacy of the regime.

Decree 681 was passed in October 1974. It included a prefacing statement regarding the purpose of the prize for literature and amended the criteria for the award introducing ideas around value, excellence and morality for the first time just as the Panamanian Junta had done. These were the ideals the regime wished to promote by associating them with literary prestige. The prize for literature would be for a 'escritor chileno cuya obra, por su excelencia, lo haga acreedor a dicha distinción' (Chilean author whose work, for its excellence, makes him worthy of this distinction) (Decree 681 1974). Literary excellence alone, however, would not suffice. Article 1 declared 'es necesario reconocer los valores en el campo de las actividades creadoras de la cultura y la ciencia' (it is necessary to recognize values in the field of creative endeavours in culture and science). Article 2 stated: 'es conveniente exaltar dichos valores mediante el otorgamiento de galardones que incentiven el cultivo de las artes y ciencias' (it is expedient to exalt said values through the awarding of prizes that incentivize the cultivation of the arts and sciences). The decision of the jury 'deberá ser fundado, destacando los méritos intelectuales y morales de los agraciados y la trascendencia de su obra' (must be grounded in and highlight the intellectual and moral merits of the winner and the transcendence of their work) (Decree 681 1974). This criterion allowed the government to cast dissenting authors and their work as immoral and effectively exclude them from the prize.

To ensure these new laws were enforced judging was brought under strict state supervision as has been typical of prizes under totalitarian regimes in Spanish America. The competition was, from 1974, presided over by the minister of education who had the deciding vote and could effectively veto any candidate. Winners now also had to be nominated by certain institutions, three or more past winners, or literature departments in specified universities. Most of those eligible to propose candidates were reliant on the state for their positions. The law thus effectively circumscribed those individuals and institutions with the authority to bestow literary prestige.

Eight awards were made during the dictatorship as the junta tried to put literary prestige into the service of the new regime.[8] Clearly aware of the risks of the prize becoming a focal point for political dissent, the first award in 1974 went to 81-year-old Sandy Zañartu. He was selected because 'su obra y su vida no constituían ninguna amenaza contra el nuevo orden' (his work and his life constituted no threat to the new order) (Moure Rojas 'Todo comenzó' 2020). Pablo Faúndez Morán likens the award to Zañartu to that for children's author Marcela Paz in 1982. In both cases, he argues, the prizes associated cultural value with 'una ideología militarista y moralmente conservadora' (a militaristic and morally conservative ideology') (2016, 218). The awards in 1980, 1984 and 1988 to Roque Esteban Scarpa, Braulio Arenas and Eduardo Anguita also rewarded ideological conservatism. While not excessively controversial because of the authors' literary credentials, the decisions had a clear political bent.

Scarpa had been removed from his role as Director of the National Library under the Allende government and was reinstated following the coup (Freudenthal 1985, 90). The national prize publicly vindicated Scarpa and marked a break with the past. Braulio Arenas went from 'un allendismo visceral antes de 1973, hasta un pinochetismo convencido y militante, luego del Golpe de Estado' (being a visceral Allende supporter before 1973 to a convinced and militant Pinochet supporter after the coup) (Moure Rojas 'Braulio Arenas' 2020). His willingness to change allegiances was rewarded and sent a clear message to those who may have been inclined to follow. On the award to Anguita, Edmundo Moure Rojas writes that there was 'un consenso transversal en lo relativo a la calidad creativa de su obra, pese a su declarada adhesión personal hacia las ideas de la derecha política' (a cross-cutting consensus regarding the quality of his work, despite his open personal adhesion to the ideas of the political right) ('Eduardo Anguita' 2020). If authors were deemed to have made a sufficient contribution to literature, they, and the award, were shielded from scandal as authors across the political spectrum strategically prioritized the illusion that literary value was paramount.

When the literary credentials of the recipient were in doubt a pretext was created which allowed those who did not recognize the state's authority in the field of literature or politics to dissent and scandal ensued. A number of awards were made in this period to writers with limited connections to literature. These awards were controversial because they seemed to negate completely the value of literature in favour of political agenda that many authors opposed. In 1976, the winner, Arturo Alduante Phillips, was an

---

[8]For a full account of how these awards played out in the media both in this period and throughout the prize's history, see Faúndez Morán (2016). See also the excellent series of articles by Moure Rojas (2020) and Gómez Bravo (2005).

engineer and the official citation emphasized his contributions to science and Chile's international reputation: 'ha sido acreedor a distinciones de indudable relieve para su Patria' (he has been worthy of distinctions of indisputable importance for his Fatherland) (quoted in Moure Rojas 'En 1976' 2020). Moure Rojas describes Alduante Phillips as a '[e]scritor sin contaminaciones de literatura social ni de sesgos sospechosos. En él no se dio la imagen del escritor deprimido, contestatrio y menesteroso' (writer not contaminated by associations with social literature nor with suspect positions. In him you did not find the image of the depressed, rebellious and needy author) (Moure Rojas 'En 1976' 2020). With so many writers dissenting and in exile, in recognizing Alduante Phillips the government used the prize to project an alternative image of the author as one who served his country and was not socially engaged.

Perhaps struggling to find authors they deemed suitable or those willing to accept the award from the regime, the trend for giving the prize to men whose main achievements lay outside the field of literature continued in 1978. Rodolfo Oroz, who won the award that year, was, first and foremost, an expert in linguistics. The award was all the more scandalous because he was the sitting president of the Academia Chilena (Chilean Academy) which had nominated him. The debate, on the surface, was about cronyism but in fact gave opponents of the government cover to air their concerns about the regime without directly confronting it (Faúndez Morán 2016, 236). The prize, which once affirmed an alliance between authors and the state, now provided a space for expressing dissent at a time when opportunities to do so were severely limited.

The final major scandal of the Pinochet years was the awarding of the prize to Enrique Campos Menéndez in 1986. Again, political motivations were perceived to overshadow literary considerations but more importantly many objected to Campos Menéndez's politics. Campos Menéndez's career calls to mind that of the nineteenth-century statesmen-writers. He was a novelist working in the diplomatic service and foreign office and when he won the Premio Nacional he was the serving Chilean ambassador in Spain. The fact Campos Menéndez claimed that the Pinochet regime was democratic in remarks when the award was announced, and that the exiled José Donoso was the main challenger for the prize, only served to aggravate the sense of outrage.[9] As will be seen in Chapter 3, Miguel Ángel Asturias was a serving ambassador when he won the Nobel Prize for Literature without this fact causing controversy. The problem with Campos Menéndez's award was not that the prize went to someone employed by the regime or that literary merit was secondary, but the prize provided a platform for opponents to air larger political grievances.

---

[9] For Campos Menéndez's full remarks on winning the prize, see Faúndez Morán (2016, 256–7).

Following the Campos Menéndez scandal, the law governing Chile's national prizes was changed again in 1986 further increasing state oversight of the award. Writers' representatives, whose presence was supposed to ensure the 'credibilidad y legitimidad' (credibility and legitimacy) of the prize, were removed (Faúndez Morán 2916, 262). These stipulations were, however, short lived as democracy was restored and new laws governing the prize introduced. The speed of change again demonstrates the importance Spanish American states attach to national prizes for literature as tools for establishing a pact with authors who can then be called upon as public intellectuals lending tacit or explicit endorsement to the regime and its values or even expressing dissent which enables the state to demonstrate its democratic credentials in contrast to earlier totalitarian regimes which only recognized those whose values aligned with their own.

The Pinochet dictatorship ended in March 1990, and, by 24 January 1991, a process had begun to create eleven new national prizes including one for literature. The new Law 19169 passed in 1992 stipulated that, in a given year, only five or six of the eleven prizes would be awarded on an alternating basis. The prizes still aimed to achieve nation-building through cultural prestige, and so Article 1 stated that the prizes should go to those Chileans who 'por su excelencia, creatividad, aporte trascendente a la cultura nacional y al Desarrollo de dichos campos de saber y de las artes, se hagan acreedores a estos galardones' (for their excellence, creativity, transcendental contribution to national culture and the development of these fields of knowledge and the arts, make themselves worthy of these awards). New, democratic values were reflected in the greater freedom given to the jury. Article 9 set out the jurors who would be responsible for each prize and reinstated the writers' representative in the person of the previous winner of the prize. The composition of the juries was amended again in 2017 to allow even greater autonomy. The Ministry for Education would oversee procedures, but jurors were no longer obliged to submit any reports justifying their selections. The jury had to consider: 'los méritos intelectuales de los agraciados y la trascendencia de su obra' (the intellectual merits of the winner and the transcendence of their work) (Article 16), but the moral criterion was removed creating the appearance of a prize based purely on literary merit. As will be seen in Chapter 3, ideas of transcendence associated with universal literature have come, through prizes such as the Nobel Prize for Literature, to be associated with liberal democratic values and for this reason were enshrined in the new Chilean awards. In the years after the dictatorship, as happened in Panama, the awards for the Chilean Premio Nacional de Literatura went to those authors, including Donoso, who had opposed Pinochet and been forced into exile representing a restoration of the pact between authors and the state and a break with the past.

Lest we think of the link between literary prizes, nation-building and the role of the public intellectual as unusual or a thing of the past, many Spanish American countries have used the inauguration of national literary prizes to mark more recent transitions to democracy. The Premio Nacional de Literatura de Uruguay (Uruguayan National Prize for Literature) was established in 1986 after the dictatorship ended in 1984. The Guatemalan Premio Nacional de Literatura Miguel Ángel Asturias (Miguel Ángel de Asturias National Prize for Literature) was established in 1988 after the Peace Accords of 1986. In 1990, following the end of the Stroessner dictatorship, Paraguay created its own Premio Nacional de Literatura y Ciencia (National Prize for Literature and Science). The first article of Paraguayan Law 97/90 declares that the intention of the legislation is to stimulate literary creation in order to 'promover la cultura en el país' (promote culture in the country) thus following the established pattern of connecting literature and nation. The link is cemented by the coming together of authors and the state as the law stipulates that the prize will be awarded by the president 'en nombre del pueblo paraguayo' (in the name of the people of Paraguay). In Paraguay, as is common in post-dictatorship contexts, the prize has been used to recognize authors who returned from political exile turning it into a symbol of reconciliation and recompense. These and other awards have led to accusations that the prize consistently 'responde más a cuestiones extraliterarias y vinculadas al proceso de democratización que a valores literarios más o menos reconocibles (responds more to extraliterary matters and those tied to the process of democratization than to more or less recognisable literary values) (Benisz 2020). Again, we see the importance of achieving a balance between literature and politics and that it may be beneficial if literary values appear paramount while political impact may be best achieved through the authors' speeches.

Scandal engulfed the Paraguayan prize in 2017 when the state initially refused to recognize an author writing in Guaraní as the winner despite having previously approved Guaraní as an official language therefore making entries in that language eligible for consideration. Indeed, alongside the creation of the Paraguayan national prize, the new government had also recognized Guaraní as an official language. In 2017 Guaraní author Susy Delgado won the prize. However, she only received it four months after it had been announced and did so at a private event at which the president, in contravention of the law, was not present. The actions of the government were, not surprisingly, interpreted as a snub ('González Delvalle' 2018). The president's refusal to meet his obligation was interpreted as a rejection of the multicultural, multilingual state envisaged by the prize statutes. The national prize for literature in Paraguay, as happened in Panama and Chile, thus became the site of negotiation over who should be part of the nation.

Brokering international relations with state-sponsored prizes

Literary prizes proved such effective political tools for nation-building that some Spanish American states have also used them to broker international relations. Again, the prizes were created to address moments of transition and crisis. In the immediate aftermath of the Cuban Revolution the cultural institute, Casa de las Américas, was established and with it a number of literary awards open to authors writing in Spanish regardless of nationality. The first prizes were for novels, poetry, drama, short story and essays. In the 1970s the categories of *testimonio* and children's literature were added, and the awards expanded to include Brazilian authors, those from the English-speaking West Indies and the French-speaking Caribbean. Initially, the prizes, like the Revolution itself, were enthusiastically embraced by authors from across the continent. The prizes were outward looking and aimed to consolidate the Cuban government's position in the face of US opposition to its communist politics. As Pamela Smorkaloff writes, '[a]ll of the Latin American governments, with the exception of Mexico, had severed relations with the island, thus the extreme importance of keeping a range of channels and mechanisms for international exchange open' (1997, 131). In this context, the prizes took the place of official diplomatic channels with prizewinning authors acting as ambassadors and go-betweens for Cuba and the rest of the region.

The link between the Casa de las Américas prizes and politics was well established, and so later when some Spanish American authors wished to express dissatisfaction with the Castro regime following the Padilla Affair, the awards fell out of favour. Supporters of the regime, meanwhile, expressed ongoing solidarity through their continued participation in the prizes.[10] In 1968, Cuban Heriberto Padilla's poetry collection *Fuera del juego* won the Premio Julián del Casal awarded by the Unión de Escritores y Artistas de Cuba (Union of Cuban Artists and Writers). The organization initially refused to honour the decision of the jury because of the 'contenido ideológico del libro de poemas' (ideological content of the poetry collection) ('Declaración de la UNEAC' 15 November 1968). Ultimately, the text was published with the proviso that the Union's declaration denouncing the work was included in the published editions. In 1971, following a speech to the Union in which he criticized the Castro regime, Padilla was arrested. In response authors from across Spanish America, including the now internationally famous authors of the Boom Carlos Fuentes, Mario Vargas Llosa and Julio Cortázar, as well as others from outside Spanish America, wrote in protest. Padilla

---

[10]For detailed discussion of the Padilla Affair, see Weiss (1977) and Abreu Arcia (2007).

recanted, many assumed under duress, and was released, but the damage to Cuba's reputation and the Casa de las Américas prizes had been done.

As authors became disillusioned with the Cuban Revolution, the Premio Rómulo Gallegos, established in Venezuela in 1964, emerged as a beacon for Spanish American democracy until it too went into crisis at the turn of the twentieth century. The Premio Rómulo Gallegos was intended to act as a 'contrapeso' (counterweight) to the Cuban awards by curbing the influence of the Casa de las Américas and communism in the region (Guerrero 2015). Anadeli Bencomo reports that, shortly before the first Premio Rómulo Gallegos was awarded, Venezuela had submitted a complaint against Cuba to the Organization of American States (2006, 766). The timing of the new prize was, therefore, no coincidence as Venezuela sought to diminish Cuba's political power by reducing the prominence of the Cuban prizes and thence Cuba's influence over Spanish American intellectuals. In this context, the choice of Mario Vargas Llosa as the first winner in 1967 was particularly astute. Vargas Llosa, as the 1962 winner of the Premio Biblioteca Breve discussed in Chapters 2 and 5, was at the forefront of the Boom which brought Spanish American authors to the attention of readers around the world. He was also, at the time, an ardent supporter of the Castro regime. At the award ceremony Simón Alberto Consalvi, president of the Venezuelan Instituto Nacional de Cultura y Bellas Artes (National Institute for Culture and Fine Arts), underscored that this award was made on literary merit without consideration of the author's politics (Bencomo 2006, 766). In so doing, the Premio Rómulo Gallegos tried to set itself apart from the overtly politicized Casa de las Américas prizes (Bencomo 2006, 766). This tradition of consecrating authors regardless of political beliefs as a way of underscoring the difference between the Premio Rómulo Gallegos and the Cuban awards continued as Venezuelan editor of the French publishing house Gallimard Gustavo Guerrero wrote in 2005 that the Premio Rómulo Gallegos used to recognize 'conservadores, marxistas o socialdemócratas, aquellos representaban, año tras año, un vivo e impecable ejemplo de pluralismo y diversidad' (conservatives, Marxists and social democrats, who represented year after year a living and impeccable example of pluralism and diversity) (2005 n.p). Of course, the award was simply making another kind of political statement.

In accepting state-sponsored prizes authors may make speeches criticizing the awarding administration or its values. Such a move can actually reflect well on the state because it is seen to be tolerant and to allow dissent and thus to be democratic. Thus, when Vargas Llosa was awarded the Premio Rómulo Gallegos and declared his freedom as an artist and his support for Cuba, he actually served the purposes of the organizers well. In his speech, entitled 'La literatura es fuego' (Literature is fire), Vargas Llosa said that although states were now trying to 'conferirle [al escritor] una especie de estatuo oficial' (confer [on the author] a kind of official status), they must be warned that 'la literatura es fuego, que ella significa inconformismo y rebelión, que la razón del ser del escritor es la protesta, la contradicción y la crítica' (literature is fire, that it represents non-conformity and rebellion and that the raison d'être of the writer is protest, contradiction and criticism) (1986, 134). He went on to fulfil the role of dissenting author to perfection by expressing his wish that all Spanish American countries would become like Cuba. In Venezuela, as later in Panama and Chile, democracy was increasingly associated with authors who had greater independence from the state as opposed to the earlier author-statesmen. Authors who continued to speak out, as Vargas Llosa did, thus became almost more beneficial to the state's democratic agenda than those who simply endorsed its values

In addition to challenging Cuban influence in the region, the Premio Rómulo Gallegos was intimately connected to Venezuela's nation-building goals. The prize sought to re-establish Venezuela's position as a democratic country on the international stage following a period of dictatorship. The Premio Rómulo Gallegos was created by President Raúl Leoni in 1964. Administration of the prize was placed in the hands of the newly created Centro de Estudios Latinoamericanos 'Rómulo Gallegos' (CELARG) which was akin to the Casa de las Américas. Naming the prize after the author turned politician and the first democratically elected president of Venezuela is indicative of the desire to use the prize to associate literary prestige with democratic values. Initially bestowed every five years, from 1991 the prize became biennial. The award is given to the author of the best text written within the given period. The prize is open to Spanish American, Spanish and Filipino authors but, as a rival to the Premio Casa de las Américas and its given role as a focal point for a debate on 'un modo de ser latinoamericano' (how to be Latin American), the majority of early winners were Spanish American (Bencomo 2006, 771). By 1989, any author writing in the Spanish language could compete regardless of nationality or country of residence. In a format similar to that used by the Nobel Prize for Literature and the Premio Cervantes, both discussed in Chapter 3, a central jury used to reach its decision based on the nominations received from relevant institutions across the Spanish-speaking world. This procedure made the prizes all the more effective in creating regional and international ties, a sense of a pan-Hispanic community, and the appearance of a democratic process. Information about the prize was disseminated to institutions via a substantial brochure, a copy of which I found in the Centro Nacional de Literatura archive in Mexico City ('Premio Internacional de Novela Rómulo Gallegos' 1982). In 1982 the cover bore a portrait of Gallegos and contained a detailed biography alongside the prize criteria reminding the nominating bodies of the ideal link between literature and politics embodied by the former president.

In 1982 the Premio Rómulo Gallegos offered the winner 100,000 bolívares which was the equivalent to US$22,223 at the time, a gold medal, and a certificate ('Premio Internacional de Novela Rómulo Gallegos' 1982). The awarding of prize money was another way to differentiate the Rómulo Gallegos from the Casa de las Américas prizes which offered publication but no financial recompense. The financial incentive was intended to 'assurer l'indépendance matérielle de l'écrivain pendant des années' (ensure the material independence of the author for years) (Delprat 2005, 233). The state-sponsored prize ironically wished to liberate authors from the need for further state subsidy or, more accurately, sought to ensure that they were indebted to the values of the Venezuelan state. The Instituto Nacional de Cultura y Bellas Artes (National Institute for Arts and Culture) in Venezuela reserved the right to publish 25,000 copies of the winning text. This large print run was an attempt to rival that offered by the Premio Casa de las Américas. It is not clear, however, if the Venezuelan government was in a position to make these books available for free as did the Casa de las Américas. The prize would be awarded on 2 August, the birthday of Gallegos, just as the Casa de las Américas prizes coincided with the anniversary of the Cuban Revolution, in both cases strengthening the link between the prizes, politics and the nation.

The list of early winners of the Premio Rómulo Gallegos reads like a who's who of Spanish American literature. In the first iterations of the prize the Boom authors dominated. Vargas Llosa won for *La casa verde* in 1967, Gabriel García Márquez won for *Cien años de soledad* in 1972 and Carlos Fuentes won for *Terra Nostra* in 1977. Their rising stars no doubt helped to lift the award and its associated institutions just as much as the prize served to consolidate their prestige. Today, barely a newspaper article is written about the prize that does not mention the names of these early winners reminding readers of the prize's illustrious heritage.

The Boom authors went on to become the jurors for the Premio Rómulo Gallegos as the winning author was appointed to lead the jury the next time it was awarded. In 1982, for example, Fuentes, fellow Boom author Julio Cortázar, and Carlos Barral, of the Seix Barral publishing house whose name was so associated with the Boom, all served on the jury. Winning authors thus acted as guarantors of the prize's ongoing significance and status. They were also more likely to favour works that were aesthetically similar and evidenced shared values. As will be seen in Chapters 5 and 7, the ability of a prize to consecrate a body of literature with common aesthetics and interests is one way in which literary prestige becomes associated with particular traditions and marginalization is perpetuated in the literary field.

By the turn of the twentieth century, Venezuelan politics had changed dramatically and the Premio Rómulo Gallegos became a battleground for competing visions of the nation.[11] Scandal is now commonplace. Having

---

[11] For a history of the prize between 1967 and 2003 see Bencomo (2006).

been at the forefront of rehabilitating the country's image as a modern democracy, the prize was indelibly linked to politics. President Hugo Chávez (1999–2013), however, wished to leave behind the liberal democratic politics with which the prize was associated. To this end under Chávez: '[o]ld elites and system beneficiaries were replaced by new actors and constituencies with different interests, cultures, and priorities' (Buxton 2011, x). Some of the cultural institutions associated with the previous government were closed, others subject to closer control and others still sidelined through the creation of parallel institutions. In 2008 CELARG, the institution responsible for organizing the Premio Rómulo Gallegos, was brought under the auspices of the Ministerio del Poder Popular para la Cultura (Ministry of Popular Power for Culture) which had been established in 2005 (Decreto 6.414 la Gaceta No. 39.037. 14 October 2008). CELARG retained responsibility for the prize, but neither it nor the prize was in keeping with the new regime's cultural politics and so both have been gradually sidelined and replaced even though such moves have led to the prize becoming a site for wider debates about the place of literature in present-day Venezuela.

Whereas literature had enjoyed special status as seen, for example, in the way it was invoked for the purposes of nation-building through national prizes for literature, in contemporary Venezuela, literature has been replaced by other forms of cultural production. The 1999 Venezuelan Constitution thus stated: '[t]he folk cultures comprising the national identity of Venezuela enjoy special attention' (Article 100 of the 1999 Constitution). This focus on popular culture continued under President Nicolás Maduro (2013–) who introduced the Ley Orgánica de Cultura (Law of Culture) in 2014 which 'defines Venezuelan culture in restrictive and traditionalist terms as "cultures that create nationhood" (indigenous, afro-descendant, popular, rural and urban creole cultures)' (Kozak Rovero 2019, 27). The only reference to literature in this law was to that written in Patua, the creole language of Venezuela, which is identified as part of Afro-Venezuelan heritage (Article 3.18). There was no reference to CELARG or to the Premio Rómulo Gallegos.

As the rejection of elite culture has seen the Premio Rómulo Gallegos fall out of favour, the government has established other prizes which are more in tune with its new popular agenda. These awards expand the prize network making alternative positions in the literary field available and viable and reflecting new political positions and agendas. The Premio Nacional del Libro de Venezuela (Venezuelan National Book Prize) was created in 2002. This biannual prize is almost the antithesis of the Rómulo Gallegos as it is aimed at 'aquellas instituciones, agrupaciones, páginas web, blogs, autores y autoras, editoriales y programas de radio o televisión que hayan contribuido significativamente con la producción, promoción y difusión del libro y la lectura' (those institutions, associations, web pages, blogs, authors, publishers, radio and television programmes that have significantly contributed to the production, promotion and distribution of books and reading) ('República Bolivariana de Venezuela. Ministerio. Informe de Gestión' 2014, 62). The government's support for literacy over literature and popular culture over elite culture is reflected in the prize once again demonstrating the link between political agenda, prizes and literary prestige.

The problem, however, was not just that the Premio Rómulo Gallegos represented elite culture when the new regime wished to promote popular culture, but that the Premio Rómulo Gallegos was tied to a rejection of Cuba and communism at a time when Venezuela was aligning itself with the Castro regime and Marxist politics. For this reason, two further new prizes were created. In 2005 the Ministry for Culture announced the creation of the Premio Internacional de Poesía Víctor Valera Mora (Víctor Valera Mora International Poetry Prize). This award was for a poetry collection published that year. It was endowed with the same prize money as the Premio Rómulo Gallegos and, like the Premio Rómulo Gallegos, was open to anyone writing in Spanish. Another prize that has emerged as a competitor to the Rómulo Gallegos is the Premio Internacional de Novela Monte Ávila Editores (Monte Ávila Publishers International Novel Prize). This prize is also connected to the Ministry for Culture and the state-funded publisher Monte Ávila. In 2020, the fourth edition of the prize offered the winner 40,000 euros (nearly US$50,000) and publication. It too was open to authors of any nationality writing in Spanish. Given that the Premio Rómulo Gallegos has been beset by financial problems, it is hard to disagree with Tulio Hernández's assessment in *El Nacional*, a Venezuelan newspaper that has been consistently critical of the regime, that the government is trying to sabotage the Rómulo Gallegos prize through the creation of other international literary prizes (2016). The political motivations are clear. By undermining the Premio Rómulo Gallegos, the government seeks to set a new national agenda, present itself as an ally and not a rival to Cuba and distance itself from the past.

Despite the state prioritizing popular culture and establishing competing awards, the twenty-first-century trajectory of the Premio Rómulo Gallegos is not straightforward. The long history and international reputation of the prize have doubtless contributed to its survival. The status of the prize may be such that cancelling it would be too damaging to the government. A managed decline seems to have been a favoured approach. Against this backdrop of new rivals and unfavourable cultural policy, the Premio Rómulo Gallegos has become a battleground within a highly polarized intellectual community.

One strategy that seems designed to undermine the Premio Rómulo Gallegos has been to threaten to withdraw funds. Since Chávez took office there have been constant financial threats to the prize which, critics claim, damage the country's international reputation. Authors who oppose the regime have sought to protect the award because it secures for them potential income, prestige and the role of public intellectuals relevant to the nation's future but, perhaps more importantly, because it is a symbol of a different Venezuela to which they wish to return. Since 2001, the Premio Planeta awarded by the Spanish publisher Planeta has also overtaken the Premio Rómulo Gallegos in terms of prize money. The Premio Rómulo Gallegos had derived some status from being the best-endowed award for literature in Spanish, a fact mentioned in almost all press coverage prior to 2001, and so the failure of the Venezuelan government to maintain the prize money is an indication of how it is not a priority and it is even using the award to demonstrate its break with the past. At the prize ceremony in 2001 juror Sergio Ramírez advocated for the financial future of the prize to be guaranteed ('Venezuela-Literatura' 2001 and 'Enrique Vila-Matas defiende' 2001). Financial problems continued to plague the award as payments to judges and the winner were severely delayed in 2003 ('Retrasan pago' 2001). Venezuela's economic situation at this time was more precarious so, while detractors may have seen the delay as deliberate sabotage, it is possible that it was the result of genuine economic difficulties. Whereas oil prices had been high in the early years of the prize, under Chávez they were falling. An attempted coup, general strike and the exodus of foreign capital had destabilized the economy. Viewed in the broader context in which new awards were funded, however, the financial difficulties encountered by the prize and CELARG look to have been strategically inflicted or at least the result of official indifference as their priorities lay elsewhere.

Problems with payments have not been restricted to the Chávez regime. Pablo Montoya, winner in 2015, had not received his prize money by January 2016 ('Ni impaciente'). In 2017 the situation had deteriorated to the extent that the prize was cancelled. Writing in *El País* former winner Enrique Vila-Matas noted that 'para muchos es una prueba más de la destrucción del área pública que gestiona el arte y la cultura en Venezuela' (for many it is another proof of the destruction of the public sphere which manages art and culture in Venezuela) (2017). The official line was that the cancellation was due to budget cuts and would only be temporary (DPA Caracas 2017). In 2020 the prize was restored, but Rodrigo Blanco Calderón (quoted in EFE 2020) argues that the restoration was also politically motivated as if to say 'que una especie de normalidad ha regresado a Venezuela' (that a kind of normality has returned to Venezuela) following a period in which the United Nations had denounced human rights abuses, Venezuela had been subject to international sanctions, people had gone into exile and opposition was repressed. In the controversies surrounding the late and non-payments the nation and the state's international reputation is brought into play by its opponents wishing to shame the government into meeting its commitments. The government, in response, has claimed that its detractors are using the prize to undermine it. At the same time, the state diverts resources to initiatives that are more in line with its alternative vision for the nation. At stake are competing views of the nation, national pride and Venezuela's status in the international arena.

In the eyes of the government, elite authors are no longer useful for building the kind of nation they wish to create. This breakdown of relations between (some) authors and the state became visible when, from 2001, Chávez ceased attending the Premio Rómulo Gallegos prize ceremony. The president's presence maximizes the political significance of the award and its literary prestige. Chávez's absence, like that of the Paraguayan president discussed earlier in the chapter, was, unsurprisingly, seen as a snub to the prize and the community of authors that value the Premio Rómulo Gallegos and the type of literature it consecrates. This impression was compounded by his reported remarks about the winning novel. An article in *El Nacional* reported that

> no solo ha dejado plantado al ganador, el novelista Enrique Vila-Matas, sino que reemplazó el protocolario discurso del anfitrión con un disciplente y chocarrero comentario transmitido de viva voz al ganador por boca del ministro de Educacion, Cultura y Deportes: 'Te manda a decir Chávez que lo excuses porque anda muy ocupado y que esa novela te quedó del carajo' (not only has he left the winner, the novelist Enrique Vila-Matas, in the lurch, he also replaced the customary speech by the host with a distasteful and vulgar comment spoken out loud to the winner by the Minister for Education, Culture and Sport: 'Chávez says to ask you to excuse him because he's very busy and this novel was rubbish'). (quoted in Mora 2003)

Chávez never attended the ceremony throughout his time in office. His place was taken by another, more junior, official. The state was still represented, but the honour of receiving the award from the president was withheld thus diminishing the prize's profile and prestige.

Another strategy the Venezuelan regime has employed to reduce the importance of the Premio Rómulo Gallegos in the literary field and cut the ties between the award, nation-building and the brokering of international ties has been to replace nominations by sister institutions from across Spanish America with nominations by publishers. This strategy has led to recent winners being those already published by major houses such as Alfaguara (Bencomo 2006, 773–4). In 2001 CELARG president Rigoberto Lanz expressed concern about this new role for publishing houses saying that the prize had become 'un regalo para las casas editoriales' (a present for the publishing houses) which would prioritize sales over all else ('Enrique Vila-Matas gana' 2001). These changes to the nominations process threaten the international bonds between CELARG and other cultural institutions across the Spanish-speaking world who had been responsible for nominating authors for the consideration of the jury. As will be seen in the final chapter and briefly in Chapter 2, public–private partnerships are one of the latest trends in the prize network reflecting the neoliberal turn in Spanish America. This case is different. Instead of private companies sponsoring prizes administered by the state and offering the opportunity for authors to publish with a publisher with access to many markets, the Premio Rómulo Gallegos is now essentially awarded by the publishers to their own pre-existing product and so is, in effect, free marketing at the state's expense. Authors are left to fend for themselves as they are no longer wanted as the public intellectuals of the new regime. Independence in this context is difficult to reconcile with Bourdieu's conceptualization of the ideal position of the author in relation to politics.

In addition to financial problems, jury scandals have become a feature in the debates surrounding the prize post 2000. Unlike in Anglophone contexts though the accusations revolve around judges prioritizing politics over literary value rather than around accusations of cronyism and flawed literary judgements. In 2005 little-known Spanish author Isaac Rosa won the Premio Rómulo Gallegos and the prominent Mexican critic Christopher Domínguez Michael wrote an article entitled 'El fin de un premio literario' (The End of a Literary Prize) (2005). Domínguez Michael, who had previously been caught up in a non-payment scandal when he was a juror, wrote that the prize 'destacaba no solo por la calidad canónica de los galardonados, sino por la pluralidad estética e ideológica de los jurados que lo otorgaban' (used to stand out not only for the canonical quality of its winners but also for the aesthetic and ideological plurality of the jurors who made the award) (2005). In 2005, however, Domínguez Michael scathingly claimed that the jurors were all 'de rancia obediencia revolucionaria'(of long-standing revolutionary obedience) and that '[l]a misión del jurado [. . .] fue premiar en Rosa a un amiguete español de la dictadura cubana y un cuadro bien dispuesto a pasearse en procesión revolucionaria por las ruinas de Venezuela, bailando al son del teniente coronel que Castro tiene como deseadísimo sucesor' (the mission of the jury [. . .] in nominating Rosa was to give the prize to a little Spanish friend of the Cuban dictatorship and a person who was well disposed to walk in revolutionary parades through the ruins of Venezuela, dancing to the song of the lieutenant colonel who Castro has appointed as his much desired successor) (2005). The fact that Fernando Vallejo, the winner the year before, had caused a scandal by criticizing Fidel Castro in his acceptance speech and was not on the jury, as was customary, lends some credence to these claims. The problem, Domínguez Michael continued, was not Rosa's beliefs, since true democracy tolerates all beliefs, but the fact that his victory signalled the end of 'una institución literaria cuya liberalidad honraba al mundo de habla hispana' (a literary institution whose liberalism was an honour to the Spanish-speaking world) (2005). Liberal values are presented as politically neutral and associated literary prestige, but what is really at stake in this controversy is a struggle between two political ideologies.

The perception that the Premio Rómulo Gallegos is now destined for supporters of the regime has led some Venezuelan authors to boycott the prize and to call for others to do likewise. Calls for a boycott are based on the understanding that, although the prize is ostensibly a literary award, because it is awarded by the state, acceptance implies a tacit endorsement. Michelle Roche Rodríguez in *El Nacional* reported that five Venezuelan authors withdrew in 2009. That year, Venezuelan author Ana Teresa Torres also declined to be a juror (Rivero 2009). In 2013 Roche Rodríguez in *El Nacional* claimed that more and more Venezuelan authors were refusing to have their works submitted (Rodríguez 2013). In 2020, in response to criticisms from CELARG that authors were politicizing the prize, an article, printed in *El Universal*, rightly declared '[e]ste premio nació, pues, politizado' ([t]his prize was born politicized) ('Denuncian campana' 2020). Moreover, the authors' claim that they had the right to politicize the prize, but the organizers should not provides an insight into the perceived rules of the game whereby the authors are the ones who should define the politics of the award they are accepting. In many ways, the function of acceptance speeches could be to fulfil this purpose. That year, Argentine author Perla Suez was widely criticized for accepting the award. She naively denied that her participation represented an endorsement of the government as the press clearly interpreted acceptance of the award as approval of the regime ('La escritora Argentina' 2020). As Katie Brown concludes, '[w]hat emerges from these debates is that, regardless of whether juries are making decisions based on politics or not, it has become impossible to separate the literary field from politics in public opinion' (2019, 444). The future of the prize remains uncertain. The state has oscillated between trying to put an end to the Premio Rómulo Gallegos, attempting to sever the ties between the prize and the state and using it to recognize authors who are aligned with its values. The changes to the prize and resulting scandals have made the politics of the award more visible but, as with other state-sponsored awards for literature in Spanish America, it was born political.

Conclusions

Laws which created state-sponsored prizes make plain the politics of literary prestige. State-sponsored national prizes call on authors to contribute to nation-building. Prizes offered by states to authors from Spanish America or the Spanish-speaking world have similarly been used to foster international relations and set a political agenda for the region. An examination of the laws which created these awards reveals how Spanish American states understood their purpose and sought to harness literary prestige to serve political agenda. Early debates focused on how literature could be best harnessed for the good of the nation, what kinds of literature promoted nation-building, and how to establish the nation's reputation as modern and democratic. Disavowal of the exchange between symbolic and political capital, understood as specifically the kind of power wielded by politicians and institutions of the state, has been strategically beneficial for democratic states, but that does not make the exchange any less real. For publisher-run prizes, which will be discussed in the next chapter, the transaction between politics and prestige may be further concealed and disavowed, but it is ever present. In periods of crisis and transition, when authors wished to express dissent, these prizes, already imbued with political significance, became battlegrounds on which the struggle for the nation played out. Regime change, for example as a result of military coups, consistently results in the laws governing prizes being changed. Spanish America's totalitarian regimes have been all too aware of the symbolic and political power of the awards and the potential threat they represent as they open up a space for dialogue between the state and authors acting as public intellectuals. Once they have created a platform for authors to act as public intellectuals, states struggle to take it away when it suits them. Backlash against state-sponsored prizes usually claims that the award is motivated by politics rather than literature as if this were not always the case. After all, democratic regimes do not tend to give awards to fascist authors.

2

Peninsular publishers, Spanish American authors and prizes for literature in Spanish

From the 1940s onwards prizes funded by publishing houses and open to authors writing in Spanish regardless of nationality became a significant feature of the Spanish American literary landscape. In the 1950s two Argentine publishers, Emecé Editores and Editorial Losada, launched the Premio Emecé (1954) and the Premio Losada de Novela (1958). Other publisher-run prizes originated in Spain, among them the Premio Biblioteca Breve (1958) and the Premio Planeta (1952), and later the Premio Herralde (1983), and the Premio Alfaguara (1968). Commercial imperatives were, and remain, key as publishing houses vie for market dominance, but politics are also in play.

The nation-building politics of state-sponsored prizes are more immediately apparent, but we must also recognize the politics, understood as specifically political endowments, of literary prestige when it comes to publisher-run prizes. These prizes were part of the battle between Francoist Spain and its opponents who rejected the ideology and isolationism of the regime. Contemporary publisher-run prizes are tied to the politics of globalization with its centres of power rooted in Europe and the United States. Today, the major publisher-run prizes for literature in Spanish in terms of prize money, number of entries and their potential to reach audiences across national boundaries are those which originated in Spain. Even though the old publishing houses and the prizes they established are no longer Spanish-owned, their reputations and the resulting prestige are tied to the peninsular. The structures of the contemporary publishing industry and prizes for literature in Spanish contribute to an increasingly interconnected, transnational Spanish-speaking literary field that is nevertheless rooted in

Spain and in established hierarchies and networks of prestige that stretch back to colonial times. The rewards for Spanish American winners of such prizes are significant, but the prestige attached to them is no less politically charged than when it comes to state-sponsored awards even if it is better concealed.

This chapter locates early publisher-run prizes on both sides of the Atlantic within the context of the commercial struggle for control of the Spanish American book trade and the struggle against Franco and fascism. It uses papers from the archive of Spanish publisher Carlos Barral of the publishing house Seix Barral to understand events from the publisher's perspective. The second part of the chapter shows that the struggle for market share continues when it comes to the major publisher-run prizes for literature in Spanish today. The frequency with which some of these prizes go to Spanish American authors is striking. The press coverage of statements by Alfaguara employees reveals the way in which the publisher associates these prizes with a globalized literature in Spanish. The experience of Siglo XXI Editores in Mexico suggests that Spanish American–based publishers have notably less success in establishing major awards as many Spanish American authors opt for awards which promise access to European networks of prestige. The final part of the chapter looks at how publisher-run prizes have led to changes in the role of the author in contemporary society suggesting that, in contrast with state-run prizes, these awards prioritize the visibility of authors over their role as public intellectuals. Again, drawing on Barral's archive it shows how the Premio Biblioteca Breve was already positioning the Boom authors as celebrities. Today, the publishers aggressively promote the author as a celebrity through book tours, via their YouTube channels and other social media. Spanish American authors, however, are still prone to be called upon to perform the well-established role of the postcolonial author as spokesperson or interpreter who can explain Spanish America to a foreign audience.

Publisher-run prizes and the struggle against fascism

The Premio Emecé was the first of its kind in Argentina followed shortly after by the Premio Losada de Novela. From a commercial point of view, the prizes were a way to kick-start the catalogues of these new publishing ventures with the publishers having the option to publish not only the winning text but other quality submissions as well. Losada in particular was also committed to using the prize as a political tool and both publishers had strong ties to Spanish exiles and republicanism. Sent to Argentina by peninsular publisher Espasa-Calpe, the founder of Editorial Losada,

Gonzalo Losada, split with his former employer over political differences (Fuster 2016, 4). His new venture 'dio forma a un catálogo con un fuerte componente ético y político, en el que predominaban de forma muy clara los autores de ideología republicana y liberal' (gave rise to a catalogue with a strong ethical and political component, in which liberal republican authors very clearly dominated) (Fuster 2016, 4). The political underpinnings of the Losada catalogue were such that for a long time it was banned under Franco (Fuster 2016, 4). In terms of their complexity and innovative style and technique the books recognized by the prize had much in common with the Boom novels which positioned Spanish American authors at the forefront of contemporary literature in Spanish, but they were more determinedly politically engaged (Larraz 2016, 68). In Fernando Larraz's assessment politics was always the overriding concern for the prize (2016, 68). The official history of the publishing house, available on their website,[1] boasts that the Premio Losada was open to 'todo el mundo hispanohablante' (all the Spanish-speaking world) (41). The prize's open criteria, an invitation to authors in the Spanish-speaking world to reject the isolationism of the Franco regime, as well as the prizewinning texts selected, reflected Losada's politics.

The founding of Editorial Losada was part of a wider shift as the centre of gravity of the hispanophone publishing industry moved from Spain to Mexico City and Buenos Aires. Republican exiles brought their expertise to Spanish America and came to occupy key roles in existing publishing houses and founded new ones including Emecé and Sudamericana in Argentina and Joaquín Mortiz in Mexico. This change provoked concern among peninsular publishers and the Franco regime whose commercial and economic goals sometimes aligned where their politics did not. To help peninsular publishers to compete with their Spanish American counterparts in Spain imports of books were restricted and the domestic book industry was given special status. A change in the law in Spain in 1966 also meant that censorship became less of an issue for those looking to export because 'many works by Latin American writers were authorized for printing as long as they were not distributed in Spain' (Herrera-Olaizola 2007, 3). As well as receiving government support and protection, peninsular publishers developed their own initiatives. At almost the same time as Editorial Losada founded its award in 1958 Carlos Barral of Barcelona-based publisher Seix Barral likewise looked to a literary prize to address both commercial and political concerns.

In 1959 Barral was among a group of authors, critics, translators and publishers who gathered at the Hotel Formentor on the island of Mallorca for the first Coloquio Internacional de Novela (International Colloquium

---

[1] http://www.editoriallosada.com/quienes-somos.

on the Novel). The colloquium culminated in a meeting to select the first winner of the Premio de Novela Biblioteca Breve awarded by Seix Barral. The criteria for this prize explicitly embraced ideas that went 'against the grain of officialist Spanish cultural politics' (Santana 2000, 141). The prize was therefore open to 'unpublished novels [written] in any of the romance languages used in the Iberian Peninsula and any of their American variants' (quoted in Santana 2000, 141). Barral's subversive politics in relation to peninsular regional identities, which were repressed by the Franco regime, and Spanish American linguistic variants, deemed a threat to the purity of the language by Franco's censors, were again evident when, following his split with Seix Barral, he founded Barral Editores and the Premio Barral de Novela in 1971 which also adopted open criteria.

A year after the first Premio Biblioteca Breve was awarded, a spirit of openness and international collaboration prevailed as Carlos Barral and a group of like-minded foreign publishers established two more prizes, the Prix Formentor and the Prix International des Éditeurs. In addition to Víctor Seix and Carlos Barral of Seix Barral, Claude Gallimard of Librairie Gallimard in France, Giulio Einaudi of the eponymous Italian publisher, Georges Weidenfeld of Weidenfeld and Nicolson of London, Heinrich Ledig-Rowohlt of Rowohlt-Verlag in Germany, and Barney Roset of Grove Press, New York, were all involved in the creation of the prizes. Such was the success of the endeavour and the two prizes that, over time, publishers in other countries including Portugal, Sweden, Denmark, Oslo, Canada, Holland, Finland and Japan joined the group. The Prix International was to be awarded to an imaginative work published in the last three years in any language by an author of any nationality. In 1961 the first Prix International des Éditeurs was won jointly by Samuel Beckett and Argentine author Jorge Luis Borges. The Prix Formentor was for an unpublished work, and the winning text would be published simultaneously by each of the publishing houses involved. The ethos of these awards and the thinking beyond national borders they embodied reflected a post-Second-World-War internationalism and the belief that a shared literary culture would contribute to the spread of democracy. The same spirit informed the creation, in 1948, of the UNESCO Collection of Representative Works which 'was intended to foster cross-cultural understanding and help the bases of lasting world peace' (Brouillette 2019, 21). In this sense the connection between Barral's prizes and post-war politics was not unusual but, in his case, of course, there was the added commercial dimension.

Doubtless the collaboration was commercially advantageous to Seix Barral as Spanish American publishing houses had emerged as serious competitors for the rights to publish foreign works in Spanish, but Barral's motivations were not purely commercial. Ideologically, he saw the prizes as a means to combat Spain's isolationism and to contribute to the creation of a shared culture in Europe and the Spanish-speaking world which would act as protection from extremist politics. Barral was concerned that Spain, communist Eastern European countries and, to a lesser extent, Portugal were being separated from 'la actualidad literaria internacional' (the international literary present) to their own detriment ('La experiencia que un editor literario' 1962). The Prix International and the Prix Formentor both had the potential to help reconnect these countries with the literary present and thence to the political mainstream. Looking back at the first few years of the prizes, Barral wrote with considerable pride that reports in the Spanish and foreign press had commented on the 'inmensas repercusiones' (immense repercussions) the prizes could have (Text sense titol incl. 'Los años 1959 y 1960' 1962). Specifically, the prizes were said to be able to contribute 'a la progresiva internacionalización de la cultura occidental' (to the progressive internationalization of Western culture) (Text sense titol incl. 'Los años 1959 y 1960' 1962). In the context in which Barral was writing the phrase 'internationalization of western culture', while redolent of a Eurocentric and even colonial outlook, speaks to a rejection of repressive, isolationist regimes as exemplified by Spain at the time.

The Franco regime seems to have been keenly aware of the political implications of Barral's activities and sought to curb them. The threat of censorship loomed large for Barral. In his report on the 1959 and 1960 awards he bemoaned the fact that, despite regularly sending information to the Spanish press, articles about the Prix Formentor were censored (Text sense titol incl. 'Los años 1959 y 1960' 1962). In 1962 Barral wrote of his belief that there was 'consigna oficial de que Formentor sea totalmente ignorada por la prensa española' (an official decree that Formentor should be completely ignored by the Spanish press) (Text sense titol incl. 'Michel Mohrt y' 1962). The government denied these allegations, but journalists confirmed to Barral that they had their reports censored following submission (Text sense titol incl. 'Los años 1959 y 1960' 1962). Barral's notes from that year further suggest that three policemen were spying on the colloquium (Text sense titol incl. 'Michel Mohrt y' 1962). Earlier reports referred to the presence of four civil servants from the Dirección de Seguridad (Directorate General for Security) in the hotel (Text sense titol, incl. 'Los años 1959 y 1960' 1962). In addition, some of the foreign publishers encountered difficulties in securing visas from the Spanish government to allow them to attend. Such interference meant that, in later years, when the group was forced to relocate its annual meeting outside Spain, Barral was unable to attend as he was refused permission by Spanish authorities who would not validate his passport ('Protesta Intelectuales' 1965). Faced with the denial of Barral's visa to travel to meetings of the prize committee the other publishers proposed placing articles hostile to Spain in their national press (Text sense titol, incl 'Michel Mohrt y' 1962). It is not clear if they carried out their threat, but they certainly did not succeed in securing permission for Barral to travel. Nevertheless, the spirit of international solidarity and cooperation in the face of isolationist and repressive regimes that the prizes sought to foster was alive and well among its creators.

Political dissidence brought commercial risk. Censors could withhold permission to publish the prizewinning texts that Barral had committed to publish under the terms of the Prix Formentor. If the winning text was written in a language not accepted by the censors, then the financial risk to Seix Barral was even greater as a translation had to be commissioned in order for it to be submitted to the censors ('La experiencia' 1962). In 1962 Barral described how he had been able to overcome some difficulties with the censors thanks to a letter signed by all of the publishers involved in the Formentor prize (Text sense titol, incl 'Michel Mohrt y' 1962). Ultimately, Barral's commercial goals were sufficiently aligned with those of the Franco regime that he became 'the most important publisher in Spanish in this century' (Saval 2005, 206). He did not, however, shy away from using literary prizes to further an opposing political agenda.

The hierarchies of contemporary global literature in Spanish

The collaboration Barral organized between major publishing houses from around the world in some ways anticipated the contemporary publishing context even as the politics underpinning these relationships have changed significantly. Barral perceived that there was a 'convergencia de culturas nacionales' (convergence of national cultures) which he believed made propositions such as the Prix International and the Prix Formentor viable ('La experiencia' 1962). Equally, the prizes helped to consolidate the sense of shared culture which he believed was necessary for the spread of democracy and future peace. Today, international cooperation has been replaced by a culture of mergers and takeovers. The result is a Spanish-language publishing context that is increasingly concentrated in the hands of a few publishing houses with historical roots in Spain but now part of larger conglomerates and owned by companies elsewhere in Europe. These companies seek to harness the literary prestige of Spanish American authors, through prizes, for profit, but the politics underpinning the awards are the same as those that create unequal relationships within the context of globalization.

Towards the end of the twentieth century, as the founders of independent Spanish and Spanish American publishing houses retired, they often sold their businesses to larger publishing houses looking to expand and find new markets. The result in the Spanish-speaking context was the same as that described by John B. Thomspon with reference to the Anglophone world

> where there had once been dozens of independent publishing houses, each reflecting the idiosyncratic tastes and styles of their owners and

editors, there were now five or six large corporations, each operating as an umbrella organization for numerous imprints, many of which still bore the names of previously independent houses that were now part of a larger organization, operating with varying degrees of autonomy depending on the strategies and policies of the corporate owners. (2010, 102)

Prizes created by the original publishing houses were usually retained and sometimes revived, but the politics that underpinned them changed within their new context. The size of these businesses enables them to offer significant prize money, the guarantee of simultaneous publication across the Spanish-speaking world and in the United States as well as enhanced possibilities for authors to have their works translated into other languages. As the prizes continue to be open to authors across Spain and Spanish America, they still contribute to a sense of a shared culture, but it is one that is increasingly deterritorialized and makes strategic use of nationality or regional identity only where it is expedient for marketing purposes.

Today, there are five major publisher-run prizes for literature in Spanish all of which have their roots in peninsular publishing and have shown varying degrees of interest in recognizing Spanish American authors. They are the Premio Planeta, the Premio Nadal, the Premio Biblioteca Breve, the Premio Herralde and the Premio Alfaguara. The Grupo Planeta, one of the major publishing and media groups in the Spanish-speaking world, is behind the first three of these awards. These prizes are now associated with peninsular letters and seldom recognize Spanish American authors. Only seven Spanish American authors have received the Premio Planeta since it was established in 1952. First awarded in 1944, only five Spanish American authors have won the Premio Nadal.

Even the Premio Biblioteca Breve, the prestige of which derived from its association with the Boom in Spanish American literature quickly turned away from Spanish American authors when it was revived in 1999. In 1982 Grupo Planeta had bought Seix Barral, and in 1999 literary director Basilio Baltasar decided to mark the twenty-fifth anniversary of the Premio Biblioteca Breve by reinstating it. The Spanish press diverged in their understanding of the reasons behind the revival. Some saw it as directed at recognizing the new generation of up-and-coming Spanish American authors and others as a celebration of Spain's literary heritage as the prize originated there (Ullerhaus 2020, 36). These apparently diverging interpretations were, however, somewhat consistent with Barral's original vision of the prize as being connected to the preservation of both the Spanish publishing industry and Spain's position at the forefront of recognizing new trends in Hispanic literature. The prize's association with Barral's values was, however, lost and so too was its position in relation to Spanish American literature.

In the early years, the resurrected prize seemed to pick up where its earlier incarnation had left off with the choice of Mexican Jorge Volpi as the first winner suggesting that the prize was on a path to consecrating on the international stage the new 'crack' generation, of which Volpi was part, just as it had contributed to the earlier consecration of the Boom authors. The award to Volpi marked a watershed moment which allowed Spanish American literature to move on from the Boom in the eyes of international readers (Sánchez Prado 2018, 102–4). Longer term, the Premio Biblioteca Breve did not pursue its interest in the 'crack' authors. Nor did it pick up on the contemporaneous McOndo movement. In the first few years it did favour younger Spanish American authors but soon shifted focus to more established figures before turning away from Spanish American authors altogether. Since 2011 no Spanish American author has won the Premio Biblioteca Breve.

One reason Spanish American authors may be increasingly overlooked by the Premio Bibliteca Breve is because prizes are no longer a significant part of Grupo Planeta's strategy in attracting and marketing Spanish American authors of literary fiction. Instead, their approach in the region is based on taking over prestigious Spanish American publishers. They have acquired Joaquín Mortiz and Editorial Diana in Mexico and Emecé in Argentina. In 1992 Joaquín Mortiz and Planeta established the Premio Planeta-Joaquín Mortiz. Joaquín Mortiz was in a strong position to confer prestige in the form of a literary prize. In his excellent 1996 study of the publishing house Danny J. Anderson observed that 'the joint prize aims for public visibility and strategically exploits Joaquín Mortiz's cultural authority as an arbiter of value' (27). In the event, the prize was not a success and was short-lived. Perhaps fearing overlap with the revived Premio Biblioteca Breve, the Premio Joaquín Mortiz was awarded for the last time in 2001 with no winner having been declared for the previous two years. In 2006 when Planeta bought Editorial Diana, they showed no inclination to revive the Premio Literario Internacional de Novela *Novedades*-Diana that ran between 1986 and 1992. After Argentine Emecé Editores was bought by Planeta in 2000 the Premio Emecé similarly appears to have lapsed from 2012 onwards.

Another reason why Spanish American authors are no longer associated with the Premio Biblioteca Breve could be because, in Spanish American eyes, the prestige of the Premio Planeta, and by extension other prizes run by Grupo Planeta, may have become especially tainted. Preselection processes whereby jurors are only presented with shortlisted titles are common to many contemporary awards and not just those run by Grupo Planeta. Spanish critic Jorge Carrión has suggested that, in some cases, preselection can be done in such a way as to sway the jury in a certain direction (reported in Mattio 2020). An experienced juror also told Fernando González Ariza that publishers typically only give jurors copies of the shortlisted books and a list of titles and pseudonyms of the remaining entries which the jury can request to read if they wish (2004, 33–4). In 2005, however, this system broke down as Spanish novelist Juan Marsé resigned from the jury of the Premio Planeta because he was not permitted to see details of all of the submissions (Mattio 2020). That year Argentine author Gustavo Nielsen also won a legal case against Planeta after he had been a finalist in the 1997 contest but lost out to Ricardo Piglia. The judgement declared that there was a 'predisposición del premio en favor de la novela de Piglia' (predisposition of the prize in favour of Piglia's novel) because the author's book was already under contract with Planeta ('Nielsen: el juicio "fue una cuestión de honor"' 2005). These causes célèbres have given credence to misgivings about publisher-run prizes that revolve around the extent to which the prizes, while seeming to be open to new talent, are in fact closed shops. These awards boast of attracting thousands of entries per year, but they are seldom won by unknown authors. The judges typically already have some connection to the publisher rather than being truly independent, and the prizes tend to recognize authors who have previously published with the sponsoring publisher.

In contrast with prizes run by the Grupo Planeta, the two other major prizes for literature in Spanish, the Premio Herralde, offered by Anagrama, and the Premio Alfaguara, run by Alfaguara Editorial are today frequently won by Spanish American authors. The result is that much of the symbolic and economic profits from the work of contemporary Spanish American authors continue to be located in Europe and associated with Spain. Spanish American authors who wish to access these prizes and international prestige have to produce fiction and present themselves in ways that meet the demands of this market. The prizes value literary bestsellers and middlebrow fiction and are crucial in the publishers' efforts to boost sales and to attract authors. Since the turn of the twenty-first century, these two publishers and their prizes have been competing to become heirs to Seix Barral and the Premio Biblioteca Breve. Locane (2017, 103) and Bencomo (2006, 16) suggest that Anagrama and the Premio Herralde are winning this battle.

Both publishers originated in Spain and have historical political ties to the left which they try to balance with commercial imperatives (Locane 2017, 103). Anagrama was founded by Jorge Herralde in 1969 but was sold to the Italian publishing and media company Grupo Feltrinelli in 2010. The choice to sell to the group founded by a left-wing activist associated with the historically prestigious Italian publishing house, Giangiacomo Feltrinelli Editore, as opposed to a larger conglomerate, is indicative of Herralde's values. Anagrama initially focused on publishing essays and established the Premio Anagrama de Ensayo (Anagrama Essay Prize) to develop its catalogue. From the 1980s, however, Anagrama began to develop its fictional lines. One line focused on literature in translation and the other on literature in Spanish. The Premio Herralde, established in 1983, was intended to support the latter. In the first decade the prize was associated with peninsular literature, but, from the turn of the century, Anagrama began to develop its interests in the Spanish American market.

Prior to 2003, there were only three Spanish American winners of the Premio Herralde, but in the period 2003–20 eleven Spanish American authors have won. Most have been from Mexico or Argentina. The average age of the Spanish American winners in this timeframe was forty-four. They were not first-time novelists, had often previously published with Anagrama and had usually won other prizes earlier in their careers. Several were named in the Bogotá 39 list of 'outstanding writers under 40' which was published by the UK-based Hay Festival in 2007 when Bogotá was World Book Capital. The list, available on their website,[2] was revised in 2017. Inclusion in the 2007 list gave the authors significant visibility leading to invitations to participate in events as part of the World Book Capital year and to attend Hay Festivals around the world and perhaps bolstering their chances of winning awards. Only two Spanish American women have won the Premio Herralde which has a poor track record in recognizing women authors that, as will be seen in Chapter 6, is as typical as it is disappointing.

The Premio Alfaguara first ran between 1968 and 1972, and Carlos Droguett, in 1970, was the only Spanish American winner in this period. In 1980 Alfaguara was bought by another peninsular publishing group Grupo Santillana as it sought to expand into fiction. At the same time, the director, Juan Cruz, reoriented the Alfaguara catalogue to focus on Spanish American literature (Sánchez 2008, 123). Alfaguara signed and bought up the back catalogues of Boom authors. Uruguayan Juan Carlos Onetti's *Cuando ya no importe* (1993) was published simultaneously in Spain and the Americas (Palacios Goya 1997). This project 'Alfaguara Global' (Global Alfaguara) was launched and at the ceremony announcing the creation of the Premio Alfaguara Cruz declared, 'lanzamos la idea de globalizar la publicación en lengua castellana' (we are launching the idea of globalizing publishing in the Castillian language) (quoted in Ramos 1997).[3] He continued: 'los escritores que publican en este sello "son de un país y de un lugar, pero son también, y sobre todo, patrimonio irrenunciable de una cultura variada y única"' (the writers who publish with this imprint 'are of one country and one place, but they are also, and above all, the enduring heritage of a varied and unique culture') (quoted in Ramos 1997). Cruz's global strategy has been referred to as the 'alfaguarización' (alfaguarization) of Spanish American literature.[4] This somewhat disparaging term alludes to the homogenization of narrative caused by authors seeking to be part of this phenomenon and readers who want more of the same. Of course, it is also a reference to Alfaguara's dominance and colonization of Spanish American literature.

---

[2] https://www.hayfestival.com/bogota39/home.
[3] For a discussion of the 'Alfaguara Global' project and its website, see Pohl (2001, 271–4).
[4] The term was first used by Víctor Barrera (2002).

Under Santillana, and in keeping with the new direction inaugurated by Cruz, the Premio Alfaguara was relaunched in 1998 just a year before Planeta revived the Premio Biblioteca Breve. In 2000 Santillana was bought by the PRISA media group who own Spanish newspaper *El País* before being sold again in 2014 to Penguin Random House now belonging to German media group Bertelsmann. The type of symbiosis between publisher-run prizes and newspapers, seen while Alfaguara was owned by PRISA, has longstanding roots stretching back at least to the creation of the Premio Lanz Duret by *El Universal* in Mexico in the 1940s. It was also evident in the Editorial Diana collaboration with *Novedades* for the Premio Internacional de Novela *Novedades*-Diana and today as seen in Argentina's contemporary Premio Clarín and the eponymous newspaper. The way these prizes position authors may differ from other publisher-run prizes because it is potentially more useful to the newspapers to recognize authors who can contribute to editorials, for example, as public intellectuals. In the case of Spanish American winners of the Premio Alfaguara they were often already writing in *El País* acting as spokespeople as will be discussed later in the chapter.

Since its relaunch in 1998, and in keeping with the 'Alfaguara Global' strategy, the Premio Alfaguara, like the Premio Herralde, has shown a strong propensity to recognize Spanish American authors. An incredible twenty out of the twenty-five winners have been Spanish American. The author profile is similar to that of the Premio Herralde. Most authors are from Mexico or Argentina. The average age of the Spanish American winners is forty, many have previously published with Alfaguara, this is not their first literary prize and several were named in the Bogotá 39 lists. Five Spanish American women have received the award.

The success of the Premio Alfaguara in attracting Spanish American authors can be measured not only in terms of the number of Spanish American winners but also with reference to the number of submissions. In 1998 the prize received 602 submissions of which 257 were from Spain, 115 from Argentina, 52 from Mexico, 31 from Colombia, 24 from Venezuela, 22 from Chile and 21 from Peru ('Carlos Fuentes anunciará . . .' 1998). Other entries came from an additional eleven countries ('Carlos Fuentes anunciará . . .' 1998). In 1999 435 submissions were from Spanish America compared to just 185 from Spain ('620 obras compiten' 1999). The Alfaguara press release rightly described this number as 'sin precedente' (unprecedented) (quoted in 'Mañana se da a conocer . . .' 1999).

Alfaguara's commitment to the concept of 'Alfaguara Global' and a global literature in Spanish was such that the new prize was announced simultaneously in Mexico City and Madrid in a move that at least nodded to decentring the old colonial relationship. The plan was for the result to be announced every year in a different country starting with Spain, then Mexico and Argentina (Velázquez Yebra and Anabitarte 1997). Submissions would be accepted at the Alfaguara offices in Spain, Mexico, Argentina and

Colombia (Velázquez Yebra and Anabitarte 1997). Today this fact may not seem so significant, but submissions were in hard copy and postage could be expensive and unreliable. Alfaguara were doing all they could to both advertise and make this prize accessible to Spanish American authors. The award promised publication in 16 Spanish-speaking countries, including the United States, and an average print run of 2,000 copies as well as US$175,000 prize money (Abelleyra 1997). The judges would come from both sides of the Atlantic and so offered Spanish American authors additional opportunities to enhance their status and profile.

The theme of a global literature in Spanish featured prominently at the launch event. Patricia Velázquez Yebra and Ana Anabitarte (1997) reported in Mexican newspaper *El Universal* that the official aim of the prize was to 'premiar la creación literaria en lengua española y ayudar a unificar las dos orillas para lograr que los textos sean universales' (recognize literary creativity in the Spanish language and help to unite the two sides so that the texts can become universal) (1997). Here, as we will see again in Chapter 3, universal literature is associated with prestige. In another Mexican newspaper, *La Jornada*, Angélica Abelleyra reported that Selatiel Alatriste, head of Alfaguara in Mexico, 'habló de este "premio global para una literatura global"' (spoke of this 'global prize for a global literature') (1997). This global literature prize, he said, would be 'un reconocimiento "en defensa de la lengua española"' (a recognition in defence of the Spanish language) (quoted in Abelleyra 1997). The same vocabulary was still being employed in 2020 and 2021 by Nuria Cabutí, CEO of Penguin Random House when the awarding of the prize was broadcast on the Penguin España YouTube channel. She said that one of the main aims of the prize was to 'conectar culturalmente todo el territorio de la lengua Española' (culturally connect all of the territories of the Spanish language) (2021) and referred to 'esta lengua que nos une' (this language which unites us) (2020). The statements by Alfaguara representatives in the press and now on social media portray an idealized view of the Premio Alfaguara and the 'Alfaguara Global' strategy implying a relationship of equals within the Spanish-speaking world, but this global literature is centred in a company based in Europe which is harnessing the symbolic and economic profits of Spanish American authors for its own benefit. While they offer the illusion of freedom from political agenda, the Premio Alfaguara and the Premio Herralde continue to associate Spanish American authors and literary prestige with Spain.

Alfaguara and Anagrama are no longer Spanish-owned companies, but the publishers and their respective prizes are tied to Spain. Like their spiritual precursor, the Premio Biblioteca Breve, these awards are in keeping with Spain's long-standing goal to retain the authority to consecrate literature in Spanish. In the words of Mario Santana, '[i]n various forms, both liberal and conservative (panhispanismo, hispanoamericanismo, iberoamericanismo), and particularly in the twentieth century, the ideal of a Spanish cultural tutelage over its former colonies has remained in theory a constant topic of foreign policy, even though in practice it has often been contradicted by an also persistent lack of action and initiative' (2000, 35–6). The Spanish state also continues to recognize the role played by privately owned publishers in securing a Spain-centred pan-Hispanic culture. Thus, in 1998, when the Premio Alfaguara went to the Nicaraguan author Sergio Ramírez, *El País* reported that the Minister for Education and Culture Esperanza Aguirre congratulated the publisher for providing an 'ejemplo de iniciativa privada al servicio de la cultura' (example of a private initiative in the service of culture) (Castilla and Mora 1998). In return for this service, Spanish publishers have recently sought to combat the growing influence of English-language fiction by seeking the support of the Spanish state in the creation of a 'mercado común del libro en lengua española' (common Spanish-language book market) (Gallego Cuiñas, 240). As happened with Seix Barral under Franco, state and private interests coincide when it comes to securing profits and prestige for Spain on the backs of Spanish American authors.

On the one hand, the transcultural, transnational pan-Hispanic identity created and envisaged by the Premio Alfaguara is a counter-discourse to 'una globalización entendida como aculturación anglosajona' (a globalization understood as Anglo-Saxon acculturation) (Pohl 2001, 275). It nevertheless remains a discourse of globalization rooted in Europe. The open criteria of the original Premio Biblioteca Breve spoke to the prize's inclusive and internationalist politics even as they also helped to further the goals of the Franco regime and Barral's commercial aims. The same prize criteria of the Premio Alfaguara and the Premio Herralde, now owned by major publishing conglomerates, in the latter twentieth century and early twenty-first century speak to a peninsular politics that still sees Spain as the locus for the consecration of all literatures in Spanish. Internationalism is based on reciprocal relationships. Globalization is not. In accepting the Premio Alfaguara or the Premio Herralde contemporary Spanish American authors, wittingly or otherwise, align themselves with the idea of a global literature in Spanish and a global culture and trade run by multinational corporations where profits, both symbolic and economic, more easily accrue outside Spanish America.

Just because these companies are now multinational, we cannot ignore '[t]he relationship between a worldwide, media-supported commercial culture and its imperial past' which is 'not direct, but still persists in an increasingly sublimated form' (Buell 1994, 293). Argentine author Ricardo Piglia certainly identifies with this perspective when he says '[e]n este momento la situación de las editoriales y de cierta tradición colonial de España en su manera de actuar con América Latina, pareciera que es España la que decide sobre la legitimidad de los escritores en América Latina, porque los premios más importantes están en España' ([a]t this moment with the situation of the publishing houses and a certain colonial tradition in Spain when it comes to its dealings with Latin America, it would seem that it is Spain that decides when it comes to the legitimacy of Latin American writers because the most important prizes are in Spain) ('Entrevista al autor argentino Ricardo Piglia . . .' 2013).

To view the relationships created between European-based publisher-run prizes and Spanish American authors as neo-colonial, however, may be overly simplistic. In particular, this view risks overlooking the benefits Spanish American authors derive from these prizes which lead to new opportunities for them within Spanish America. We might boldly claim, as José Manuel García-García does, that contemporary Spanish American authors are involved in 'una especie de retro-colonización (¿cáracter postcolonial?) en la que, regla no dicha, primero hay que publicar en España o ganarse algun premio de alguna valía, para luego venir a invertir en tierras mexicanas el místico valor de uso de ese prestigio acumulado' (a kind of retro-colonization (with a postcolonial character?) in which, the unspoken rule is that first you have to publish in Spain or win some kind of prize which has some value, to later come and invest in Mexican lands this accumulated prestige) (2002, 513). This optimistic assertion, however, overlooks the fact that the winners of the Premio Alfaguara and Herralde are already to some extent established. Indeed, as Sánchez Prado has noted, what these publishers often do is capitalize on the state's prior investment in these authors as many come through government-funded programmes for young writers (2018 *Pierre Bourdieu*, 205). The Spanish American recipients of the Premio Alfaguara and the Premio Herralde have also often already been integrated into the prize network at a national level, but the authority to recognize these authors in the wider, international network remains, at least symbolically, in Spain.

To understand the power dynamics created by publisher-run prizes we may alternatively turn to other concepts including the 'Hispanic Atlantic' proposed by Joseba Gabilondo (2001) or to Stephanie Dennison's suggestion, made in relation to Spain and Latin American film, that we view the relationship as symbiotic (2013, 7). Yet, Gabilondo acknowledges, '[i]n the end, global capitalism in its manifold organizations [. . .] lingers over the Atlantic as the ultimate horizon as the organizer of a new postnationalist and neoimperialist condition' (2001, 111). Sarah Brouillette similarly reminds us with reference to Anglophone postcolonial literatures that '[i]f "contemporary writing is produced in a postnational, global flow of deteritorialized cultural products appropriated, translated, and recirculated worldwide," as [Paul] Jay states, that "flow" is not untapped, but is instead checked by observable hierarchies' (2007, 58). Whichever way we look at it these prizes conceal and continue a legacy of unequal relationships.

The fact that hierarchies remain intact within an increasingly globalized culture explains why the success of multinationals based in Europe has not been matched by publishers in Spanish America. The Premio Internacional de Narrativa Siglo XXI-UNAM (International Prize for Narrative) was created in 2003. It was jointly sponsored by the Mexican National Autonomous University (UNAM) and the established publisher with a presence across Spanish America Siglo XXI. The prize sought to occupy a similar place in the prize network to the Premio Alfaguara and the Premio Herralde. The award targeted literary fiction, and the publisher and university were associated with left-wing politics.[5] The prize, when it was launched, consisted of US$20,000, compared to the US$175,000 and 600,000 euros then offered by the Premio Alfaguara and the Premio Planeta, and was, like these awards, open to all Spanish-speaking authors. The prize ceremony was to take place as part of the Feria Internacional de Libro de Minería (Minería International Book Festival) giving the prize and its winner greater visibility. Despite the reputations of both publisher and university, the submissions were far fewer than the hundreds received by the Alfaguara or Herralde. Forty-eight texts were submitted in 2008, 59 in 2011, 113 in 2014 and 43 in 2018.[6] The attraction of this award for Spanish American authors would seem to be substantially less than that of the Premio Herralde or Premio Alfaguara because these prizes have helped to consolidate the perception that the authority to consecrate Spanish American literature on the international stage must lie outside Spanish America.

Publisher prizes, the celebrity author and the author as spokesperson

Publisher-run prizes keep the mechanisms for creating literary prestige, and most economic profits, outside Spanish America using Spanish American literature in a way that is akin to the way in which raw materials are extracted from the region. They also create a different role for the author in society compared to national state-sponsored prizes and prizes for Spanish American literature based in the region. Publisher-run prizes are often seen as liberating the author to become a professional who, no longer beholden to state-funding, can be independent. As Bencomo notes, however, this attitude is anachronistic as the author, now dependent on the publisher, becomes 'un producto dispuesto a ser descubierto y explotado por el editor sagaz' (a product ready to be discovered and exploited by the astute publisher) (2006, 15). This product can be marketed through publicity in a process that Locane calls the 'espectacularización de la literatura' (turning of literature into spectacle) (2017, 101). The author goes from public intellectual in

---

[5]On the history of Siglo XXI and its ties to left-wing politics through its founder Arnaldo Orfila Reynal, see the entry in the *Enciclopedia de la literatura en México*: http://www.elem.mx/institucion/datos/1494.
[6]Statistics are taken from: 'Premian ensayo' (2008), Figueroa (2014) and Díaz (2018).

dialogue with the centres of power present at the awarding ceremony to being a visible commodity. The politics of prestige thus becomes entwined with the culture of celebrity.

The Premio Herralde and the Premio Alfaguara are literary awards of the kind Frank Wynne says, 'confer a degree of celebrity' (2016, 591). They are in contrast to 'commercial prizes' which 'merely tend to confirm pre-existing celebrity' (Wynne 2016, 591). The Premio Herralde and the Premio Alfaguara clearly position themselves as literary awards. At the Mexico City launch of the latter, Selatiel Alatriste insisted on this point. He said: 'estamos conscientes de que es preciso que la calidad se imponga en el mercado y no al revés' (we are aware that quality has to impose itself on the market and not the reverse), 'aquí lo que se califica es el oficio literario' (here what we mark is the literary craft) and 'premiaremos la calidad de una obra' (we will reward the quality of the work) (quoted in Ramos 1997). The Premio Biblioteca Breve and now its two successors have thus been pivotal in turning Spanish American authors into celebrities.

In their texts the Boom authors grappled with the changing role of the Spanish American writer who went from being narrator to author to superstar as they were confronted by 'the irresistible glamour of the superstar and the predominance of the image' (Franco 1999, 167). Barral and the Premio Biblioteca Breve were instrumental in bringing about this change in the status of Spanish American authors. From Barral's papers we can see that he was obsessed with securing press coverage of the events he organized at the Hotel Formentor. Meetings were open to the media and talks were recorded for a radio and television broadcast (Espinas 1959). In a less than modest report from 1961 Barral stated, 'Tanto la prensa nacional, ampliamente representada, como la radio, la televisión y el Nodo, así como la abundante prensa extranjera que había enviado corresponsales dieron amplia cuenta de lo acaecido en Formentor' (Both the national press, who were well represented, and radio, television and news and documentaries, as well as the abundant foreign press that had sent correspondents witnessed what happened in Formentor) (Text sense titol, incl 'Los años' 1962). In 1962 permission was granted for the director Pablo Runyanto to make a documentary about the meetings that year ('Agreements' 1962). Even the way the first winner was flown in at the last minute speaks to Barral's understanding of how to maximize publicity for the winning author and the prize.

Newspaper articles, many from the French press, which Barral preserved for his archive show how successfully he stage-managed events around the Premio Biblioteca Breve to produce maximum visibility and star appeal. Famous authors are pictured relaxing in swimming trunks and sipping drinks on the terrace in images that would not be out of place in a glossy magazine. Details were given of their trips to the beach, walks in the woods, the games they played and the food they ate. Henry Green, it was noted, drank wine at breakfast! Details of their outfits were described as many wore dinner jackets in the evening. Summaries of the literary debates that took place were offset by reports which emphasized the drama of multiple rounds of voting. The prizes thus capitalized on and helped to create the first generation of Spanish American literary celebrities.

For publisher-run prizes today, media coverage continues to be a priority. Instead of the author setting or at least negotiating the agenda through their acceptance speech, as in the case of the prizes discussed in Chapters 1 and 3, questions may be vetted in advance by the publisher; the interviewer steers the direction of the conversation and edits the piece according to their priorities. The homogeneity of reporting about these prizes suggests a strong reliance on press-briefing materials prepared and distributed by the publisher. Photographs of the author are commonplace and extracts from the text are rare. The successful contemporary author 'se ha convertido en una marca que se vende' (has become a brand to be sold) and is someone who promotes themselves and their work (Gallego Cuiñas 2018, 236). In modern publishing editorial policy and aesthetics have been replaced by communication strategies (Gallego Cuiñas 2018, 245). It is no coincidence then that, as Burkhard Pohl observes, the rules of the Premio Alfaguara stipulate that the author must commit to a promotional book tour (2001, 270). The importance of this requirement can be judged by the fact that Alfaguara only launched the work of Colombian author Fernando Vallejo after he reluctantly agreed to this condition (Pohl 2001, 270). These tours are extensive and gruelling with Spanish author Espido Freire, winner of the 1999 Planeta Prize, reporting that she gave up to sixteen interviews a day when she travelled to Latin America (Henseler 2013, 138). These events are not just significant for commercial reasons though. They shape expectations of how the role of the author will be performed in society. The result is that literary prestige is now increasingly equated with the kind of visibility that publisher-run prizes facilitate.

In recent years, the announcement of the Premio Alfaguara has been broadcast on the Penguin España YouTube channel maximizing the potential for publicity and the visibility of the author. The CEO of the Spanish-language section of Penguin Random House, as well as others who work for the publisher, are present alongside the members of the jury and past winners. The head juror describes the deliberation process and reads the decision revealing the name of the winner. The winner is then contacted via video-link to capture the emotion of the occasion and maximize the sense of spectacle. In 2021 Colombian author Pilar Quintana, who was identified as one of the Bogotá 39, won the prize. The jury took turns to say what they had appreciated about her book and to ask her questions. Journalists from across the Americas were then invited to pose their questions in keeping with the prize's agenda to reach audiences across the Spanish-speaking world. She did not deliver an acceptance speech.

The questions asked and the context suggest that the press was not given a copy of the unpublished manuscript. This event is more about the author than the text. Quintana was asked about her choice of pseudonym for her winning entry, her sources of inspiration and influence, the research she had done for the book, whether she found it difficult to write after her previously successful novel *La perra* (2017), and about the settings of her novels. The most political questions she was asked were about her position as a woman author and about motherhood, which was a theme in the novel. There were no questions which invited her to discuss politics beyond gender politics, but she was offered the chance to act as a representative of her gender. Her main role in this exchange was to be present as part of the show and to perform the role of the author divulging her craft.

In what seems to have been a first for Anagrama, the winners of the 2020 Premio Herralde were also presented live on Facebook and the broadcast posted to the publishers' YouTube channel. The event was introduced by Silvia Sesé of Anagrama. The winner, Spaniard Luisgé Martín, and the runner-up, Argentine Federico Falco, were interviewed by the journalist Lara Hermoso and questions were put to them that were sent in from the live online audience. The questions were in a similar vein to those put to Quintana with the difference that Hermoso had definitely read the prizewinning books in advance and so was able to ask some more detailed questions about the texts. The readers who submitted questions, of course, had no access to the books. The authors were asked about the autobiographical or autofictional aspects of their novels, about the settings for their novels, the writing process, their reasons for writing and their sources of inspiration. They were also invited to comment on sections of the texts. Overall, the roles Martín and Falco played in this exchange were the same as that of Quintana – to be visible and writerly with their packed bookshelves behind them on screen.

In the Premio Herralde prize ceremony, there was the briefest of moments when politics was introduced into the conversation, but Martín said it was not the right time for him to enter the debate about prostitution in Spain. There were no follow-up questions. Later in the interview Martín described himself as being very 'politizado' (politicized). Yet he did not present himself in this way in the context of this prize. Political debate was easily sidestepped illustrating the freedom authors have to negotiate their position when it comes to publisher-run prizes because their value to the awarding body comes from their visibility and not from their political endorsement as is the case for state-run awards. Winners of publisher-run prizes can expect fewer questions about their politics and are less likely to be pressed on the matter. This claim may be particularly true for peninsular writers such as Martín. The role of Spanish American literary celebrity is not, however, incompatible with making certain kinds of political statements because they are still sanctioned as spokespeople for their countries.

In the context of publisher-run prizes based in Europe, Spanish American authors can combine their celebrity role with that of spokesperson called upon to talk about specific issues. Pablo Sánchez (2008) has shown that many

Spanish American authors who contributed to the opinion pages of *El País* also won the Premio Alfaguara when both were owned by the same company. In the newspaper these authors were called upon to explain political events in their countries but not to defend revolutionary upheavals (Sánchez 2008, 124). In the context of the prize this role continued to be available to them.

Within certain constraints Spanish American authors can construct their public image. They have agency. In many cases they can choose whether or not to submit their work for consideration for publisher-run and state-sponsored awards. Writers wishing to participate in the market may also seek to set their own terms for this participation (Sánchez Prado 2018, 146). They may try to use the prize network to achieve their goals and negotiate their way between different positions in the literary field. In other words, they may deliberately assume roles depending on the type of prize and its audiences. We may consider, therefore, that Spanish American authors have adopted what Sánchez Prado has termed 'strategic occidentalism' or a 'cosmopolitan stance' to try to take over the field of literature in Spanish (2018, 18). Strategic occidentalism entails adapting to the preferences of the European-based prizes and requirements of the market in order to reap the symbolic and economic rewards. The fact that Spanish American authors dominate the lists of recent winners of the Premio Alfaguara and Premio Herralde suggests that they have had considerable success in adapting. The main goal of strategic occidentalism, however, is to avoid the established roles for Spanish American authors in the West as being 'merchants of authenticity' or 'native informant' (Sánchez Prado 2018, 20). It is not clear that the winners of these awards have successfully sidestepped this pitfall. The cosmopolitan stance, or what Sánchez (2008, 122) terms their 'enfático internacionalismo cultural sospechosamente adecuado para funcionar en el nuevo mercado global' (emphatic cultural internationalism suspiciously well suited to functioning in the global market), is readily co-opted. While Spanish American authors benefit from these prizes, therefore, they leave established hierarchies and centres of power and literary prestige not only intact but stronger than ever. The question critics and the authors must ask is to what extent it matters where the centre of cultural consecration lies when it comes to Spanish American literature. The matter is pressing because the propensity for Spanish American authors to favour European-based publishers combined with the neoliberal turn mean that the prize network is evolving, and the coexistence of state-sponsored and publisher-run prizes may be unsustainable. For those Spanish American countries where the state is withdrawing for ideological reasons, or where the state is unable to provide incentives for culture for financial reasons, public–private partnerships that are fully aligned with a neoliberal model are proving popular. The Premio Nacional de Bolivia (National Prize of Bolivia), and similar awards discussed in the final chapter of this book, may be a sign of things to come. Established in 1998 the prize was a joint venture between the government and Alfaguara/Santillana with each party providing a portion of the prize money. The prize is akin to state-sponsored national awards discussed in Chapter 1 in that it is only open to Bolivian nationals and was referred to as the Premio Nacional de Novela Alfaguara, but the neoliberal politics of the prize is clear. As new political positions emerge so too do new types of awards which could fundamentally alter the composition of the prize network and change the role of Spanish American authors at home as well as abroad depriving them altogether of their role as public intellectuals.

3

Spanish American authors on the world stage[1]

State-sponsored institutions in Spanish America invest economic capital in literary prizes to confer prestige on authors and further their agenda at national and regional level. The authors' acceptance of an award and their presence at prize ceremonies confirm their allegiance and legitimize the state, its authority and values. State-sponsored awards, such as those discussed in Chapter 1, and the Premio Cervantes, studied in this chapter and awarded by the Spanish Ministry of Culture to an author writing in Spanish, typically call upon authors to deliver substantial acceptance speeches. The same is true of the Nobel Prize for Literature which, although not state-funded, is awarded by the Swedish Academy. Appointments to this body are approved by the king who is the Academy's patron, and he presents the awards. Authors do not, as we have seen in Chapter 2, usually give acceptance speeches for publisher-run prizes. When it comes to national prizes, the Premio Cervantes and the Nobel Prize for Literature, however, the authors' speeches are a crucial part of the exchange which the prize entails. These speeches are made in the presence of presidents, monarchs or ministers creating an ideal opportunity for authors to speak about politics as much as about literature. On the world stage, as recipients of the Premio Cervantes and the Nobel Prize for Literature, therefore, Spanish American authors take on the role of spokesperson to an even greater extent than they do in the context of publisher-run awards. At the same time, they use

---

[1]This chapter draws substantially on arguments that appeared in relation to the Premio Cervantes and Spain's transition to democracy in Bowskill, S.E.L. (2012), 'Politics and Literary Prizes: A Case Study of Spanish America and the Premio Cervantes', *Hispanic Review* 80(2): 289–311.

the platform offered to them by these prizes to 'talk back' and challenge the political and literary marginalization of Spanish America and its authors.

This chapter studies the prize ceremony acceptance speeches made by Spanish American winners of the Nobel Prize for Literature and the Premio Cervantes.[2] Their words reveal that recipients and awarding bodies have been broadly aligned in their understandings of the significance of the awards which valued the Spanish American authors as defenders of democracy. At the same time, what has been largely overlooked is the way that these prizes open up a site of negotiation and so Spanish American authors use the opportunity they provide to talk back to European centres of power, to advocate for new, more equal relationships and resist Eurocentric notions of universal literature.

The prize ceremonies constitute 'rituals of symbolic exchange, requiring all participants to acknowledge and show respect for the conventions attendant upon the giving and receiving of gifts' (English 2005, 218). The speeches form an important part of this symbolic exchange. Just as the authors may display their gold medals, the awarding bodies display their 'winnings' in the form of the author's presence at the ceremony and by publishing the authors' speeches on their websites. In other words, the intraconversion of capital is materialized in these objects. As well as an exchange of capital, the ceremonies create a space for discourse which involves the negotiation of power and the possibility of resistance (Foucault 1998, 93). The speeches of Spanish American authors are therefore both the counter gift in a symbolic exchange and a tool for the negotiation and resistance of power. Analysing the speeches will enhance our understanding of the politics of literary prestige as a two-way process involving not just the agenda of the awarding body but that of the author too.

At stake in these speeches is the shared understanding of what a writer can and cannot say about literature and politics without damaging their symbolic capital which, Bourdieu suggested, 'is to be understood as economic capital or political capital that is disavowed' (1993, 75). When it comes to the Nobel Prize for Literature and the Premio Cervantes, however, political capital does not have to be disavowed. When it comes to Spanish American authors receiving prizes from European institutions different rules apply. To understand 'what artists and writers can say and do', Bourdieu writes, 'one

---

[2] The speeches of the winners of the Nobel Prize for Literature, the presentation speeches and citations for each winner are on the website: https://www.nobelprize.org/prizes/lists/all-nobel-prizes-in-literature/. The speeches of the winners of the Premio Cervantes are on the website of the Spanish Ministry of Culture: http://www.culturaydeporte.gob.es/premiado/busquedaPremioParticularAction.do?action=busquedaInicial&params.id_tipo_premio=90&layout=premioMiguelCervantesLibro&cache=init&language=es. English-language quotations from the Nobel speeches are taken from the published translations on the Nobel Prize website. All other translations are by the author unless otherwise stated.

must always take into account their membership of a dominated universe and the greater or lesser distance of this universe from that of the dominant class' (1993, 166). We must also consider the type of award and how it positions the author in relation to politics. Thus, to some extent, different rules apply to all of the prizewinners of the Nobel Prize for Literature and the Premio Cervantes when compared to publisher-run awards. For Spanish American winners in particular their political capital is well established as most are already author-states(wo)men or at least public intellectuals. The success of these authors beyond Spanish America may depend on their ability to take on the similarly politicized role of spokesperson interpreting their countries of origin and the region for foreign audiences. In other words, they are called upon to be not just '*representers* of culture' in their texts but also to be 'bona fide cultural *representatives*' (Huggan 2001, 65). In the context of the Premio Cervantes and the Nobel Prize for Literature, far from damaging their symbolic capital, politicized speeches may serve the Spanish American authors just as much as the awarding body.

Even if an author does not speak about politics, and therefore, does not take the opportunity to negotiate the meaning of the award, acceptance of the Premio Cervantes or the Nobel Prize represents a tacit endorsement of the politics and authority of the bestowing institution. Jean-Paul Sartre recognized this fact when he rejected the Nobel Prize for Literature because he saw the award as 'a way of saying, finally he's on our side' (Sartre quoted in Feldman 2000, 78). For Spanish American authors, declining to speak about politics in the context of these awards is to resist the role of spokesperson and defend their specifically literary prestige. For some, the need to affirm their literary credentials may be particularly acute as the Nobel Prize for Literature is widely understood as politicized when it comes to non-European authors in a way that is more pronounced than when it is given to Western European authors. In opting not to speak about politics, as Borges did when he accepted the Premio Cervantes, the Spanish American authors still meet their obligations because their presence is endorsement enough of the awarding body. Having some authors not talk about politics may even be helpful to counterbalance perceptions that the political goals outweigh literary concerns which could damage the prize as we saw in Chapter 1 happened in Chile under Pinochet. Be that as it may, with the exception of Gabriela Mistral, whose speech was very brief, Spanish American Nobel laureates have taken the opportunity to talk back to power in front of worldwide audiences, to institutions at the centre of the world republic of letters and to former colonial powers. They have equally unfailingly also talked about literature.

The Nobel Prize for Literature, established in 1901 by the will of the inventor and entrepreneur Alfred Nobel, is given to 'the person who, in the field of literature, produced the most outstanding work in an idealistic direction' ('Alfred Nobel's will'). The interpretation of Nobel's will is in the hands of the Swedish Academy and has evolved over time. The Academy receives nominations which, since 1969, have been evaluated by the Nobel Committee, before the Academy makes the final selection.[3] The winner is announced in October and the award ceremony takes place on 10 December in Stockholm. To date, there have been six Spanish American winners of the Nobel Prize for Literature: Gabriela Mistral (1945), Miguel Ángel Asturias (1967), Pablo Neruda (1971), Gabriel García Márquez (1982), Octavio Paz (1990) and Mario Vargas Llosa (2010). All of the Spanish American winners came post-Second World War when the prize became more international because the Swedish Academy 'aspired far more actively to the role of literary United Nations' (Lovell 2006, 65). This change was in keeping with wider post-Second-World-War shifts towards 'una nueva internacionalidad en la comunicación cultural' (a new internationalism in cultural communication) (Klengel 2018, 133). This new ethos, as seen in Chapter 2, underpinned the Premio Biblioteca Breve and the UNESCO Collection of Representative Works, as well as the changes in the Nobel Prize for Literature.[4] It is in this political context of international cooperation following the war that we can understand the awarding of the Nobel Prize for Literature to Mistral. Over time, the concept of an 'idealistic direction' came to be further associated with free speech and valuing otherness. For Asturias and García Márquez, it is widely assumed that their connection to magical realism played a role in their nominations (see, e.g. Müller 2018, 166). What they offered, it is suggested, was a marketable form of representing the Other even as their works, as they were interpreted in the West, confirmed preconceptions of Spanish America as exotic. Graham Huggan coined the term 'postcolonial exotic' to refer to this type of literature, which has proved particularly successful in the Booker Prize selling exotic postcolonial authors and their exotic texts to Western readers while keeping symbolic and economic profits in the colonial centre (2001, 8 and Chapter 4). From a political point of view, the selection of Asturias also reflected anti-American feelings following US intervention in Vietnam and Latin America (Menton 1969, 32). In each case, when a Spanish American author won the Nobel Prize for Literature, politics has been seen to have informed the selection even if literary merit was also recognized. In their Nobel lectures Spanish American authors accepted the political significance attributed by the organizers to their awards but also sought to challenge the view of Spanish American literature as exotic.

The Premio Cervantes was established in 1976 at a pivotal moment in the history of intercontinental relations between Spain and Spanish America as

---

[3] On the process, see Nomination and selection of Literature Laureates. NobelPrize.org. Nobel Media AB 2021. Sun. 13 June 2021. <https://www.nobelprize.org/nomination/literature/>. On the change to the process, see Espmark (1986, 166).
[4] On the UNESCO translation initiatives, see Brouillette (2019) and Klengel (2018).

Spain negotiated its transition to democracy and return to the international arena post-Franco. The prize aimed to restore Spain's status and secure the country's continued authority when it came to consecrating all literature in Spanish. Each year, the winner of the Premio Cervantes is announced in November or December. The award ceremony takes place the following year on 23 April, the anniversary of the death of Miguel de Cervantes, at the university in the town of his birth Alcalá de Henares, Spain. According to the website of the Spanish Ministry for Culture which administers the prize, the award is for Spanish or Spanish American authors whose work has 'contribuido a enriquecer de forma notable el patrimonio literario en lengua española' (contributed to the substantial enrichment of the literary heritage of the Spanish language) ('Presentación'). The Premio Cervantes is regularly referred to as the Spanish Nobel and is widely recognized as one of the major awards for literature in Spanish. The prize money, currently in the region of 125,000 euros, is exceeded by few prizes other than the Nobels. To date, the Premio Cervantes has been awarded on twenty-two occasions to Spanish American authors.[5] As in the case of the Nobel Prizes, some of these awards, such as the award to Augusto Roa Bastos, have been especially timely in the way they have coincided with transitions to democracy in various Spanish American countries. The winners' acceptance speeches have often emphasized democratic values as well as focused on the relationship between Spain and Spanish America.

In any given year debates around the Nobel Prize for Literature and, to a lesser extent, the Premio Cervantes raise questions about whether authors have been overlooked for their politics or other extra-literary reasons and whether the right balance has been struck between literary and political concerns when it comes to the choice of laureate. The awards and pronouncements of the Swedish Academy often reveal a tension between recognizing authors as representatives of a national community or particular values and literary merit measured with reference to the universality of their works. The Nobel Prize has also regularly been accused of Eurocentrism, a charge the Premio Cervantes tries to ward off by awarding the prize to a Spanish American author in alternate years conveniently overlooking that this arrangement still significantly favours Spain. These debates largely focus on the motives of the institutions and the biography of the person receiving the award rather than on the content of the winners' acceptance speeches. The speeches are the authors' chance to respond to the discussions that have surrounded the award and to the way in which the award seeks to position them in the literary field. The speeches given by Spanish American authors

---

[5]Mario Vargas Llosa is counted here and earlier in relation to the Nobel Prize as a Spanish American author, but in fact he won the prize Premio Cervantes in 1994 having been given Spanish citizenship in 1993 and the Nobel in 2010.

and analysed in the rest of the chapter, therefore, include political remarks and reflections on the authors' relationship to universal literature.

A licence to talk about politics

In their speeches at the prize ceremonies for the Nobel Prize for Literature and the Premio Cervantes Spanish American authors have frequently introduced politics into an ostensibly literary event. They have licence to do so because of the nature of the awarding institutions and because they are already established author-states(wom)men or public intellectuals at a national level. On the international stage they assume the accepted role of the 'third-world' author as spokesperson.

Political content in speeches by Spanish American winners of the Nobel Prize for Literature and the Premio Cervantes is not scandalous. Nor is it scandalous when Nobel literature laureates of other nationalities speak about politics. Many do so. In 2018 Polish author and winner of the Nobel Prize for Literature Olga Tokarczuk referenced the Cambridge Analytica affair, the way the internet is controlled by the market and by monopolies, and the spread of fake news. In 2015 Ukrainian author Svetlana Alexievich spoke about the impact of the Second World War and Chernobyl in her country and the war in Afghanistan. Egyptian Naguib Mahfouz in 1988 spoke about famine in Africa, the conflict in the West Bank and Gaza and the challenge of finding peace to write in the third world. In 1986 Nigerian Wole Soyinka spoke about Hola Camp, the murder of the progressive prime minister of Mozambique, Samora Machel, and Apartheid.

The propensity to talk about politics may be stronger among authors who are not from Western Europe or the United States. Those who are may be less used to the role of public intellectual and are not called upon to act as representatives and spokespeople in the same way as Spanish American and postcolonial authors are. They may, however, still act as representatives of their gender or ethnicity or opt to discuss politics. Patrick Modiano in 2004 spoke about how being born in Paris under German occupation in the Second World War marked his writing, in 2008 fellow Frenchman Jean-Marie Gustave Le Clézio also talked about the war in 2008 and Italian Dario Fo, in 1997, described his shock that young people were unaware of Turkish fundamentalism in the context of the massacre in Sivas and proposals in the European Parliament 'to allow patent rights on living organisms'. British playwright Harold Pinter entitled his Nobel lecture in 2005 'Art, Truth and Politics'. When Pinter won, he was an outspoken critic of the Iraq War and US foreign policy leading the journalist Alan Jenkins to remark 'There is the view that the Nobel literature prize often goes to someone whose political stance is found to be sympathetic at a given moment' (quoted in Smith

2005). In many cases, and certainly when it comes to Spanish American winners of the Nobel Prize, it would be hard to argue with this statement.

Politicized speeches at other award ceremonies have caused scandal. The case of John Berger, described by English, is a case in point (2005, 203–4). Scandal arose because Berger accused the Booker organization of engaging in 'cultural money-laundering' in other words deliberately trying to use literary prestige to distract from the company's politics and past (English 2005, 199). In contrast, in the case of the Nobel Prize and the Premio Cervantes, the awards are designed to draw attention to the liberal and democratic politics of the awarding bodies and the authors, and so politicized speeches are not only not scandalous they are welcomed as part of the pact or exchange between awarding body and recipient.

The political significance of the Nobel Prize and the Premio Cervantes is not concealed but ostentatiously displayed at the prize ceremonies which are carefully orchestrated events designed for maximum literary and political impact. The ceremonies explicitly bring together the domains of literature and politics. The presence of Sweden's monarch at the Nobel ceremonies is described by Burton Feldman as 'symbolically indispensable' and carrying 'a vestige of the vanished aristocratic past when princes rewarded artists or political favourites' (2000, 10). The king of Spain attends the Premio Cervantes ceremony, as does the minister for culture. The presence of King Juan Carlos when he was king was frequently remarked upon by winners who recalled his role in restoring Spanish democracy. The importance of this public meeting of the worlds of politics and literature is underscored by the fact that all but one of the Spanish American winners of the Premio Cervantes attended the ceremony in person. Nicanor Parra, then aged ninety-seven, understandably sent his grandson to read a speech on his behalf in 2011. The Nobel laureate forfeits the award if s/he does not attend in person.

As discussed in Chapter 1, in Spanish America, the role of author-statesman combining literature and politics and that of the author as public intellectual are well established. Spanish American authors may not be exceptional in making politicized acceptance speeches, but they are particularly well placed to do so readily transitioning to international spokesperson on the world stage. The Spanish American winners of the Nobel Prize all perfectly fit the profile of author-states(wo)man and public intellectual. All bar one of the Spanish American Nobel laureates had held political office when they won the award. The exception was García Márquez, whose role as public intellectual was well established through his committed form of 'advocacy journalism' (Bell-Villada 2010, 17). His political commitment as a journalist was referenced in the award ceremony speech given by Lars Gyllensten. Gabriela Mistral worked with José Vasconcelos on educational reform in Mexico and was named Chilean consul for life in 1935 having begun her career in this role in 1932.⁶ Miguel Ángel Asturias campaigned against the dictatorship of Manuel Estrada Cabrera.⁷ From 1952 he worked in the Guatemalan Embassy in Paris as *ministro consejero* (advising minister) but had to give up the position in 1962 due to regime change. A year before he won the Nobel Prize, he was named Guatemalan ambassador in Paris.

Pablo Neruda held diplomatic posts in Buenos Aires and Barcelona. Like Mistral, he was consul in Madrid and later in Paris and Mexico City. In 1945 he was elected Senator for the Chilean Communist Party before being forced into exile when the Communist Party was outlawed in 1948. When Neruda won the Nobel, he was serving as ambassador in Paris (1970–3) under the government of Salvador Allende. Octavio Paz, who has been described as 'uno de los miembros más conspicuos del Servicio Exterior Mexicano' (one of the most conspicuous members of the Mexican Foreign Office) represented Mexico as a diplomat from 1945 until 1968 when he resigned in protest at the Tlatelolco massacre (Asiain 2015).

Like fellow Boom author García Márquez, Vargas Llosa initially performed his role as public intellectual through journalism before going on to try to become an author-statesman. As the editor of *Democracia* he critiqued the dictatorship of Peruvian president Manuel A. Odría, and he wrote favourably about the Cuban Revolution when he was sent by Agence France-Presse to cover the missile crisis.⁸ The most intensely political phase of his career began when he wrote a letter to Peruvian president Alan García (1985–90) in 1987 and culminated in his narrowly unsuccessful run for president in Peru in 1990 (Williams 2014, 71). It would be two decades after this campaign before he won the Nobel.

The case of Vargas Llosa points to the possible limits of mixing literature and politics because the extent of his political activities was such that it is has been suggested that they prevented him from winning a Nobel earlier in his life. Raymond Leslie Williams notes that, from the 1980s, Vargas Llosa 'occasionally appeared on unofficial but well-informed short lists for the Nobel Prize for Literature' (2014, 50). At this time though he was very much politically active. Dominic Moran similarly suggests that the Nobel Committee initially overlooked Neruda in 1963 due to his 'extreme political position' and an 'aggressive smear campaign' backed by the CIA (2009, 155). What was and was not acceptable to the Nobel judges in terms of political positions and activities was, however, less than consistent except when it came to the rejection of fascism which was justified with

---

⁶On Mistral's biography and diplomatic career, see 'Hitos de la vida de Gabriela Mistral' Gabriela Mistral: primera cónsul chilena - Museo Gabriela Mistral de Vicuña (mgmistral.gob.cl) Accessed 18 March 2021.
⁷This biography is based on Dumas (1969).
⁸These details are based on the biography of Vargas Llosa in Part 1 'An Intellectual Biography' by Williams (2014).

reference to the criteria of 'idealism'. Feldman (2000, 76–9) clearly demonstrates the inconsistency of the politics of the award in his analysis of the Cold War years when awards went to authors who did and did not support the Soviet regime perhaps as part of the Committee's strategy of trying to appear neutral. Kjell Espmark, a member of the Swedish Academy, too notes that the competing political agenda have led to unpredictable results (1986, 203). Espmark nevertheless suggests that there has been a tendency to favour authors who demonstrated independence in the face of totalitarian regimes as was the case for Neruda and García Márquez (1986, 203). The Nobel Committee does not always shy away from politically outspoken authors or decisions that may be interpreted as being influenced by politics, but they do try to avoid situations where politics is seen as the only concern.

Given the backgrounds of the Spanish American Nobel winners as established author-states(wo)men or public intellectuals, it was not surprising that in their acceptance speeches the laureates combined literature and politics. Most of the winners of the Premio Cervantes were similarly positioned. They often held political appointments and had spent years in exile having been vocal opponents of dictatorships. Carlos Fuentes worked in the Ministry of Foreign Affairs and served as Mexican ambassador to France (1975–7). Sergio Pitol was also a member of the Mexican Foreign Service holding several posts as a cultural attaché in Eastern Europe before becoming ambassador to Czechoslovakia. Fernando del Paso was cultural attaché and Consul General in Paris, and Jorge Edwards served as Chilean ambassador in Havana and as ambassador to UNESCO. The highest office was held by Sergio Ramírez. In his acceptance speech he referred to having had to step back from literature to be part of a revolution to overthrow a dictator (2017, 1). Ramírez supported the Frente Sandinista de Liberación Nacional (FSLN) against President Anastasio Somoza Debayle and went on to be vice-president of Nicaragua (1985–90). In 2017 he won the Premio Cervantes.

In the broader context, Spanish American authors, like other writers from outside Western Europe and the United States, are further licensed to talk about politics as recipients of the Premio Cervantes and Nobel Prize because of the ready acceptance in the West of the 'third-world' author as spokesperson. As noted in Chapter 2, the author as spokesperson is called upon to interpret events in Spanish America for foreign, Western audiences. In this context, talking about politics in acceptance speeches is not scandalous, but what they say may be conscribed by what Paja Faudree terms a 'politics of voice' which limits them to being heard only insofar as they are representing their nation or culture (2015, 9). That Spanish American prizewinners are viewed by bestowing institutions as representatives is apparent from the presentation speeches given by representatives of the Swedish Academy at the Nobel Prize ceremony. Anders Österling, permanent secretary of the Swedish Academy, began his award ceremony speech in 1967 describing Asturias as 'a messenger from Latin America, its people, its spirit and its future'. Espmark, also member of the Swedish Academy, similarly described Paz as one of the 'most brilliant representatives' of writers from the Spanish-speaking world. Neruda's citation commended him as a representer of Spanish American culture 'for a poetry that with the action of an elemental force brings alive a continent's destiny and dreams' (1971). García Márquez's citation similarly suggested that his works reflected 'a continent's life and conflicts' (1982). For Spanish American prizewinners on the world stage, whose role as representers and representatives is at least as important to the awarding bodies as their role as authors, not only are they licensed to speak about politics, but it is to some extent expected.

The speeches given by the Spanish American Nobel laureates reveal that they all understood their allotted role. In her Nobel acceptance speech Mistral identified herself as a representative when she said: 'I am the direct voice of the ports of my race and the indirect voice for the noble Spanish and Portuguese tongues' and 'My homeland [...] has sent me here to accept the special honour you have awarded to it' (1945). Alejo Carpentier's speech on winning the Premio Cervantes was generally apolitical, but he nevertheless accepted the award 'en nombre mío y en el de mi pueblo' (in my own name and in that of my people) (4). Similarly, Roa Bastos viewed the award as 'un doble galardón a mi obra y a la cultura de mi patria' (a double award for my work and the culture of my homeland) (1989, 2). Sergio Ramírez likewise thanked the king of Spain for giving the award to Central America through him (2017, 14). Jorge Edwards saw the award as 'un reconocimiento que se hace a través mío de la literatura chilena en su tradición y en su rica diversidad' (a recognition made through my work of the tradition of Chilean literature in its rich diversity) (1999, 1). In receiving these awards Spanish American authors acknowledge and accept that they do so as representers and representatives of their homelands and region.

Defenders of democracy

As authors and representatives of the state meet to exchange gifts during prize ceremonies, they are embedded within a negotiation of power which impacts both the fields of literature and politics. At the prize ceremony a politico-literary space is established where each party is given a degree of licence to talk about the field of the other. The presentation speeches made by members of the Swedish Academy when Spanish American authors have won the Nobel all included reference to the authors' politics positioning them as spokespeople on these issues and opening the door for the authors to respond.

The speeches of the Spanish American Nobel and Premio Cervantes winners cover the period 1945–2018 from Gabriela Mistral winning the Nobel Prize for Literature to Ida Vitale becoming the last Spanish American winner of the Premio Cervantes. This timeframe encompasses periods of military dictatorships in Spain and Spanish America. The timing of awards to Spanish American authors who were outspoken critics of totalitarian regimes was no coincidence as the Swedish Academy and the post-Franco Spanish state sought to defend liberal values and democracy. Many Spanish American authors, no doubt conscious that they had the opportunity to speak to powerful people and wide audiences, used the opportunity to denounce dictatorship and align themselves with the values of the awarding bodies.

In 1945, shortly after the defeat of former dictator General Carlos Ibáñez in the 1942 Chilean elections, Mistral described herself in her Nobel acceptance speech as 'a daughter of Chilean democracy' and praised 'the Swedish democratic tradition'. In 1967 Asturias received the Nobel Prize just a year after Julio César Méndez Montenegro was elected as a civilian president of Guatemala promising to deliver democracy following long periods of military rule. The political significance of the prize was made clear in the presentation speech when both Asturias and Österling described Asturias's experience of going into exile following the 1954 military coup which installed Carlos Castillo Armas as president. Österling also noted that Asturias's novel *El Señor Presidente* 'criticizes the prototype of the Latin American dictator who appeared in several places at the beginning of the century and has since reappeared, his existence being fostered by the mechanism of tyranny which, for the common man, makes every day a hell on earth'. Again, Asturias's award was an endorsement for democracy in Spanish America as much as for his contributions to literature.

In his Nobel lecture, delivered on 13 December 1971, Neruda referenced his experience of dictatorship and exile as did the presentation speech by Karl Ragnar Gierow. Neruda described the journey he undertook to escape from Chile to Argentina in 1948 when communism was outlawed in Chile and a warrant was issued for his arrest by President Gabriel González Videla. The description of the journey is striking as it balances a sense of national pride in the magnificent surroundings with his fear of dying on such a treacherous path and his sadness at having to go into exile. Speaking at the award ceremony just a year after President Salvador Allende assumed office, Neruda described his pride in having contributed to the democratic transformation of Chile. He was subsequently invited by Allende to deliver his Nobel lecture again at the National Stadium in Santiago confirming his role as public intellectual at home and spokesperson for the nation abroad.

Reflecting on the current situation in Latin America in his 1982 Nobel lecture, García Márquez reported that, since Neruda had won the Nobel, '[t]here have been five wars and seventeen military coups; there emerged a diabolic dictator who is carrying out, in God's name, the first Latin

American ethnocide of our time'. He referred specifically to the practice of taking children from their mothers and illegally putting them up for adoption during the Argentine dictatorship. Such was the scale of the problem, he said, that '[t]he country that could be formed of all the exiles and forced emigrants of Latin America would have a population larger than that of Norway'. He even ventured to suggest that these circumstances may have been part of the reason why he was nominated: 'I dare to think that it is this outsized reality, and not just its literary expression, that has deserved the attention of the Swedish Academy of Letters.' The presentation speech, made by Gyllensten, was not so forthright, but it did make brief reference to García Márquez as an engaged author stating that he 'is strongly committed politically on the side of the poor and the weak against oppression and economic exploitation'. No references were made by Gyllensten to specific events or countries undergoing political, social or economic upheaval in a speech that was noticeably less politically charged than the one delivered by the laureate himself. This imbalance did not lead to controversy though as García Márquez was still fulfilling the role of spokesperson.

The most recent Spanish American Nobel laureate in literature, Vargas Llosa, finally had cause for optimism as he reported that most Spanish American countries were free of dictatorships and had established democratic rule. He nevertheless focused on the ongoing threats to democracy. He expressed his concerns about Cuba and Venezuela and, to a lesser extent, Bolivia and Nicaragua. He denounced the failure of democratic governments to act in solidarity with those who stand up to dictatorships in Spanish America and beyond including Aung San Suu Kyi, Liu Xiaobo, Las Damas de Blanco in Cuba and those who stood up to the regime in Venezuela. In broadening his frame of reference outside Spanish America Vargas Llosa underscored the fact that Latin America is not unique in suffering from dictatorships and thus avoided making Latin America seem like the problem and an exception. He also refused to be limited to his role as spokesperson.

Like several of his predecessors, Vargas Llosa had experienced exile as a result of dictatorship and recalled in his Nobel lecture his time living in Barcelona under the Franco regime at the start of the 1960s. He praised Spain's transition to democracy and denounced the threat nationalism posed to 'this happy tale'. He also described how, during the last dictatorship in Peru, he had asked for sanctions to be imposed against the regime causing him to almost lose his citizenship and leading him to take Spanish citizenship in 2007. He defended his actions saying that he would do it again if another coup threatened what he termed 'our fragile democracy'. Dictatorship, he said, 'represents absolute evil for a country' and should be challenged by any means necessary. Underscoring Vargas Llosa's credentials as a defender of democracy in his presentation speech Per Wästberg paid tribute to the author as someone who 'has fought for freedom of expression and for human rights regardless of geography and has done so with a passion for liberty and with political courage and common sense'.

Dictatorship and democracy were also recurring themes in speeches delivered by winners of the Premio Cervantes. Again, many had first-hand experience of exile, and the timing of the awards was often opportune. Augusto Roa Bastos (1989) expressed his joy at receiving the Premio Cervantes just as the dictatorship in Paraguay had ended the year before thus hinting at the link between recognizing his literature as a means of indirectly endorsing this change. Juan Gelman spoke about his time in exile from the dictatorship in Argentina and the pain it caused him every time he heard about a friend or someone he knew having disappeared (2007, 2). As many Spanish American countries, including Argentina, struggled with the legacies of dictatorship, Gelman also celebrated the way in which post-Franco Spain had engaged in recovering historical memory as part of a process of reconciliation describing it as the 'único camino para construir una conciencia cívica sólida que abra las puertas al futuro' (only way to build a solid civic consciousness able to open the doors to the future) (2007, 4). Uruguayans Juan Carlos Onetti (1980) and Ida Vitale (2018) also talked about their experiences of exile and military regimes, and Onetti thanked Spain for providing a home for so many Spanish Americans fleeing dictatorships.

Winners of the Premio Cervantes receive the award from the reigning Spanish monarch. For many years the award was made in the presence of King Juan Carlos who was pivotal in securing Spain's transition to democracy not least during the events of 23 February 1981. Many Spanish American authors receiving the Premio Cervantes praised the king for having upheld democracy. Ernesto Sábato began his speech in 1984 by saying it was an honour to receive the award 'de las manos de un hombre que los partidarios de la libertad admiramos y respetamos' (from the hands of a man who all supporters of freedom admire and respect) (1984, 1). Onetti also referenced the role of the king of Spain in guaranteeing the freedom of Spanish people today.

Recently, several Mexican winners of the Premio Cervantes have taken the opportunity to talk about the escalating violence in their country and the problems of narcotrafficking and gender-based violence both of which had attracted the attention of the world's media. José Emilio Pacheco in 2009 referred to the 'la inusitada violencia que devasta a países como México' (extraordinary violence that is devastating countries like Mexico) (2009, 3). When Elena Poniatowska won in 2013, she cast light on the violence against women as she referred to the femicides in Ciudad Juárez. In 2015 Fernando del Paso again had cause to speak about 'los atracos, las extorsiones, los secuestros, las desapariciones, los feminicidios, la discriminación, los abusos de poder, la corrupción, la impunidad y el cinismo' (highjacking, blackmail, kidnappings, disappearances, femicide, discrimination, abuses of power, corruption, impunity and shamelessness) as he said the situation in Mexico continued to worsen (2015, 2). He left his audience in no doubt about the political intent of his speech as he went on to denounce the new Ley Atenco (Atenco Law), which he saw as a threat to democratic values because of the powers it gave the police in dealing with protestors. In speaking about issues in Spanish America the prizewinners consistently use the platform they are afforded to align themselves with democratic values extending their role of national public intellectual to become international spokespeople representing and representatives of their country and their region on the world stage.

Spanish American authors talk back

The acceptance speeches also gave Spanish American authors an opportunity to negotiate the kind of politics with which they wished to be aligned. A closer examination of the speeches reveals that Spanish American authors' views were not perfectly aligned with those of the awarding bodies even as they broadly endorsed the liberal, democratic values that underpin the awards. Spanish American authors can, and do, exploit the expectations of them to their own advantage. It is not enough, therefore, to say that the Spanish American laureates talk about politics without causing scandal because of the dominated positions they occupy in the literary field. They talk back. They demand new, less euro-centric political relationships and a place within a decentred universal literature. The Nobel and Premio Cervantes award ceremony speeches provide an ideal opportunity to make such demands. This negotiation is often overlooked when the Spanish American authors, like others from beyond Western Europe and the United States, are labelled as spokespeople. For this reason, the rest of the chapter considers how the Spanish American authors advocated for new kinds of global relationships in literature and in politics even as they also accepted their allotted role of spokesperson.

Spanish American prizewinners do not just denounce dictatorships and defend democracy. They share concerns that are relevant to their global audience as they address issues outside and within Spanish America. In this sense, they do not strictly adhere to their role of continental spokesperson, but nor do they step significantly out of their prescribed role and remain well within the parameters of a public intellectual. Global issues of poverty and inequality were addressed by Paz in his Nobel lecture as he denounced unequal global relations whereby some countries are 'islands of abundance in the ocean of universal misery'. On receiving the Premio Cervantes Gelman reminded his audience that we live in 'un mundo en el que cada tres segundos y medio un niño menor de 5 años muere de enfermedades curables, de hambre, de pobreza' (a world in which every three and a half seconds a child under five years old dies from curable illnesses, hunger and poverty) (2007, 1). The threat posed by nuclear weapons was mentioned by

Vargas Llosa and Paz in their Nobel lectures. Far from being a coincidence, these references need to be understood in the context of the Nobel prizes which were established by the inventor of explosives, including dynamite, and a man who profited from arms and munitions. It was his remorse that he would be remembered for so much death and destruction that led Nobel to create the prizes (Feldman 2000, 36). In his Premio Cervantes speech Gelman compared Cervantes' time when sword fighting was the norm to modern warfare which happens at a distance and the impact of which is more wide reaching. He referenced the civilians killed at a distance in Hiroshima and now in Iraq referencing the Iraq war which was ongoing when he spoke in 2007. Reflecting the changing nature of warfare Vargas Llosa's Nobel speech also referenced the threat posed by fanatics and suicidal terrorists which he said had replaced that posed by totalitarian regimes.

When they speak at these European award ceremonies, Spanish American authors are keenly aware of the opportunity they have to talk back to former colonial powers and hold them to account. Their proclamations are designed to unsettle their hosts and the balance of power while not offending. They often speak about creating new, fairer global relations. García Márquez challenged stereotypes of Latin America as 'uncivilized' by providing reminders of less 'civilized' aspects of Europe's past and urged Europe to change the way it viewed Latin America. Rather than hollow expressions of solidarity he argued that Europe should respond with 'concrete acts of legitimate support for all the peoples that assume the illusion of having a life of their own in the distribution of the world'. He cautioned against the tendency for tolerating originality in Latin American literature but not allowing Latin America to choose its own unique path towards social change.

In his Premio Cervantes speech Roa Bastos referred to the problems caused as a result of Latin America's 'dependencia y sometimiento a los centros mundiales de decisión' (dependence and subjection to the world's decision-making centres) and saw external intervention as the 'causa central de sus problemas internos, de su inmovilismo, de su atraso, de su desaliento' (main cause of internal problems, of stagnation, backwardness and depression) (1989, 2). He acknowledged the work done by Spain rectifying the legacies of colonialism and saw the future as being one of integration 'en una comunidad orgánica de naciones libres' (as part of an organic community of free nations) (1989, 2). Clearly, he looked forward to a new more equal relationship.

Paz and Asturias both advocated in their Nobel speeches for a pan-American identity that was less oriented towards Europe. Throughout his speech Asturias referred to America, American literature and American identity building on a tradition stretching back to José Martí's essay 'Nuestra América' (1891). Following Martí's example, Asturias invoked a pan-American identity opposed to either European or US hegemony. In a similar vein, Paz proclaimed, 'We are Europeans and yet we are not Europeans' and emphasized the common ground shared by the countries of the Americas appealing to a continental identity that was part of, but also in opposition to, European identity.

In the case of the Premio Cervantes Spanish American authors were keen to establish an egalitarian relationship with the former colonial power based on a shared language and literary heritage. Ana Gallegos Cuiñas notes that these concepts were at the heart of Spanish state discourse at the time of the quincentenary (2018, 239). As seen in Chapter 2, these discourses have often been part of a peninsular agenda to secure control of the market for literature in Spanish and the authority to consecrate it. It is significant, therefore, that Spanish American authors chose specifically to endorse these values in their speeches even as they emphasized a decentred Spanish language and literature by emphasizing Spanish American contributions.

When Fuentes won the Premio Cervantes in 1987, he probably already had the upcoming quincentenary of the conquest in mind. Instead of a straightforward celebration of this moment which united Spain and Spanish America, he talked about 1492 as 'una fecha inquietante' (a worrying date) (1987, 1). As if to move on from the colonial relationship of subjugation Mexican winners have often referred to a very different moment in the shared past when Mexico offered a home to exiles from the Spanish Civil War. Elena Poniatowska, for example, recalled that the first woman to win the Premio Cervantes, María Zambrano, had been in exile in Mexico. Contact between Spain and Latin America in this later period served as a counterpoint in the speeches of Poniatowska, Fuentes and Pitol to the earlier contact of the conquest and a timely reminder of the need for more equal relationships.

Reclaiming universal literature and creating a genealogy of male authors

Not only do Spanish American authors use the world stage to negotiate more equal political relationships between Europe and Latin America, they also take the opportunity to associate themselves with universal literature. Almost all prizewinning authors of the Nobel Prize and the Premio Cervantes described how they came to writing emphasizing their literary background and credentials. In so doing they confronted any suggestion that they were only worthy of a politicized form of literary prestige. When Spanish American authors in their acceptance speeches align themselves with universal literature, they challenge Western ownership of universal literature and the two-tier system according to which 'literature from the Western canon is selected for its "universal" qualities, while non-Western literature is included for its local, refreshingly pluralistic value' (Lovell 2006, 66). In their Nobel lectures Neruda referenced the French poet Arthur Rimbaud and García Márquez referenced 1950 Nobel laureate William Faulkner. Vargas Llosa described learning from the masters Flaubert, Faulkner, Martorell, Cervantes, Dickens, Balzac, Tolstoy, Conrad, Thomas Mann, Sartre, Camus, Orwell and Malraux. Similarly, when he won the Premio Cervantes, he listed all those with whom he thought he should share the prize (Malraux, Melville, Hemingway, Kipling, Kafka, Victor Hugo, Stendhal, Faulkner, Johanot Martorell, Balzac, Flaubert and Tolstoy) because they inspired him and without them, he said he would not have become a writer (Vargas Llosa 1994, 6).

As much as they exalted universal literature, their speeches show some awareness of it as problematic for the way in which '[i]t simultaneously holds out the false promise of equality for all and validates those at the top of the hierarchy as the possessors of the "universal" culture' (Buell 1994, 266). This hierarchy has tended to prioritize Eurocentric values because 'agency for inventing universal cultural models has lain within the West, in the hands of theorizers and architects such as Goethe (1749–1832), Marx (1818–83), and Alfred Nobel (1833–96), who have tended to overlook or perpetuate various forms of Eurocentrism' (Lovell 2006, 27). The Spanish American authors decentred literary prestige by insisting on the valuable contributions of Spanish American authors to the literary patrimony of the Spanish language. In their speeches the Spanish American authors laid claim to a tradition of literature in Spanish but challenged any sense of Spain as owners of the language, literature or even Cervantes. Guillermo Cabrera Infante imagined a dialogue between himself and Cervantes in which he referenced the fact that Cervantes himself longed to go to the Americas. Had Cervantes gone, Cabrera Infante playfully noted, 'su gran libro hubiera escrito no en España, sino en la Nueva España' (his great book would have been written not in Spain but in New Spain) (1997, 1). Sábato claimed Cervantes as 'el antepasado de todos los que hoy escribimos en castellano, sea en España como en las remotas tierras que alguna vez integraron el vasto imperio' (the ancestor of all those who today write in Castillian Spanish, as much in Spain as into the remote lands that once made up the vast empire) (Sábato 1984, 1).

The language was also wrested from the sole control of the peninsular when Fuentes spoke of 'un idioma compartido, con mi patria, con mi cultura y con sus escritores' (a language that is shared with my homeland, with my culture and with its authors) which has become 'una lengua universal' (a universal language) (1987, 2). He continued: 'La lengua imperial de Nebrija se ha convertido en algo mejor: la lengua universal de Jorge Luis Borges y Pablo Neruda, de Julio Cortázar y Octavio Paz' (The imperial language of Nebrija has become something better: the universal language of Jorge Luis Borges and Pablo Neruda, of Julio Cortázar and Octavio Paz) (1987, 2). Ramírez similarly spoke about how, having received the language from Cervantes, a language much transformed and enriched in Spanish America was sent back via the work of Nicaraguan poet Rubén Darío (2017, 3).

Even as the Spanish American winners positioned themselves as the heirs of authors writing in Spanish regardless of nationality, they emphasized the importance and uniqueness of Spanish American literature often with reference to the legacy of indigenous cultures. In his Nobel lecture Vargas Llosa described how, in Barcelona in the 1960s, Spanish and Latin American authors socialized 'recognizing one another as possessors of the same tradition'. Yet he also spoke about his pride at being 'heredero de las culturas prehispánicas' (heir to the prehispanic cultures). In this way, and in common with many of the other Spanish American prizewinners of the Nobel and Premio Cervantes, he laid claim to a dual literary heritage. In his Nobel lecture Paz described how works from Latin America are 'literatures written in transplanted tongues', but he asserted the independence of Latin American literature from Spanish literature because '[o]ur literatures did not passively accept the changing fortunes of the transplanted languages: they participated in the process and even accelerated it. They very soon ceased to be mere transatlantic reflections: at times they have been the negation of the literatures of Europe; more often, they have been a reply.' In his presentation speech for Paz Espmark failed to differentiate between authors from the 'Spanish-speaking world' and only connected Spanish American literature to European traditions. Paz's remarks represent a firm rebuttal of such misconceptions.

Asturias similarly resisted literary Eurocentrism in his Nobel acceptance speech thus challenging the discourse and assumptions of the awarding institution. Österling's presentation speech linked Asturias to European literary heritage crediting it as foundational in his work by noting that '[v]ery early, he came under the influence of the new tendencies appearing in European literature; his explosive style bears a close kinship to French surrealism'. Asturias's own literary genealogy, however, departed significantly from this European tradition. Asturias replaced the more commonly referenced Cervantes as the originator of literature in Spanish with indigenous literatures. He traced the roots of Latin American literature to the Maya, Aztec and Incan cultures. He argued that indigenous literature influenced European literature as is evident in the work of the conquistador and chronicler Bernal Díaz del Castillo and suggested that, via the work of Andrés Bello and Rafael Landívar, indigenous literatures became part of world literature. Bello and Landívar, as well as the nineteenth-century novelists José Marmol and Domingo Faustino Sarmiento, were also described as the founding fathers of 'American literature'. Continuing into the twentieth century, Asturias named other American authors including the poets Rubén Darío and Juan Ramón Molina but prioritized naming a long list of novelists as he boldly stated: 'Nobody doubts that the Latin American novel is at the leading edge of its genre in the world.' In his speech Asturias was thus able to reshape the canon of world literature making it less Eurocentric than it was in the imagination of the awarding body.

García Márquez used his Nobel speech to resist having his work appropriated by Western readers. The citation for his prize focused on the magical and exotic aspects of his work stating that it was 'for his novels and short stories, in which the fantastic and the realistic are combined in a richly composed world of imagination, reflecting a continent's life and conflicts'. The presentation speech by Gyllensten similarly aligned García Márquez with the postcolonial exotic described by Huggan as he noted that '[i]n his novels and short stories we are led into this peculiar place where the miraculous and the real converge. The extravagant flight of his own fantasy combines with traditional folk tales and facts.' García Márquez's readability, as opposed to his writerly skill more often associated with literary prestige, was emphasized as he was praised as a 'rare storyteller' with 'almost overwhelming narrative talent' and in possession of a 'narrative gift'. In response, García Márquez challenged the assumptions that the extraordinary aspects of his work did not speak to a Latin American reality and denounced the contemporary state of Latin American politics. He described the challenge facing Latin American writers as they try to capture 'aquella realidad desaforada' (that outrageous reality) and said that 'el desafío mayor para nosotros ha sido la insuficiencia de los recursos convencionales para hacer creíble nuestra vida' (the biggest challenge for us has been the fact that conventional resources have been insufficient to make our reality believable). In a further reproach to Western audiences, García Márquez suggested that the extraordinary reality of Latin America had left said readers 'sin un método válido para interpretarnos' (without a valid method for interpreting us). They needed, he said, to deploy different interpretative strategies to those used to understand their own contexts. In this way García Márquez used his speech to repoliticize his work so that it was less ready for assimilation and consumption as entertainment by Western readers.

In 2013 Poniatowska used her speech to resist the male-dominated nature of the canon the Premio Cervantes has helped to create. The repeated namechecking of male writers in the speeches of the male prizewinners serves to create a kind of family tree. As a rule, women authors do not feature in the lists of authors male winners routinely cite as their influences. Gonzalo Rojas, speaking in 2003, was a rare exception in referencing Gabriela Mistral. Literary history, like family history, is patrilineal. As Anne McClintock has observed, the family tree 'represents evolutionary time as a *time without women*. The family image is an image of disavowal, for it contains only men, arranged as a linear frieze of solo males ascending towards the apogee of the individual *Homo sapiens*. Each epoch is represented by a single male type, who is characterized in turn by visible anatomical stigmata' (1995, 39). In the same way, the literary genealogy produced by the prizewinning speeches positions the men delivering the speeches as the heirs of Cervantes, past winners and a Eurocentric tradition of world literature. Generation after generation of male authors are enshrined ascending to the present moment and the crowning of the speaker himself. As the same names are repeated from one year to the next, the association between these men and literary prestige is affirmed and strengthened to the detriment of women authors.

Against this long tradition of male winners reinforcing a connection between universal literature and male literary prestige, Poniatowska set out an alternative tradition. In so doing, she used her platform on the world stage to raise the profile of other women authors for whom prizes had proved an impossible dream. Poniatowska mentioned the three prior women winners of the Premio Cervantes María Zambrano, Dulce María Loynaz and Ana María Matute before speaking at some length about Sor Juana Inés de la Cruz contrasting with male prizewinners who usually spoke about Cervantes (2013, 1). She referenced the women she had written about Jesusa Palancares, Tina Modotti, Leonora Carrington (Poniatowska 2013, 4). Finally, she listed the Mexican men who had won the Premio Cervantes and the Mexican women who were overlooked: 'Los mexicanos que me han precedido son cuatro: Octavio Paz en 1981, Carlos Fuentes en 1987, Sergio Pitol en 2005 y José Emilio Pacheco en 2009. Rosario Castellanos y María Luisa Puga no tuvieron la misma suerte y las invoco así como a José Revueltas' (Four Mexicans have preceded me: Octavio Paz in 1981, Carlos Fuentes in 1987, Sergio Pitol in 2005 and José Emilio Pacheco in 2009. Rosario Castellanos and María Luisa Puga did not have the same luck and I invoke their names as well as that of José Revueltas) (Poniatowska 2013, 6). As will be discussed in Chapter 6, women authors do not always feel able to use their platforms to speak out about the gendered politics of literary prestige for fear of being pigeonholed so it is noteworthy that, having won one of the major prizes for literature in Spanish, Poniatowska seized the opportunity.

Spanish American prizewinning authors accepting the Premio Cervantes and the Nobel Prize for Literature are free to talk about literature and politics and to try to redress the balance of power when it comes to both of these fields. There is, however, one thing they are not free to talk about. Money. To speak of money, and especially the significant sum they will receive as a result of winning the Nobel Prize for Literature or the Premio Cervantes, remains taboo. Only the smallest of references to the financial struggles of being a writer is tolerated. Roa Bastos talked about how choosing to be an 'artisan', as opposed to a professional writer, meant that '[e]ntre estos momentos creatives intermitentes del escritor no professional se interponen los obstáculos del propio vivir, los imperativos de la subsistencia' (between those intermittent creative moments of the non-professional writer are interposed the obstacles of real life, the imperatives of subsistence) (1989, 6). Pacheco also commented on the financial hardship common to authors: 'Casi todos los escritores somos, a querer o no, miembros de una orden mendicantes' (Almost all writers, whether we want to be or not, are members of a mendicant order) (2009, 3). These, as can be seen, are the merest allusions to the financial challenges of being a writer. Few though are so daring as to even broach the subject of money which, it seems, would forever taint their literary prestige.

Conclusions

On the world stage at moments when their symbolic capital is at its zenith, Spanish American winners of the Nobel Prize for Literature and the Premio Cervantes consistently spoke about politics. In so doing they affirmed their roles as national public intellectual and spokespeople for international audiences without causing scandal but also without bowing down to the centres of world literature and the former colonial power. In many ways their agenda coincided with that of the awarding institutions as they endorsed a modified version of universal literature, the rich literary heritage of the Spanish language and democratic values. At the same time, the prizewinners insisted on the shared nature of literatures in Spanish and on the unique contributions made by Spanish American authors, they resisted readings of their work as exotic and argued for European accountability and equal global relations. The awarding institutions may be exercising their power to consecrate literature on the world stage, but Spanish American authors got something more than prize money in return, namely a chance to talk back, redress the balance, claim equality and articulate their own politics of literary prestige. The prizes opened up a dynamic site of negotiation. Yet even as the prizewinning male authors used their platform on the world stage to talk back and challenge the marginalization and devaluation of Spanish American literature, including its indigenous roots, in their references to their literary heritage they also unintentionally revealed and consolidated the gendered politics of literary prestige which will be the subject of Chapters 5 and 6.

4
Roberto Bolaño, Carmen Boullosa and Fernando Iwasaki find their voice in the prizes game

Authors who win the Premio Cervantes or the Nobel Prize for Literature give speeches and 'talk back' to the awarding institutions. Publisher-run prizes do not offer the same opportunity. Authors can, of course, make their views known in interviews, but they are not in full control of the printed text and risk appearing overly invested in the prize, believing too much in its significance, or being excessively critical. Faced with a literary field in which prizes are proliferating, but the role of the public intellectual is in decline, some Spanish American authors have decided to explore the politics of literary prestige in their fiction. Their experience, like that of the Anglophone cultural commentators studied by English, suggests that they can reap potential rewards if a balance between constructive critique and apparent disinterest can be struck (2005, 213–16). This chapter analyses the critical reception of texts about prizes by Spanish American authors, the strategies the authors deployed in the prizes game and attitudes towards prizes within the texts to reveal how Roberto Bolaño, Carmen Boullosa and Fernando Iwasaki balanced these competing demands.

Roberto Bolaño's short story 'Sensini' was published in 1997 in the *Llamadas telefónicas* collection after it won the Premio Ciudad San Sebastián. Carmen Boullosa's novel *El complot de los románticos* was published in 2009 after it won the Premio Café Gijón and Iwasaki's *España, aparta de mí estos premios* was also published in 2009 but did not win a prize. These texts are not a straightforward representation of reality and nor are they an unmediated reflection of the authors' views about prizes. Yet it would be fair to say that the texts represent the most sustained, and perhaps the most critical, interventions made by Spanish American authors about literary prizes. Their very existence, their content, the fact they were published by peninsular-based presses, that two of them won awards in Spain, that they were all written by authors living outside Spanish America and were mostly, if not wholly, located in Spain, tells us much about the politics of literary prestige and prizes for Spanish American literature.

These texts are significant because they mark a shift in the discourse surrounding literary prizes in Spanish America. Commentary surrounding prizes in the Spanish American press does not typically adopt a tone which English describes as one of 'amused complicity' (2005, 215). Humour, if not exactly 'amused complicity', however, is a feature of the Spanish American fiction about prizes. For English this tone is associated with a literary field no longer structured around the opposition between high and low culture (2005, 221). The emergence of these texts, therefore, may point to the development of a less polarized literary field in Spanish America. But, a note of caution is required because peninsular commentary diverges from that in Spanish America. Noting the contrast, Chilean novelist Marcela Serrano observed: 'En España, al contrario que en América Latina, los premios suscitan una gran suspicacia' (In Spain, unlike in Spanish America, prizes provoke much suspicion) (quoted in Anabitarte 1998). *España, aparta* and, to a greater extent, *El complot* allude to prizes being rigged. Iwasaki's novel and 'Sensini' portray authors who manipulate the prize system for financial gain. Spanish critics also bemoan the excessive quantity of prizes on offer (González Ariza 2004, 20). Such remarks are rare in Spanish American criticism yet 'Sensini' and *España, aparta* reflect on the consequences of this proliferation as Bolaño and Iwasaki were perhaps struck by this feature of the peninsular literary field while living there. We cannot assume that these hereto rare examples of fictional texts by Spanish American authors reflect wider attitudes particularly when it comes to prizes based within Spanish America but as exceptions they test the rules of the prizes game.

Analysing the portrayal of literary prizes in these texts casts light on the limits of what can and cannot be said particularly as we might assume that fiction provides some cover for authors to push boundaries. The texts include authors adopting cynical attitudes and behaviours when submitting work to awards, inept judges, as well as literary fields which systematically disadvantage Spanish American and women authors. Criticism does, however, have boundaries even in fiction. It is directed towards the margins of the prize network and not at authors who are simultaneously victims whose genius is not adequately recognized or rewarded, and victors who outsmart a flawed system.

Operating outside Spanish America may have given these authors a different perspective and some leeway. Nevertheless, they still had to strike the right balance in their portrayal of the prize network. According to English, in the prizes game, the right balance entails resisting 'outright denunciation or implacable opposition' while appearing to be 'above such stakes as are at issue in the prize economy' (2005, 215). Establishing a critical distance from the prize economy through their fiction Bolaño, Boullosa and Iwasaki were able to accrue 'both the rewards of the game and the rewards due to those who are seen as standing above the game' (2005, 215). In other words, they deployed what Bourdieu termed 'strategies of condescension' which are 'those symbolic transgressions of limits which provide, at one and the same time, the benefits that result from conformity to a social definition and the benefits that result from transgression' (1991, 123). Thus, even as the texts exposed the questionable inner workings of some awards, prizes per se were not threatened and the authors' reputations were bolstered.

The texts studied here are part of a wider tradition so we may posit that the expanding prize network is giving rise to its own sub-genre of literature about prizes. This sub-genre connects to a related body of work, identified by Gallego Cuiñas, which emerged in the 1990s and in which texts expose the modes of cultural production (2018, 236). Examples include *Dejen todo en mis manos* (1994) by Mario Levero, 'Ars poética' (1999) by Jorge Volpi, *La vida nueva* (2007) by César Aira, *Efectos secundarios* (2011) by Rosa Beltrán, *Sudor* (2016) by Alberto Fuguet and 'Sensini' (1997) by Bolaño. Texts specifically about prizes, including 'Sensini', as well as *El complot* and *España, aparta* are related to this broader trend. The Spanish American texts in this sub-genre of literature about prizes postdate their peninsular counterparts. González Ariza identifies three much earlier peninsular novels about literary contests: *La llaga* (1960) by Luis Junced, *El premio* (1961), by Juan Antonio Zunzunegui and *Los importantes* (1962) by Francisco Candel (2004, 14). Manuel Vázquez Montalbán's *El premio* (1995) is the most recent addition to this peninsular tradition predating the earliest Spanish American example by two years.[1]

Critical reception and prizewinning strategies

Writing about the inner workings of literary prizes in an irreverent way, as do Bolaño, Iwasaki and Boullosa, is to risk censure for being too critical or too invested in prizes. The reception of these texts, however, indicates that they were well received, and that humour was key to their success. Bolaño and Boullosa's texts about prizes won awards prior to publication. Obituaries for Bolaño often referenced the San Sebastián prize for 'Sensini' demonstrating the significance retrospectively attributed to it in his career. *El complot* was well and widely reviewed in the Mexican press where the novel's humour was a focal point for discussion. Alejandro Flores (2009) and Nicolás Alvarado (2009) highlighted the novel's playfulness suggesting that it should be seen as

---

[1]For an analysis of prizes in *El premio*, see López Abaida (2001).

entertainment. Flores described *El complot* as 'una novela entretenida, con el acierto y jocosidad que le da la oralidad, lo cual la hace al tiempo una novela carnaval, una novela polifónica, una novela para pasar el rato, una novela ligera, simpática y con gran sentido de humour' (an entertaining novel, with the impact and jokeiness of its spoken style, which makes it at the same time a carnival novel, a multivocal novel, a novel to pass the time, a nice easy read with a great sense of humour). We might pause to wonder whether these comments are influenced by the gender of the author as one tactic for dismissing women's writing has been to associate it with entertainment so that it is taken less seriously. Lest the reader be in any doubt about how to interpret the text, they are explicitly cautioned not to connect fiction to reality: 'muy poca le interesa meterse con la realidad "real"' (the novel has little interest in 'real' reality) (Flores 2009). The text's ebullience and engaging humour were thus pivotal for the positive reception of *El complot* as they allowed critics not to take it, or its criticism of the literary sphere, too seriously.

Even for those critics willing to acknowledge the more serious aspects of the novel, humour was still identified as a noteworthy feature. Yanet Aguilar Sosa in *El Universal* recognized how humour and a serious message could coexist. She foregrounded the novel as entertainment but did not see this as diminishing the significance of the way it unmasked the inner workings of awards as she described it as 'una novela cabaret, un festín literario carnavalesco que desvela los entretelones de los premios literarios, al mismo tiempo que rinde un homenaje a escritores universales canónicos' (a cabaret novel, a carnivalesque literary feast that draws back the thick curtains on literary prizes, at the same time as it pays homage to universal canonical writers) (2009). *El complot*'s literariness, commented upon by Flores (2009) and Alvarado (2009), could have led to the novel being accused of being dry and inward looking, but humour offset such criticism. Iwasaki stated that if he had not used humour in *España, aparta*, he would have been accused of being an 'intelectual amargado' (embittered intellectual) (quoted in Rubio 2009). Had Boullosa not used humour, she too could have been accused of being an embittered intellectual. As it was, Boullosa and Iwasaki were rewarded because they successfully stood above the prize game without denouncing it outright.

Unlike Bolaño and Boullosa, Iwasaki did not win any awards for *España, aparta* but nor did he suffer from any critical backlash either. When *España, aparta* was published, many interviews with the author were printed, and he presented the book at the Guadalajara Feria Internacional del Libro (Book Fair) (FIL) in Mexico and went on a widely reported book tour. Most interviews were in the Spanish press as the book is set in Spain and, although from Peru, Iwasaki has lived in Spain since 1989. In interviews it is possible to detect a certain nervousness on Iwasaki's part as he repeatedly insisted that he was not belittling prizes of the kind featured in the novel which are ubiquitous in Spain and run by local government or private organizations. He said: 'no es un libro para ridiculizar a los premios, solo pretende ironizar, o satirizar. La literatura de humor tiene que divertir y también hacer pensar' (it is not a book that ridicules prizes. It only aims to ironize or satirize. Humorous fiction has to entertain and make you think) (quoted in 'La literatura de humor' 2009). To underscore his point he continued: 'Pero no es una burla, insisto, los premios cumplen una muy buena función' (But it is not a joke, I insist, prizes have a very important role) (quoted in 'La literatura de humor' 2009). In another interview (Carrasco 2010) Iwasaki was again careful to avoid outright denunciation or opposition which would be deemed inappropriate in the prizes game. He listed respected authors, including Bolaño, who had made a living from this type of prize indicating that not even they could ignore the financial stakes at issue in the economy of prestige. He praised the abilities of the authors who could survive on the income from awards because 'conocen el oficio y los lugares comunes' (they know the tricks of the trade) (Carrasco 2010). The true target of the novel's critique, Iwasaki insisted in *Sur*, was not prizes, nor Spain, but 'la sociedad del espectáculo, el "reality show" que suplanta a la sociedad civil por la audiencia' (the society of the spectacle, the reality show that is replacing civil society with an audience) (Sotorrío 2009). Despite his justifiable insistence that the main target of his satire was not prizes, he was keenly aware of the risk he had taken and concluded that 'se ha "descalificado como concursante"' (he had excluded himself as a competitor) (*Sur* 2009). The risk, however, was a calculated one which, if it did not bring him any prizes as it did for Bolaño and Boullosa, did not harm his reputation either as he subsequently won prizes for other works.

Bolaño and Boullosa, unlike Iwasaki, saw entering their texts about prizes to a prize competition as a logical extension of the text and part of what Boullosa termed 'un juego literario' (a literary game) ('Boullosa gana premio Café Gijón' 2008). Paratexts about their victories were added to the fictional texts giving them a new dimension. As prizewinning texts 'Sensini' and *El complot* were officially sanctioned as legitimate strategies of condescension, recognized as part of the game. The prizes which Bolaño and Boullosa entered were similar to those which feature in all three texts in other words not what Iwasaki refers to as part of the grand slam (Iwasaki quoted in Carrasco 2010). Both the Premio de Narración Ciudad de San Sebastián sponsored by the Kutxa Foundation that Bolaño won and the Premio Café Gijón won by Boullosa had long traditions from which they derived most of their status. Though not attached to the major publishing conglomerates they offered prize money and publication as reward. Akin to book fairs, the prizes were created to associate places with cultural prestige enhancing the status of the host locations as cultural hubs and bringing the associated economic benefits.[2]

---

[2] Details of the Premio Café Gijón and the Premio de Narración Ciudad de San Sebastián can be found on their websites at Premio Café Gijón | Web de Gijón (gijon.es) and Premios Literarios Kutxa Ciudad de San Sebastián – (kutxakultur.eus).

'Sensini', as part of the *Llamadas telefónicas* volume, was under contract with Jorge Herralde at Anagrama when Bolaño, unbeknown to Herralde, submitted the text to the San Sebastián competition. Under the terms of the award the copyright of the winning text, 'Sensini', passed to the prize organizers, the Kutxa Foundation. After he won, Bolaño wrote to Herralde apologizing and explaining: '[l]a tentación de enviar el cuento a un concurso literario de verdad y de ganármelo, tal como pasa en el cuento, era excesiva' ([t]he temptation to send the story to a real literary contest and win it, as happened in the story, was too much) (letter from Bolaño to Herralde quoted in the article 'Tras la tenue pista' 2013). Bolaño also tried to justify his entry saying that he did not think he would win. Herralde eventually secured the rights to include 'Sensini' in the collection as planned.

The risks taken by Bolaño were arguably greater. Not only was he in breach of the prize regulations and his contract with Anagrama; he was also less established than Boullosa and Iwasaki when they wrote their fictional texts about prizes and so in theory less able to deploy strategies of condescension appearing above the prize game while reaping its rewards. As his somewhat grovelling letter to Herralde reveals, he had a lot to lose. Of course, starting from a relatively low point, he had everything to gain as well. In retrospect, Bolaño was at a turning point in his career when he won the Premio Ciudad de San Sebastián for 'Sensini' in 1997. The prize improved his precarious financial situation. Yet Bolaño's prestige was not secured until a year later when he won the Premio Herralde and the Premio Rómulo Gallegos for *Los detectives salvajes*. These later awards were the ones that were transformational, but the earlier prize was a significant first step.

For Boullosa and Iwasaki their established positions in the literary field meant that they were better placed to deploy strategies of condescension playing and seeming to be above the game while benefitting from it. When Boullosa published *El complot*, she was a well-known author. Her early novels including *Mejor desaparece* (1987), *Antes* (1989), *Son vacas, somos puercos* (1991), and *Duerme* (1994) were very successful commercially and among feminist critics. She was associated with the *boom femenino* in Mexico, although not to the extent that she was subject to the kind of critical backlash directed at Laura Esquivel and Ángeles Mastretta for producing 'literatura light'.[3] Boullosa's early work was published with the prestigious publisher ERA with its reputation for literary fiction. She had a Fondo Nacional para la Cultura (FONCA) (National Culture Fund) grant in 1998, often seen as a steppingstone to acclaim in Mexico and won the state-sponsored Premio Xavier Villaurrutia for *Antes* in 1989.

---

[3]On the issue of 'literatura light', see Finnegan 2000.

In 2009 Iwasaki was an established author with numerous collections of short stories to his name. As Iswaski and other Spanish American authors have pointed out, the short story genre is often seen as being less prestigious in Spain than Spanish America, but Iwasaki had carved out a name for himself and had a good relationship with the independent publisher Páginas de Espuma. *España, aparta* was the fourth book he published with them. He had also published *Un milagro informal* with Alfaguara (2003). In addition, Iwasaki was a regular contributor in the Spanish press having been a columnist for *Diario 16*, *El País* and *La Razón* as well as for *Milenio* in Mexico and *El Mercurio* in Chile. From their secure positions Boullosa and Iwasaki were able to write about prizes in a way that showed them to be above the fray, 'in the know' about the inner workings of the prize system and able to differentiate between prizes and genuine prestige. They could afford to 'play with the rules of the cultural game' and benefitted from doing so (Bourdieu 1991, 125).

'Sensini'

'Sensini' is the story of two Spanish American authors living in exile in Spain writing to one another about literary prizes after they both enter the same prize competition. It is said to be based on Bolaño's friendship with Argentine author Antonio di Benedetto, Sensini in the story. The two authors became acquainted after they both entered the I Premio Alfambra de Cuentos organized by Valencia Town Hall in 1983 in the same way that Sensini and the narrator meet through a similar, fictional award.[4] The small provincial prizes the characters discuss, and that are the focus of 'Sensini', are so disconnected from the field of culture that the narrator reports that the announcements for submissions appear next to the weather or sports pages in newspapers 'ninguno, claro, en las páginas culturales' (none, of course, in the cultural section) (Bolaño 1997, 17). Many other aspects of literary prizes are criticized in the story. The narrator questions prizes as effective mechanisms for recognizing literary value because, in his view, the best text, written by Sensini, did not win. The usefulness of the awards is further undermined because they do not generate publicity. The winning entries are published in edited collections the impact of which is so limited that the narrator refers to them as 'aquellos libros invisibles' (those invisible books) (18). Awarding bodies, which include local councils and savings banks as well as the state railway company, are described as 'esa buena gente que cree en la literatura' (these good people who believe in literature) (18).

---

[4]On the autofiction and autobiographical elements in 'Sensini', see Herralde (2005, 30–1), Bagué Quílez (2010, 836) and Salas Oliva (2018).

The narrator really doubts the sincerity of the comment and is sceptical of the motives of said institutions in sponsoring the awards.

Jurors are portrayed as inept at appreciating the work of Spanish American authors. Jury membership is described as 'un oficio singular que en España ejercían de forma contumaz una pléyade de escritores y poetas menores o autores laureados en anteriores fiestas' (a unique role that is persistently performed in Spain by a pleiad of minor writers and poets and authors who had previously been prizewinners in earlier events) (19). Such an incestuous system, run by authors who are ironically referred to as a 'pleiad', excludes 'outsiders' like the narrator and Sensini. The problem faced by the Spanish American authors is particularly acute as peninsular critics fail to value their work on its own terms and instead impose European models. Spanish critics, therefore, view Sensini as 'una especie de Kafka colonial' (a kind of colonial Kafka) (14). The critics in the story are, to borrow from Casanova, guilty of reducing 'foreign works of literature to their own categories of perception, which they mistake for universal norms, while neglecting all the elements of historical, cultural, political and especially literary context that make it possible to properly and fully appreciate such works' (2004, 154). The result is that Spanish American works, such as those by Sensini, are always seen as being derivative and do not receive the recognition they deserve.

In these impoverished margins of the literary field the main function of prizes is to provide essential income for struggling writers and so the story does not present an outright denunciation of the prizes game. For Sensini entering prizes is a job like any other, a matter of economic necessity rather than creativity. He no longer holds to romantic ideals about being a writer and adopts a voracious and business-like approach to entering these prizes asking the narrator to share announcements about new contests to maximize his income. To minimize effort, he enters the same text in different contests using different titles. This deceit, Sensini explains, is all part of playing the game. In *España, aparta* Iwasaki shows just how effectively this strategy can be deployed. The texts Sensini submits are humorously likened by the narrator to a rabbit being used as a test subject for a new vaccine. The critique of the system, which results in a story the narrator admired being reduced to a money-making experiment and an author he respected turned into a trickster, is thus offset by humour.

The nicknames Sensini's daughter and wife give to him point to the dubiousness of his approach and the absence of the disinterested attitude supposedly appropriate to the true artist who would uphold the 'negative correlation between temporal (notably financial) success and properly artistic value' (Bourdieu 1993, 164). His daughter calls her father 'un profesional' (a professional) while his wife, perhaps half-jokingly, refers to him and the narrator as 'los pistoleros o los cazarrecompensas' (the gangsters and the bounty hunters) and 'los cazadores de cabelleras' (scalp hunters) as if they were cowboys in the wild west of the prize network (Bolaño 1997, 28).

The metaphor recurred in Bolaño's novel *Monsieur Pain* (1999) in which he referred to the minor prizes portrayed in 'Sensini' as 'premios búfalo' in other words, prizes which provided food for impoverished authors (quoted in Iwasaki 2009, 11). 'Sensini' thus contributes to a general theme Felipe A. Ríos Baeza identifies in Bolaño's work which is the 'desacralización del oficio de escritor' (deconsecration of the trade of being a writer) (2013, 96–7).

Far from condemning their cowboy antics we are encouraged to empathize with Sensini and the narrator who describes himself as 'más pobre que una rata' (poorer than a rat) (Bolaño 1997, 13). By the end of Sensini's first letter to the narrator, in which he educates him on how to play the prize game, the narrator feels that he has been trapped in a nightmarish scenario. In this degraded and degrading new Borgesian world into which he is inducted by the old master, prizes that the narrator initially sought as a means to validate himself as a writer have become a senseless pursuit from which he can no longer escape. He claims that 'tal vez' (perhaps) extreme poverty had first led him to enter his work for a prize (13). His hesitation is because he does not want to admit that he used to have a more idealistic view of prizes that is now exposed as naive. By the end of the story, the now jaded narrator criticizes the errors in the anthology of winning texts, complains that his text was better than the winning one and confesses that he cursed the judges (14). These are the more appropriate responses for the effective performance of the role of serious, disinterested writer. By exposing the direct intraconvertability between cultural and economic capital, the narrator could be said to undo the belief in the special aura of prizes, art and the artist. However, in portraying the two writers as victims of a system that fails to recognize true talent, the story preserves this aura and perpetuates the stereotype of the author as misunderstood genius. That they are also astute and good enough to enter and consistently win prizes is to their credit if not that of the awards.

'Sensini' ends with a footnote: 'Este cuento obtuvo el Premio de Narración Ciudad de San Sebastián, patrocinado por la Fundación Kutxa' (This short story won the City of San Sebastián Prize for Narrative sponsored by the Kutxa Foundation) (Bolaño 1997, 29). The reader may be forgiven for being uncertain as to whether the statement is fact or a final joke in the story. As Maria Martha Gigena states, the reader may view this statement with scepticism as part of 'la apuesta literaria' (the literary gamble) (2009, 3). In fact, Bolaño did win the prize. Regardless of whether the statement is understood as true or not by the reader the effect in the story is the same. It reveals that the author figure played the system and won. Speaking at the Feria Internacional del Libro (International Book Fair) in Santiago in 1999, two years after the story won the San Sebastián prize, Bolaño claimed that 'Sensini' was unpublishable were it not for the fact that it won a prize: 'la apuesta literaria no se cumplía en el texto, sino en ganar un premio *real*' (the literary gamble was not realized in the text but in the winning of a real prize)

(Bolaño cited in Gigena, 3). Herralde's willingness to publish the story prior to the award belies Bolaño's claim. Nevertheless, Bolaño's gamble paid off because he offset his critique with humour and only targeted prizes at the edge of the literary field. He had the last laugh as the recipient of a prize for a short story about literary prizes which enabled him to present himself as above the game while being a beneficiary of it.

España, aparta de mí estos premios

Iwasaki's *España, aparta de mí estos premios* takes up the challenge posed by 'Sensini' and shows how it is possible to submit variations of a single story to different literary contests. The novel thus consists of seven short stories based on a single story or '"célula madre" literaria' (literary mother cell) which is to be adapted according to the criteria of different prizes (Iwasaki 2009, 154). Each story is bookended by a parody of the rules governing such awards and the judges' statement declaring the preceding text the winner. The novel concludes with 'Decálogo del concursante consuentudianrio (y probablemente ultramarino)' (Ten Commandments for the Regular (and probably foreign) Contestant) addressed to aspiring authors advising them how to maximize their chances of winning a prize of this kind (155). The commandments and the use of the 'mother cell' story are intended to enable the aspiring Spanish American author who is the implied reader to make money with minimum effort. The novel, like 'Sensini', attaches no shame to authors who exploit the system in this way. It is the system that is flawed. The suggestion is clear, there is a game to be played and tactics should be deployed.

The prizes portrayed in the novel are akin to those in 'Sensini'. They are not those attached to major literary, cultural or political institutions and so the established politics of literary prestige remain intact. These awards are described as belonging to the 'tumulto de premios desperdigados por toda la geografía Española' (mass of prizes scattered throughout all parts of Spain) in a phrase that is taken from Bolaño's novel *Monsieur Pain* (1999) and quoted as an epigraph in *España, aparta* (Iwasaki 2009, 13).[5] In the rest of the quotation, also included in the epigraph, we find the full aforementioned quotation in which Bolaño refers to these prizes as 'premios búfalo que un piel roja tenía que salir a cazar pues en ello le iba la vida' (buffalo prizes

---

[5]Interestingly, both *Monsieur Pain* and *España, aparta* are linked by their connection to Chilean poet César Vallejo. The title *España, aparta* echoes that of Vallejo's collection of poems published posthumously about the Spanish Civil War, *España, aparta de mí este cáliz* (1939). The title is, therefore, part of the novel's running joke that to succeed in Spain one must write about the Civil War. In *Monsieur Pain* (originally published as *La senda de los elefantes*) the protagonist named in the title is asked to help treat Vallejo who is in hospital in Paris.

that a redskin [*sic*] had to go out and hunt because his life depended on it) (quoted in Iwasaki 2009, 11). Both texts therefore adopt the critique that is common in Spain, but not Spanish America, that prizes are ubiquitous and therefore devalued.

The prizes lampooned by Iwasaki's novel are presented as part of the wider problem of cultural relativism and the banalization of culture which leads to everything being turned into reality TV and spin-off books. They are a lamented feature of a literary field that is no longer polarized around high and low culture. All the prizewinning stories refer to events that are commercialized in this way. Groucho Marx's claim that '[l]os grandes éxitos los obtienen los libros de cocina, los volúmenes de teología, los manuales de "cómo hacer" y los refritos de la Guerra Civil' ([t]he bestsellers are cooking books, books about religion, self-help books and books about the Civil War) is quoted in the prologue and is the final commandment to aspiring authors who are told that these are the texts that sell and, therefore, should be reworked ad infinitum if their goal is to make money (Iwasaki 2009, 13 and 157). Quality literature, it is implied, will never sell in this impoverished environment.

In the same way that the narrator of 'Sensini' came to realize that these prizes are only useful for providing financial support, so too the first commandment in *España, aparta* disabuses the aspiring author-reader of the text of the myth that these prizes will lead to consecration: 'Los cuentos que envíes a los concursus nunca serán importantes para la historia de la literatura. En realidad, ni siquiera para la literatura' (The stories you submit to the competitions will never be important for literary history. In fact, not even for literature) (Iwasaki 2009, 155). Nevertheless, thanks to these prizes, the prologue states, 'cientos de escritores latinoamericanos y no pocos aborígenes (en este caso, españoles), pueden comer caliente, llegar a fin de mes e incluso comprarse un nuevo ordenador' (hundreds of Latin American writers and no small number of aboriginal ones (in this case, Spanish), can eat hot meals, make it to the end of the month and even buy themselves a new computer) (13). *España, aparta*, like 'Sensini', does not reject prizes out of hand because of the income they provide.

The novel reserves its harshest criticism for the awarding bodies who try to subordinate literature to a political agenda. The novel takes aim at 'the extravagant number of literary awards given throughout Spain, many of them with localist or atavistically folkloric topics, similar to those included in *España, aparta*' (López Calvo 2013, 123). Spanish nationalism is a particular target as the different prize criteria relate to the different Spanish nationalisms (Castany Prado 2016, 116). The way in which prizes try to further political agenda is highlighted by the criteria for the Premio de Relatos 'Héroes de Toledo' ('Heroes of Toledo' Short Story Prize). The regulations state that this prize is intended to 'promover la cultura y mantener viva la memoria histórica de España' (promote culture and keep

Spain's historical memory alive). The prize is organized by a surprising, but historically factual, coalition between the far-left and far-right parties in charge of Ardales Council. This combination of opposing political views leads to ridiculous prize criteria that try to satisfy the aims of both sides. For example, the rules state that the right-wing party will not accept entries that are not submitted in Spanish, but the left-wing party has agreed to translate into Spanish any submissions that arrive up to ten days before the actual prize deadline so that they will be eligible for consideration.

As in 'Sensini', prizes are organized by institutions that have little literary expertise but seek to capitalize on literary prestige. Such is the proliferation of these prizes that the sponsorship comes from Seville Football Club and organizations promoting the La Pileta Cave and Basque cuisine. Their pretensions are undercut by the text of the supposed prize regulations which mock the organizations' inflated sense of self-importance and their overly proscriptive requirements. For example, the prize offered by the body responsible for certifying the origin of Sanlúcar prawns is for a story about said prawns and the environment in which they are found. On the one hand, the organizers are mocked for their closed mindedness, for prioritizing propaganda over aesthetics and trying to turn fiction into a marketing tool. On the other, the belief these organizations place in the powerful role literature can play affirms its value and the novel does not undermine this suggestion.

The organizing bodies seek to turn authors into writers of extended adverts for their cause, but creativity and creative freedom always triumph over their bureaucratic mindset. The author figure always has the last laugh. S/he wins the prizes but subverts the criteria. This ability to refuse to submit to the prize agenda or take it too seriously and yet still emerge victorious is what makes the author figure the hero of the novel. In the Seville FC story the main character is a supporter of local rivals Real Betis. He has travelled from Japan to scatter the ashes of his friend, a Seville fan, at Seville FC's stadium. The prize judges declared the story the winner, but the inclusion of a Betis fan meant that the decision was not unanimous. The dissenting juror's objections are mocked in the declaration in which he steadfastly refuses to name Betis referring only to the '*otro* equipo de la ciudad' (other team in the city) (Iwasaki 2009, 111). For some judges, it is clear, literary merit is not the deciding factor and this is exposed in Iwasaki's novel.

Every story has a dissenting juror who is always the representative of the awarding body seeking to put politics above aesthetics. These lone voices do not prevail and, ultimately, literary criteria prevail. As Ignacio López Calvo points out, however, the other jurors are authors who may not be as immune to corruption as first appears as 'every short story is preceded by a quotation from a work by a jury member' (2013, 124). Cronyism is hinted at though not outright corruption.

Personally and politically motivated choices are criticized, but the greater risk is if substandard texts are rewarded. Even though the prizes are seen as fundamentally lacking in prestige, the awarding of any prize to an unworthy text poses an existential problem. If a flawed prize can go to a flawed text, then all awards and their winners are tainted by association. The prize criteria for the various awards in *España, aparta*, mirroring the majority of actual prize criteria, stipulate that an award must be made. The real challenges this stipulation can create were seen in Panama and discussed in Chapter 1. In the novel, this refusal to declare no winner is criticized as some of the statements suggest that the jury would have preferred to make no award. To make no award is to defend the conception of the author as rare genius, to negate the idea of prize as competition or game, and to impose 'an aesthetic paradigm in terms of which only a handful of people (genuine artists) are actually capable of producing authentic works of poetry, and the failed attempts of others cannot be said to hold any artistic value whatsoever' (English 2005, 145). The juror's statement following the La Pileta Cave Contest for Speleological Stories recommends that the criteria be changed to allow future juries to make no award. The Margarita Xirgú jury suggests making the same change or raising the prize money. The latter proposal, not disclaimed by the text, controversially implies that enhanced funding will lead to higher quality entries hinting that in the economy of prestige there is an exchange rate which equates prize money with quality. These calls to amend the regulations could be interpreted as damning indictments of the preceding winning text or, at best, indicate that there were so few good entries that jurors foresaw the need to have such criteria in the future. There is no desire, however, to put an end to the prizes. Indeed, these writer-jurors who put themselves and their reputations into the service of these narrow-minded organizations come out rather well as they are the only ones to suggest useful reform to protect literary prestige.

Improvements could be made, literature should not be made to serve political ends, but even the most culturally impoverished prizes which are a by-product of nationalist and other agenda, as they are portrayed in *España, aparta*, have a function. Spanish American authors are advised to take advantage of the money they offer without falling into the trap of equating prizes with literary value, making their art subservient to politics, or expending too much effort. In short, these implied readers should follow the guide they have been given and, like the author-narrator, should play the game and reap its rewards while appearing to be above the fray.

El complot de los románticos

Boullosa's novel *El complot de los románticos* is a carnivalesque portrayal of authors and their rivalries in which humour and exaggeration are used to bring into question the hierarchies that structure the literary world. Each year, those authors who belong to the El Parnaso association of consecrated, dead authors meet for a conference at which an annual prize, whose winner is chosen by the members of the organization, is awarded. Narrated by the living president of the association, which is based in New York, much of the novel focuses on her bizarre journey as she attempts to find a venue for the conference. Unable to hold the event in Mexico City she finally settles on Madrid. The question of the prize comes to the fore in the last third of the novel when the romantics, Byron, Coleridge, Blake, Shelley, Moore, Keats, Sir Walter Scott, José Asunción Silva and Jorge Isaacs, support the submission of a novel, written posthumously, by Ecuadorean author Dolores Veintimilla who the narrator describes as 'la Mary Shelley del Ecuador' (the Mary Shelley of Ecuador) (Boullosa 2009, 224). At the prize ceremony, the romantics are outraged when Veintimilla does not win and chaos ensues.

As in 'Sensini' and *España, aparta*, prizes are seen as poor measures of literary value. The winning text, selected ahead of Veintimilla's, is dismissively described as 'un reciclado bastante flojón' (a pretty weak reworking) (Boullosa 2009, 217). The narrator further undermines the aura of the prize by explaining its true significance: 'Cada año entregamos un premio que, por su propia naturaleza, porque es premio, no quiere decir que sea el libro mejor de todos los textos escritos en Ultratumbia ese año, sino que es precisamente el que gana el premio' (Every year we award a prize that, by its very nature, because it is a prize, does not mean that it is the best book of all those written Beyond the Grave that year, but rather that it is the one that wins the prize) (217). The prizes do, however, have a function. For this reason, far from behaving in an appropriately disinterested manner the romantics and other authors vie behind the scenes to win the award for themselves or a member of their group hoping to benefit by association. In petitioning for the award, they are motivated by self-interest and greed because the narrator reports 'él que lo recibe vuelve a estar en el gusto, los críticos se ocupan de él, salen nuevas traducciones, biografías, estudios, artefactos de la gloria' (whoever receives it comes back in fashion, critics concern themselves with him, new translations, biographies, studies and famous artefacts appear) (218). Prizes, unlike in 'Sensini', provide vital publicity even if they are not a true reflection of quality.

Yet prizes are not mere marketing tools. The stakes are much higher. Prizes can confirm or help to overturn existing hierarchies of value which are centred on dead male European authors. Judging should be taken seriously. In *El complot*, however, judges are easily swayed by authors' campaigns and petitions and by the presence of prefaces written by famous authors in the works submitted. Sometimes, the narrator reveals, judges do not even read the texts. The integrity of the prize is further brought into question as the narrator disregarded Veintimilla's text 'porque llegó firmada con un nombre que nadie reconoció' (because it arrived signed with a name that no one recognized) (Boullosa 2009, 223). Worryingly, the narrator admits that she thought that Veintimilla was used as a pseudonym. The fact that she discounted the novel because she did not recognize the pseudonym suggests that the widespread use of pseudonyms when submitting entries is ineffective in preventing prizes from being rigged because the jury is familiar with the pseudonyms of well-known authors. The reader is left with no doubt that the judging process is a farce and prizes are a thoroughly compromised measure of value.

The consequences of this flawed system are particularly serious for Spanish American women authors. The world of literature presented in *El complot* is structured in accordance with Casanova's 'world republic of letters' and 'international literary space' centred around Paris, London and New York with English and French the dominant languages. The narrator speaks out about the widespread ignorance about literatures in Spanish among El Parnaso members:

> en El Parnaso las letras anglosajonas, las francesas las italianas, las alemanas están muy bien representadas, pero de los nuestros . . . ¡¡no saben ni quién es Quevedo! ¡Ni Rubén Darío! De José Martí . . . medio saben los gringos porque es héroe político que juega a su favor. Pero no crean que le conocen demasiado. José Lezama Lima les parece nombre de fruta, de Macedonio Fernández no saben ni que existe. (159–60)

> (in the Parnassus Anglo Saxon, French, Italian and German literatures are very well represented. But as for ours . . . they do not even know who Quevedo is! Nor Rubén Darío! As for José Martí . . . the gringos know a bit because he is a political hero which works in his favour. But don't think they know him too well. They think José Lezama Lima is the name of a fruit and they don't even know that Macedonio Fernández exists).

Humour and hyperbole are used to present the situation as ridiculous and in need of change. The narrator seeks to decentre this world republic of letters by holding the El Parnaso meeting in Mexico City. Following a debacle of a trip the narrator's hopes of raising the status of Mexico City and Latin American literature are dashed in favour of the Spanish capital, but she consoles herself that at least Madrid is Spanish-speaking.

The gender politics underpinning the literary sphere generally, and prizes in particular, are also challenged as the narrator highlights the way in which Spanish American women authors are marginalized if not completely excluded. The narrator laments the fact that Mexican author Elena Garro has never attended an El Paranso meeting because no one in New York knows who she is. Rosario Castellanos's endorsement of Veintimilla's prize submission is deemed particularly useless: 'pues mujer y latinoamericana queda por fuerza relegada a un cierto rango de El Parnaso' (since as a woman and a Latin American she is by default relegated to a certain status within the Parnassus) (Boullosa 2009, 223). When the prize ceremony descends into chaos and Cuban author Gertrudis Gómez de Avellaneda defends Zorilla, the abuse she suffers is worse than that aimed at male authors pointing to the way in which women are censured when they dare speak out. Outraged at the treatment of Avellaneda, Flora Tristán denounces the treatment of women authors by the members of El Parnaso saying: 'A muchas otras ustedes las mantienen a raya por el único *defecto* de ser mujeres' (You keep many other women out when their only *defect* is being a woman) (220). Even as Tristán shouts a series of 'Vivas' (long lives) to various Spanish American women authors, the narrator reports that '[a] estas alturas ya nadie escucha, sino yo' ([a]t this point no one was listening except for me) (221). This is a tellingly ironic comment on the way in which women's voices are ignored or only heard by other women. In the hierarchy exposed in *El complot* Spanish American literature is marginalized because it is written in Spanish and it is produced away from the literary centres. However, women authors are doubly disadvantaged.

In its portrayal of the meeting of the El Parnassus association of great authors and the debacle of the prize-giving process *El complot* presents an extreme parody of the behind-the-scenes rivalries between authors and the game playing in the prize network. Events are taken to their comedic extreme so that we can finally see the flaws in the system. In its unmasking of these men (and occasional woman) the novel embraces the spirit of the carnivalesque.[6] The 'carnivalistic laughter' that is directed at these authors is an invitation to re-examine them, their status and the apparatus that enables their privilege (Bakhtin 1994, 254). They may be the residents of the Parnassus Mountain from Greek mythology reputed to be the home of poetry, music and learning, but these great authors have human foils and foibles which come to the fore when they are placed in ridiculous situations. Dante Alghieri, author of *The Divine Comedy*, for example, is forced to travel to Mexico City on the back of a rat and wears a Britney Spears baseball cap. In this way, and in contrast to *España, aparta*, *El complot* embraces the disruption of hierarchies of cultural value. The result is that canonical authors are taken down from their pedestals in the eyes of the reader. The conference in Madrid is likened to 'una fiesta de graduación de chicos preuniversitarios, en un encuentro de jóvenes escritores de provincias en una reunión de convictos fugados' (a graduation party for high-school

---

[6]While I read the process of unmasking in *El complot* with reference to Bakhtin and the carnivalesque Mauricio Zabalgoitia Herrera has connected these aspects of the novel to Octavio Paz's *fiesta* and Mexican masks in *El laberinto de la soledad* and denies a Bakhtinian connection (2012, 113–14).

students, a meeting of young provincial writers, a meeting of escaped convicts) (Boullosa 2009, 212). This description is very much in keeping with Bakhtin's description of a carnival whereby 'a free and familiar attitude spreads over everything' and the sacred and the profane, the lofty and the low, the great and the insignificant, the wise and the stupid are all combined (Bakhtin 1994, 251). The portrayal is thus both irreverent and celebratory.

The ultimate aim of carnival is renewal thus *El complot* invites us to challenge the status quo. In the ultimate expression of the carnivalesque in the novel the moment the winner is announced a fight breaks out. The romantics shout insults so vulgar the narrator cannot repeat them, and they storm the stage. The winning text and other entries are ceremonially burned. El Parnaso, we are told, never reconvened after this event. According to Bakhtin, the 'primary carnivalistic act is the mock crowning and subsequent decrowning of the carnival king' (1994, 252). This act 'proclaims the joyful relativity of all structure and order, of all authority and all (hierarchical) position' (Bakhtin 1994, 252). By selecting a winner who is immediately rejected, *El complot* exposes the inherent relativity of literary prizes as well as underscoring a view of prizewinners as interchangeable. The fire, as Bakthin points out, is a 'deeply ambivalent image' which points simultaneously to destruction and renewal (1994, 252). Thus, the final scenes of *El complot*, in which the winning text is reduced to ashes and the world's 'great' authors are involved in a fistfight, call on the reader to reflect critically on the value of prizes and the supposed greatness of the authors they consecrate.

El complot was published as a result of Boullosa winning the Premio de Novela Café Gijón in 2008. Between the title page and the list of contents there is a copy of the jury's pronouncement which states: 'El jurado destaca en la obra ganadora lo atrevido de su propuesta y el brillante uso de la cultura literaria' (The jury highlights the daring proposition of the winning work) ('Acta' in Boullosa 2009). The proclamation is signed in Madrid which is also the site of the failed awards ceremony around which the novel centres. As with Bolaño's 'Sensini', fiction and reality are blurred as the reader may wonder if the declaration is real or part of the fiction. Again, the fact that the question is asked is more important than the answer as the paratext, with a knowing wink, becomes part of a game that the text plays with the reader because, despite appearing to be above the game and questioning the politics of literary prizes, Boullosa's novel still won.

Conclusions

Writing about prizes in a way that was neither too naive nor too hostile enabled Bolaño, Boullosa and Iwasaki to present themselves as shrewd operators in the literary field and as defenders of the aura of the author.

They, we are supposed to conclude, were not fooled into thinking that all prizes were created equal or that prestige and literary prizes correlate. They used humour to deflect any potential criticism of them being embittered authors. In the cases of Bolaño and Boullosa, entering the works to prizes was another way of proving that they were expert players rather than sore losers in the prizes game and further inoculated them against criticism. If the jury could see the joke, then critics would be petty-minded if they did not. Major national, international prizes, and those run by publishers are spared any criticism. To target them could have been a step too far. Even the less well-known prizes portrayed in 'Sensini' and *España, aparta*, or those run for and by authors, as in *El complot*, which are especially prone to corruption, cliques and in-fighting, have a place and a function. There is no call in these texts for prizes to be abolished, although some reform would be welcome. Boullosa's critique of the way prizes perpetuate existing canons and marginalize women and authors writing in Spanish is the most significant. The fire at the end of *El complot* and the fact that there are no subsequent meetings of El Parnaso can be interpreted as signalling a hopeful moment of renewal and change. These fictional texts may provoke a moment of reflection, but, as shown by the reviews, they were well within the permitted rules of the game. The politics of prestige remained intact, but these Spanish American authors played the joker and won.

5

The Premio Biblioteca Breve and the forgotten women of the Boom

Two mid-twentieth-century Spanish American women authors were connected to the prestigious Premio Biblioteca Breve but did not derive from it the same recognition as the male winners of the award, many of whom achieved international renown as part of the Boom in Spanish American literature. In the twelve years between the prize's inception and Barral's departure from Seix Barral the Premio Biblioteca Breve had been awarded five times to a Spanish American author and no woman author of any nationality had ever been recognized. But that is not the full story. In 1960 Mexican Ana Mairena (1909–78) came close to winning the prize for *Los extraordinarios* (1961). As usual, the jury of five met in May at the Hotel Formentor in Mallorca. Mairena, alongside Spaniards Juan Marsé and Daniel Sueiro, was a finalist. In the end, no award was made because none of the competing texts received sufficient votes to be declared the winner.[1] Even though *Los extraordinarios* had not won the prize, the novel was published by Seix Barral in 1961 as part of its prestigious Biblioteca Formentor series. While many of the male winners and nearly winners of the Premio Biblioteca Breve, among them José Donoso and Manuel Puig, are now associated with the Boom and considered pioneering Spanish American authors, Mairena is never mentioned in histories of the Boom and, in fact, is rarely mentioned at all. In 1972, after Barral's departure from Seix Barral, Cuban Nivaria Tejera (1929–2016) became the only woman to win the Premio Biblioteca Breve in its first phase. She won the prize for

---

[1] A statement to this effect is included at the beginning of the 1961 Seix Barral edition of *Los extraordinarios*. According to text from Seix Barral reproduced in the journal *Espéculo* Marsé had the most votes. 'Premio Biblioteca Breve 40 años después (1958–1998).'

her novel *Sonámbulo del sol* (1972) which was published by Seix Barral. She too continues to be largely overlooked. The experiences of Mairena and Tejera provide compelling evidence of the way in which the politics of literary prestige and literary history are gendered in a way that consistently marginalizes women authors and their achievements. Success within the prize network, even at an international level and in a prize that acquired the stature of the Premio Biblioteca Breve, does not necessarily help women authors to overcome inequalities in the wider literary field.

This chapter showcases the value of looking back at the winners and the shortlists of literary prizes to enhance our understanding of Spanish American literary history and re-evaluate the contributions of Spanish American women authors. The chapter analyses *Los extraordinarios* and *Sonámbulo del sol* to show that they, like recognised Boom novels, combined technical innovation and social awareness and so merit a more prominent place in Spanish American literary history. Acknowledging the connections between Spanish American women and the Premio Biblioteca Breve has the potential to alter our understanding of a pivotal phase in Spanish American literature and the history of women's writing in the region as we see that the Boom was bookended by the success of two Spanish American women authors. There can be no doubt as to the importance of understanding the politics of literary prestige once we realize that our understanding of *the* pivotal period in twentieth-century Spanish American literary history would be completely different were literary prestige not so heavily gendered.

The 'Boom' is the term commonly used to refer to the phenomenon that brought Spanish American authors to the attention of international readers. The Boom was a 'boys club' centred around the 'big four' authors Colombian Gabriel García Márquez, Mexican Carlos Fuentes, Peruvian Mario Vargas Llosa and Argentine Julio Cortázar.[2] Yet this view, which associates literary prestige with a group of exclusively male authors, could have been very different. Although the dominant narrative suggests that women authors were a later arrival following the Boom, a closer examination of the history of the Premio Biblioteca Breve reveals two forgotten women of the Boom who attracted the attention of Seix Barral. Argentine Marta Traba (1930–83) also has a case to be included in the Boom, but, because she was not connected specifically to the Premio Biblioteca Breve, she is not discussed here. That these women were the exception makes them all the more significant.

Literary and extra-literary factors coincided to create the Boom. Carlos Barral, Seix Barral and the Premio Biblioteca Breve were among the main extra-literary influences. The Premio Biblioteca Breve was pivotal in

---

[2]Herrera-Olaizola refers to the 'boys' club of the 'boom' and its sequel in the '"female" Boom of the 1980s' (2007, 32). The phrase 'the big four' is taken from Swanson (2005, 62).

publicizing the works of the Boom authors and making literary prestige synonymous with the kind of texts we now associate with the Boom. As Barral sought to use the prize to reinvigorate literature in the Spanish language and find solutions to contemporary social and political problems, as discussed in Chapter 2, Spanish American authors of the Boom provided the answer. In 1962 Vargas Llosa won, Fuentes won in 1967 and Mexican Vicente Leñero and Cuban Guillermo Cabrera Infante won in 1963 and 1964, respectively.

Such is the association between the Boom and the Premio Biblioteca Breve that one method of dating the Boom is with reference to the trajectory of this prize (Swanson 2005, 61). According to this view, the Boom began in 1962 when Mario Vargas Llosa became the first Spanish American winner of the award and ended in 1970 when José Donoso would have won had Carlos Barral not left the publishing house.[3] Despite Barral's departure, Donoso's *El obsceno pájaro de la noche* was published by Seix Barral with a foreword by Barral. The Premio Biblioteca Breve was awarded twice more in 1971 and 1972. In 1972 Barral declared that 'el "boom" ya no existe más que a nivel de explotación editorial' (the 'boom' now only exists as a marketing tool for publishers) (¿Existe o no..?, nd). That year Tejera became the only woman to win the prize. Donoso, in his novel-exposé of the Boom, *El jardín de al lado*, connected the emergence of women authors with the decline of the Boom (Herrero-Olaizola 2007, 25). To date the end of the Boom with reference to Tejera's victory and the supposed arrival of women authors on the literary scene is to indulge male anxiety about competition from women authors and women's changing role in society and significantly overlooks Tejera's links to the Boom and those of Mairena. Once we associate these two women authors with the Boom it comes to be dated a year earlier, in 1961, when Mairena was nominated for the Premio Biblioteca Breve and lasts until 1972 when Tejera won.

Mairena and Tejera's critical reception and extra-literary links to the Boom

As a shortlisted candidate for the Premio Biblioteca Breve and one of only two women to be included in the 1969 Seix Barral catalogue, in the 'Latin American Novelists' section, Mairena has clear extra-literary connections to the Boom.[4] Ana Mairena was a pseudonym used by Asunción Izquierdo

---

[3]On the different ways of dating of the Boom, see Swanson (2005, 62).
[4]Herrera-Olaizola notes that Mairena and Traba were the only two women in this catalogue a fact which 'confirms the exclusionary character of the male Boom' (2007, 33).

Albiñana to conceal her writing activities from her husband, the well-known politician Gilberto Flores Muñoz.⁵ Today she is perhaps best known for her untimely death as she and her husband were murdered in their homes. However, during her lifetime she published poetry, eight novels and wrote a play which was never performed. Between 1973 and 1978 she also wrote a regular column in *El Día* called 'Crónicas al vuelo'. Despite *Los extraordinarios* being described by Vicente Leñero as better than other works published in the same year by respected, and now better-known, women authors Luisa Josefina Hernández, Emma Dolujanoff and Concha Villareal, Mairena's novel and her other works are, according to Diana Gutiérrez, 'prácticamente inconseguibles' (practically unobtainable) for today's readers (Leñero 1992, 108; Gutiérrez 2018).

A snapshot of the limited existing criticism about *Los extraordinarios* reveals that the novel was thought to have merit.⁶ It was appreciated for being socially aware, possessing signs of experimentation and innovation, and received qualified endorsement as a finalist for the Biblioteca Breve prize. Vicente Leñero, himself winner of the 1963 Premio Biblioteca Breve, in his book about the murder of Mairena and her husband, described *Los extraordinarios* as a worthy finalist for the prize (1992, 108). He also said it was, without doubt, the best Mexican novel published that year. The well-known critic of Mexican literature, John Brushwood, similarly praised *Los extraordinarios* stating that it 'is more than just a good novel and deserves its place among the finalists of the "Biblioteca Breve" prize of 1960' (1962, 140). In a later retrospective on Mexican literature between 1967 and 1982 Brushwood again praised the novel for its use of modern techniques: 'Las estrategias que emplea la autora son modernas, en el sentido general del término' (The strategies that the author employs are modern, in the general sense of the word) (1983, 103). None of the critics, however, were unreserved in their praise.

Like Mairena, Tejera has also been largely overlooked bar a few important interventions which have, to no avail, mooted Tejera's claim to be considered part of the Boom.⁷ Catherine Davies, for example, states that *Sonámbulo* 'should have been included in the "boom" of the late 1960s but

---

⁵Biographical details are based on accounts in Leñero (1992), Martínez (1995), 'Ana Mairena [Asunción Izquierdo Albiñana de Flores Muñoz]. Ana Mairena [Asunción Izquierdo Albiñana de Flores Muñoz] – Detalle del autor – Enciclopedia de la Literatura en México – FLM – CONACULTA (elem.mx) and Diana Gutiérrez (2018).

⁶This overview of criticism is based on Leñero (1992), Martínez (1995), Brushwood (1962 and 1983) and Pedro Gómez in the online *Enciclopedia de la Literatura en México* Ana Mairena [Asunción Izquierdo Albiñana de Flores Muñoz] – Detalle del autor – Enciclopedia de la Literatura en México – FLM – CONACULTA (elem.mx) and Gutiérrez (2018).

⁷On the early reception of the novel in the contemporary press, see Hernández-Ojeda (2009, 99–102). Much of this overview is based on the interview with Weiss, J. (1999), 'Descifrar al exilio. Entrevista a Nivaria Tejera', *Quimera* 183, 8–13.

passed virtually unnoticed' (1997, 127). One of the main reasons Tejera is not commonly associated with the Boom is because Barral had left Seix Barral when she became the only woman to win the award in its first phase. Yet, it is highly likely that Barral would have supported Tejera as the winner in 1972. Barral had long been an admirer of Tejera's work and tried to secure the rights to *Sonámbulo* for his new venture.[8]

It is all the more surprising that Tejera has been overlooked as the pre-eminent woman author of the Boom if we consider that, prior to winning the Premio Biblioteca Breve, in common with many of the Boom authors, Tejera had an established reputation in France. *Sonámbulo* had been published in French in 1970 as had her earlier novel *Le ravin* (1958). According to Casanova, consecration in Paris was fundamental to the success of the Boom authors (2004, 135). In Tejera's case, however, it has been suggested that her exile counted against her, and so she was not well received in Spanish America (Hernández-Ojeda 2009, 138). Just as Tejera did not benefit from the prestige of the Premio Biblioteca Breve to the same extent as her male counterparts, nor did she benefit equally from having been consecrated in Paris.

Despite the extra-literary factors connecting Tejera to the Boom, we must, nevertheless, exercise caution. Tejera distanced herself from established canons and was an outspoken critic of the Boom. In Tejera's later (autobiographical) anti-Fidel Castro novel, *Espero la noche para soñarte, Revolución* (1997), 'la narradora se refiere a Julio Cortázar como el "genio del ku-klux-klan Boom"' (the narrator refers to Julio Cortázar as the 'genius of the ku-klux-klan Boom') (Díaz-Vega 2012, 53). The objection though was perhaps to the exclusive and exclusionary nature of the Boom more than to its aesthetic preferences. Cortázar, after all, is grudgingly referred to as a genius. Tejera also rejected the 'carácter mercantil del Boom' (mercantile character of the Boom) (Díaz-Vega 2012, 52). Here again, her objection is to the Boom as a marketing phenomenon and is not a dismissal of the innovative aesthetics she shares in common with Boom novels. Moreover, her opposition to the publicity surrounding the Boom was not so great that she refused the Premio Biblioteca Breve which was one of the main mechanisms for marketing the Boom.

Another important, but non-literary, point of divergence between Tejera and the Boom authors centres on politics. The Cuban Revolution was a political focal point for the Boom authors. It provided them with what Donoso terms an 'estructura ideológica' (ideological structure), a 'sensación

---

[8] Barral's interest in Tejera's work is evident in his correspondence with Carmen Balcells about Tejera's *El ojo exiliado* ('Nota sobre *El Ojo Exiliado*' no date). Tejera stated that Barral was interested in securing *Sonámbulo* in an interview with Jason Weiss quoted in Hernández-Ojeda (2009, 99).

de cohesión' (feeling of cohesion), and what John King refers to as 'the utopian promise of uniting the artistic and political vanguards' (quoted in Díaz-Vega 2012, 48). All of the 'big four' Boom authors were, at first, ardent supporters of the Castro regime. They all visited Cuba in the immediate aftermath of the Revolution (Aguirre 2017). Carlos Barral also visited Cuba several times and signed a contract to import and export books with the department directed by the poet Heberto Padilla (Aguirre 2017). As a result of this contract, 2,000 copies of Mario Vargas Llosa's prizewinning *La ciudad y los perros* were exported to Cuba (Aguirre 2017). Tejera, however, took the Boom authors to task for being slow to denounce the curbs that the Revolution placed on artistic freedom. She broke with the regime in 1965 when she resigned her post as cultural attaché at the Cuban Embassy in Rome. For the Boom authors it was the later Padilla Affair, discussed in Chapter 1, that proved the turning point.

Tejera's long-standing opposition to the Revolution may have been a factor in the awarding of the Premio Biblioteca Breve to Tejera in May 1971 against the backdrop of Padilla's imprisonment in March 1971. The prize jury in 1971 consisted of the Spaniards Luis Goytisolo and Pere Gimferrer, Mexican Juan Rulfo and Juan Ferraté who worked for Seix Barral. Santana also lists Spanish author Jorge Semprún as a juror, but his name does not appear in the list of jurors on the opening pages of the 1972 Seix Barral edition of *Sonámbulo* (2000, 62).[9] Goytisolo had strong links with the Boom authors through his time in Paris and work with French publisher Gallimard. Following a trip to Cuba with Cabrera Infante, author of *Tres tristes tigres*, in 1967 he distanced himself from the Revolution having witnessed 'the repression against African religions, censorship and persecution of homosexuals' (Goytisolo quoted in an interview with Jaggi 2000). Rulfo was not a communist and was closely connected to the Congress for Cultural Freedom, 'the CIA's principal cultural front organisation during the Cold War' designed to combat Cuban influence (Iber 2015, 264). Semprún and Barral were signatories to the letter a group of intellectuals sent to Castro expressing their concern at the arrest of Padilla (Weinberg 2004, 37). Tejera's opposition to the Revolution predates that of some of the Boom authors, but now her views aligned with those of several jury members and three out of the 'big four'. Vargas Llosa, Fuentes and Cortázar all signed the letter of protest to Castro. The Boom authors became disillusioned later than Tejera, but her earlier rejection of the Cuban Revolution does not mean that *Sonámbulo* cannot be considered a Boom novel.

---

[9]Santana includes Semprún in the list of jurors, but Hernández-Ojeda does not (2016, 173). Semprún is also not listed as a juror on the title page of the published edition of *Sonámbulo* (1972).

One way to date the Boom is with reference to Barral's involvement in the Premio Biblioteca Breve. Another way is with reference to the Padilla Affair and the resulting split among the 'big four' Boom authors. Given that Barral was a confirmed fan of Tejera's work, that she won the Premio Biblioteca Breve and that her award was so intimately connected to the Padilla Affair then the case for her to be considered the pre-eminent forgotten woman author of the Boom is compelling. A third way to define the Boom is with reference to aesthetics. The next section will, therefore, focus on the aesthetic alignment between Mairena's *Los extraordinarios*, Tejera's *Sonámbulo* and Donald Shaw's characterization of the Boom novels as, to differing degrees, combining technical innovation in a literature which retained its social function (1981, 13).

Mairena and Tejera's aesthetic links to the Boom

When the Premio Biblioteca Breve was launched, it was common practice for Spanish publishers to create prizes as a means of adding new authors who shared the established aesthetic of the publishing house to their catalogues (Esposito 2009).[10] The Seix Barral aesthetic, which became the Boom aesthetic, combined 'la crítica social' (social criticism) with 'una preocupación por los aspectos formales de la novela que los acerca a las tendencias más novedosas de la novela moderna' (a concern for the formal aspects of the novel which aligned with the latest tendencies in the modern novel) (Esposito 2009). These priorities are evident in the aims of the Premio Biblioteca Breve as stated by the founders of Seix Barral. Víctor Seix stated: 'la principal misión del premio es estimular a los escritores jóvenes para que se incorporen al movimiento de renovación de la literatura europea actual' (the main mission of the prize is to encourage young authors to join the movement of renewal within contemporary European literature) (Planeta, 'Premio Biblioteca Breve'). Barral said: 'la obra premiada debería contarse entre las que delatan una auténtica vocación renovadora o entre las que se presumen adscritas a la problemática literaria y humana estrictamente de nuestro tiempo' (the prizewinning work should be among those which reveals an authentic vocation for renewal or among those which engages with the literary and human challenges that belong specifically to our time) (Planeta, 'Premio Biblioteca Breve'). These dual concerns were further evident in the discussions held at the Hotel Formentor in 1959 prior to the awarding of the second Premio Biblioteca Breve when debate topics for those attending the Coloquio Internacional de Novela (International Colloquium

---

[10]This was also established practice in Spanish America as discussed in Chapter 2.

on the Novel) included whether the novel should aspire to bear witness to a situation, defend an ideological stance or create an independent world (Espinas 1959). Another question participants were asked was whether the novel should portray the world as it is or if it should try to contribute to its transformation (Espinas 1959). These discussions, which took place at the same time as the prize deliberations, reflect, and are likely to have led to the further development of, a shared sense of what kind of literature would ultimately be deemed worthy of the prize.

Los extraordinarios by Ana Mairena

One of the main innovative features of Mairena's *Los extraordinarios* is its structure which is based around a series of flashbacks. The young indigenous protagonist, Jacinto, sits in the apartment of Doña Mercedes who owns the garage where he works awaiting her return. The flashbacks take us back to an earlier episode in his life arranged not in chronological order but according to their relative importance in leading to the present as we delve deeper into Jacinto's repressed consciousness. His disordered recollections reflect his struggle to understand his present predicament. In this sense, *Los extraordinarios* is akin to the Boom novels which replaced linear structures with 'otra estructura basada en la evolución espiritual del protagonista' (another structure based on the spiritual evolution of the protagonista) (Shaw 1998, 4).

The novel is also experimental in the way it subverts the conventions of the detective genre. It is a forerunner of Vicente Leñero's later novel *Los albañiles* (1964) which won the 1963 Premio Biblioteca Breve and should be seen as contributing to the development of the genre in Mexico just as Leñero's novel has been widely praised for the way it 'bouleverse les codes' (overthrows the rules) (Fell 2013, 47) and as 'una de las pocas novelas detectivescas hispanoamericanas de calidad' (one of the few quality Hispanic American detective novels) (Szmetan 1989, 70). In place of the usual 'whodunnit' the structure is altered so we are forced to ask why Jacinto has been driven to commit a crime. Detective fiction in which the crime is solved is said to reaffirm the status quo because the state can impose order (Simpson 1990, 139; Stavans 1997, 55). In *Los extraordinarios* the status quo is the problem that has to be investigated by delving into Jacinto's past. Not only is Mairena left out of the history of the Boom, but she is also wrongly excluded from the history of Spanish American detective fiction.

In analysing the root causes of criminality the novel engages in a nature versus nurture debate. On the nurture side Jacinto is presented as being as much a victim as Doña Mercedes. As Hans Beerman wrote in a brief review for *Books Abroad*, 'We follow the protagonist through his miserable childhood, the revolting experiences of his young manhood where cruelty, hatred, and injustice are his daily companions, until he finally succumbs to the insidious pressures of his environment' (1962, 61). Jacinto's actions are thus rationalized as the logical consequence of his upbringing and environment alongside his growing awareness, through his contact with Enrique, Doña Tinita and Doña Mercedes, that there is a better life which he cannot afford. Jacinto's fate is presented as being particularly tragic because, despite his lack of formal education, he is intelligent and a talented painter. These skills should help Jacinto to succeed, but they are not enough.

In the novel's exploration of what leads a man to become a criminal, however, Jacinto may not be blameless. We have glimpses into his faults and misdeeds, but these are concealed by the use of free indirect speech meaning that the reader has to try to see through the narrative of self-justification. In this way, as well as in its use of the flashback technique, the novel is reminiscent of Carlos Fuentes's classic Boom novel *La muerte de Artemio Cruz* (1962), which was published just a year after *Los extraordinarios*, and in which an ex-revolutionary tries to justify his betrayal of the Mexican Revolution on his deathbed.

On the nature side of the debate, the indigenous Jacinto is repeatedly essentialized in ways that are likely to prove problematic for contemporary readers. Ultimately, we can see Jacinto as an isolated, alienated individual motivated by greed and a sense of self-preservation. Seeing the lives of Enrique and the other privileged students known as *Los extraordinarios*, and the wealthy widow, Tinita, Jacinto glimpses the better life to which he aspires.[11] Despite his efforts, he cannot quite fit in. With Enrique he feels 'envuelto en una densa irrealidad' (wrapped up in a dense unreality) (Mairena 1961, 122). He lives a kind of double life with Enrique or Tinita by day and at the garage at night. We are told '¡Estaba harto de ser tantos Jacintos!' (He was fed up of being so many Jacintos!) and 'tenía prisa de vivir' (he was in a hurry to live) (67). It is this desire to change his life, to become what he sees as his true self, that leads him to plan the robbery and murder. In its portrayal of Jacinto's alienation *Los extraordinarios* fits in well with an interest in existentialism shared by Boom novelists including Cortázar as discussed by Harris (2009). Moreover, his quest to become his true self links to the male quest for identity that, Gerald Martin points out, was central to the Boom novels (1984, 60).

Female characters in Boom novels are rare, and when they do appear, they are generally not well rounded and significant only in so far as they relate to the male protagonists. Regrettably, the same is true of *Los extraordinarios* and Tejera's *Sonámbulo*. The significance of Jacinto's two love interests,

---

[11]*Los Extraordinarios* (the extraordinaries) are so-called because their lack of commitment to their studies means that they have to sit their exams in extraordinary circumstances, that is, during the resit period.

Cristina and Guadalupe, lies in the way his attitude and treatment of them is revealing of his character. Women are among the victims in Mairena's novel, but, unlike Jacinto, they are not the focus of our attention. Mercedes is the obvious victim, but we know almost nothing about her apart from the fact that she runs the garage and the male workers resent her in this role because she is a woman. Even when she pays for the medical treatment and funeral of the child of one of the men, this act only affords her a brief respite from the derogatory comments made behind her back. Jacinto never even sees her face. Ultimately, he attacks her not because of who she is as an individual but because she represents everything he cannot have. Her death is violent because he is overcome by rage which prevents him from executing the carefully planned robbery and escape which would supposedly have led him to becoming his true self. Feminist critics looking for something different will be disappointed by this one-dimensional portrayal of female characters, but in its portrayal of women as types who are largely incidental to a male quest for selfhood Mairena's novel is very much in keeping with the dominant trends of the Boom.

The regrettable portrayal of female characters may have led to *Los extraordinarios* attracting little attention in the context of the work of recovering forgotten women authors by feminist critics to date. The fact remains, however, that *Los extraordinarios* was the subject of some acclaim not least as a finalist for the Premio Biblioteca Breve. It also shared with many of the Boom novels an interest in providing a panoramic view of society and its ills as well as a penchant for technical innovation. Mairena's work certainly makes for a very interesting comparison with its better-known contemporaries. It is a daring step to speculate that Fuentes could have been inspired by the way *Los extraordinarios* used flashbacks when it came to reconstructing the life of Artemio Cruz from his deathbed, but *Los extraordinarios* certainly provides evidence that the characteristics that were so lauded in the works of the male Boom authors were also present in the works of a less well-known woman author. Such findings are important for our understanding of how literary history is gendered and how the study of literary prizes could help to fill in some of our blind spots in this regard.

Sonámbulo del sol by Nivaria Tejera

The early reception of *Sonámbulo* was caught up in issues surrounding the Padilla Affair, the Cuban Revolution and the split at Seix Barral. As a result, Tejera did not derive the benefit other authors had from winning the Premio Biblioteca Breve. Tejera made a statement to this effect in an interview (quoted in Hernández-Ojeda 2009, 99–100). At a distance from this context, we are well positioned to reconsider *Sonámbulo*'s relationship to the Boom novel and other winners of the Premio Biblioteca Breve focusing on the way in which it combined social awareness with technical innovation.

Critics who have championed Tejera's significance have already commented on some of the aesthetic connections between her work and that of the Boom authors. María Díaz-Vega notes: 'Es posible decir que Tejera manifiesta ciertos rasgos de la generación del Boom' (It is possible to say that Tejera shows certain traits of the Boom generation) (2012, 51). Like the Boom authors, Tejera was committed to 'la renovación de la literatura de Latinoamérica' (the renewal of Latin American literature) (Díaz-Vega 2012, 51). She, like many of the Boom novelists, was also influenced by the French nouveau-roman (Hernández-Ojeda 2009). Of particular significance in connecting Tejera to the Boom are the similarities Davies (1997, 127) and Hernández-Ojeda (2009, 85–6) have identified between *Sonámbulo* and *Tres tristes tigres* by fellow Cuban author Cabrera Infante. Cabrera Infante won the Premio Biblioteca Breve in 1964 for *Vista de amanecer en el trópico*. The text underwent 'un radical proceso de re-escritora' (a radical rewriting) due to the constraints imposed by censorship under the Franco regime (Aguirre 2018, n.p). The reworked text was published as *Tres tigres tristes* and is often associated with the Boom. Such were the similarities between the two prizewinning texts that Tejera herself stated that she believed that the two novels complemented one another (quoted in Hernández-Ojeda 2009, 86). This likeness demonstrates the full extent to which Tejera's novel aligned with the aesthetic preferences of the first phase of the Premio Biblioteca Breve.

Like *Los extraordinarios Sonámbulo* eschews linear narrative in favour of a structure that reflects the evolution of the Afro-Cuban protagonist, Sidelfiro and the subjective nature of reality. Such an approach was typical of Boom novels (Shaw 1998, 4). The short, fragmented episodes of *Sonámbulo* reflect the protagonist's fragmented sense of self. This collage of texts and fragments creates a disorienting experience for the reader mirroring Sidelfiro's sense of disorientation as he wanders around Havana of the late 1950s. In between each episode there is often a gap in time or space or a shift in perspective indicated by large blanks on the page.

Tejera, like the Boom novelists, also rejected the single, reliable, third-person narrator. The narrative of *Sonámbulo* is further broken up by the use of text in italics, in inverted commas or formatted as poetry alongside prose sections. The reader moves freely between the real-world Sidelfiro experiences on his walk, the world of his imagination and the voices of his subconscious. Boom novels likewise replaced realism with ambiguity and 'espacios imaginarios' (imagined spaces) and blurred the distinction between the real and the imagined, fantastic or magical (Shaw 1998, 4).

In keeping with the themes of incommunication, solitude and existential angst characteristic of Boom novels, Sidelfiro is alone alienated from himself, others and his environment even more so than Jacinto in *Los extraordinarios*. He vainly searches the city trying to give meaning to his life. His aimless wandering 'representa la agonía de ese anhelo capital: la voluntad de poseer su propia vida' (represents the agony of this fundamental desire: the will to possess one's own life) (Hector Bianciotti quoted in Hernández-Ojeda 2009, 90). As he walks around, he hears snippets of conversation. He witnesses scenes but is not part of them, and they make little sense to him. When he visits friends he still feels isolated. He is acutely aware that as far as his co-workers at the Ministry are concerned, he barely exists. They make racist remarks about him. He says nothing. He contemplates reacting to the women whose idle chatter he is forced to listen to by throwing himself on the floor kicking and screaming. Ultimately, however, he will never respond: 'No encontraría nunca él dentro de sí la fuerza para rebelarse verdaderamente' (He would never find within himself the strength to truly rebel) (Tejera 1972, 178). Even towards the end of the novel, when the general strike of 1958 is called by the 26 July Movement, he watches events but does not participate.

Symbolism is used throughout the novel in a way that is in keeping with the rejection of realism in Boom novels. The sun is omnipresent from the beginning of the novel. It prevents Sidelfiro from sleeping, drives him to walk the streets, burns with such intensity that Sidelfiro feels like it is burning him from the inside and represents the oppression of the Batista dictatorship from which Sidelfiro cannot escape (Hernández-Ojeda 2009, 75; Morris 2012, 88). It is also clearly reminiscent of the sun that oppresses Mersault reminding him of his subjugation in Camus's *L'étranger*.[12] The sea, which Sidelfiro gazes at longingly, represents freedom as it would allow him to escape from the island, and the rain at the end of the novel after the general strike signifies the end of the dictatorship.

President Batista (1940–4, 52–9) barely features in the novel, but through symbolism *Sonámbulo* nevertheless presents a scathing critique of the negative impact of the Batista regime on the Cuban people and especially on Afro-Cubans. Such was Tejera's interest in the effect of dictatorship that *Sonámbulo* was part of what Hernández-Ojeda has termed her 'trilogía de las dictaduras' (dictator trilogy) alongside *Fuir la spirale* (1987) and *Espero la noche* (1997) set under Franco, Batista and Castro, respectively (2009, 138). Form and content are inextricably linked as the impossibility of pinning down a single meaning in *Sonámbulo* stands in opposition to the monolithic discourses of dictatorships (Hernández-Ojeda 2009, 98). Thus, Hernández-Ojeda suggests, Tejera is seeking an anti-authoritarian form of writing (2009, 98). Such a focus on dictatorship means that *Sonámbulo* must be considered in relation to the *novela del dictador* (dictatorship novel), a genre closely associated with the Boom. Dictators feature, for example, in Miguel Ángel Asturias's *El Señor Presidente* (1946), García Márquez's *El*

---

[12]On this interpretation of the sun in *L'étranger*, see Ohayon (1983, 193). Hernández-Ojeda also make a comparison with the sun in *L'étranger* and *Sonámbulo* (2009, 86–7).

otoño del patriarca (1975), Augusto Roa Bastos's *Yo, el supremo* (1974) and Alejo Carpentier's *El recurso del método* (1974). Shaw goes so far as to suggest a later date for the end of the Boom in order to encompass these dictatorship novels (1981, 161). On this basis, Tejera and *Sonámbulo* have an even stronger claim to be considered part of the Boom.

Sidelfiro moves through the different neighbourhoods of Havana. *Sonámbulo*, however, is not a total novel to the same extent as those associated with the Boom novelists.[13] Here we do not have the same comprehensive sense of the city, its different neighbourhoods, and inhabitants seen, for example, in Fuentes's portrayal of Mexico City in *La región más transparente* (1958). Yet, as in Boom novels, we do have social commentary and a sense of a divided city as Sidelfiro cannot wander in the wealthier areas. Here, the trees remain having been removed elsewhere symbolizing how the wealthy are shaded from the worst effects of the dictatorship. Instead of a comprehensive panoramic vision across time and space, we experience the city from Sidelfiro's perspective. We are excluded from the spaces from which he is excluded on the basis of his class and ethnicity. The result is a narrative that comments on urban inequality as well as reflecting the protagonist's alienation from his surroundings.

With its focus on the male protagonist's quest for identity, central to many Boom novels, *Sonámbulo*, like *Los extraordinarios*, has failed to attract the attention of all but a few feminist critics. As Morris's (2012) analysis has shown, however, there is significant potential for analysing the novel from the perspective of ethnicity and postcolonial criticism. Indeed, part of the novel's social awareness comes precisely from its portrayal of the racism and discrimination Sidelfiro experiences. Batista's hypocrisy is denounced as he is described as 'un aspirante a blanco' (someone trying to be white) denying his own, as well as the country's, Afro-Cuban heritage and identity (Tejera 1972, 145). Sidelfiro endures the racist remarks of his co-workers, is thrown out of bars and is subjected to violence at the hands of the police because of the colour of his skin. When compared to the *neoindigenismo* of the Boom novels and the essentialism of *Los extraordinarios*, this critique of the experience of Sidelfiro in urban Havana is strikingly progressive.

Tejera won the Premio Biblioteca Breve and achieved what no other woman had. *Sonámbulo* was accomplished in its technical experimentation and shared much in common with other Boom novels. Still, even the prize, which has been central to critical narratives about twentieth-century Spanish American literary history, could not save a woman author from being

---

[13]The term 'total novel' (novela totalizadora) came to be associated with the Boom in the 1960s. These novels entail the portrayal of a complete, parallel reality which reflects the world outside the novel. These novels are defined primarily by the scale of their scope and ambition, as well as their use of this alternative universe to cast the real world in a new light. For a more detailed discussion of the total novel, see Anderson (2003) and Fiddian (1989).

overlooked. Consecration in Paris also made little difference for Tejera. The degree of critical neglect is astounding when we think of the scores of articles and monographs dedicated to the 'big four'. For women authors like Mairena and Tejera literary prestige is clearly harder won. This sad assertion is confirmed in the next chapter where we see that literary prestige in the form of prizes is more readily attached to male authors.

6

Women winning prizes: A no win situation?

The politics of literary prestige is gendered. The first part of this chapter presents statistics which evidence the extent to which Spanish American women authors have been overlooked in the awarding of literary prizes. Prizes reserved for women authors are one mechanism that is being used to enhance their access to literary prestige and redress this inequality. These prizes emerged within a broader context in which social movements in Spanish America, perhaps most famously the Madres de la Plaza de Mayo (Mothers of the Plaza de Mayo) in Argentina, were increasingly moving away from traditional political parties and instead drawing on identity politics to stake their claims.[1] The second part of the chapter examines the effectiveness of women-only prizes as a mechanism for overcoming women's marginalization in the literary sphere taking the Premio Sor Juana Inés de la Cruz awarded to the best novel published by a woman author written in Spanish as a case study drawing on comments by authors, judges and journalists in press coverage about prizes.

Much is at stake when it comes to the marginalization of women authors in the prize network. Women miss out on the prize money and in some cases the chance of publication; they lose out on the prestige and the chance to consolidate or enhance their place in the literary field. They are not interviewed or quoted in the press or given the chance to deliver speeches in the presence of those in power. Less tangibly they may not be considered for other awards, their work is not translated, they are overlooked for speaking invitations, do not receive offers to write in the press or to submit their next manuscript with the offer of a generous advance. They miss out on honorary

---

[1] For an overview of this process, see Huiskamp (2000).

posts in universities, on grants to support their writing and even on the chance to be on the jury of a major literary prize. Finally, publishers, realizing that women authors are less likely to win, may become less inclined to put their works forward for consideration thus perpetuating a vicious circle. The costs to the careers of women authors of being consistently overlooked when it comes to literary prizes should not be underestimated.

Before we look at the facts and figures let us quell some of the objections raised when it is suggested that women authors are disadvantaged in the literary sphere as a result of their gender. There is the argument that there are fewer women winners of major literary prizes because, for much of the twentieth century, there were fewer women writers. There is the fact that women's education lagged behind that of men, women were less likely to be taught to read, let alone write, and they were certainly less likely to have a degree-level education. As the primary caregivers, wives and mothers, women were also less likely to have the free time to be able to write professionally. Not marrying in order to dedicate themselves to their writing historically meant women authors exposing themselves to social stigma and financial precarity. Of course, opportunities for women transformed over the course of the last century. In the latter decades of the twentieth-century women readers outnumbered men and women writers became increasingly commercially successful (Castillo 1998, 33). Women's commercial success was such that critics have spoken about a *boom* in women's writing comparable to that experienced by male authors in the late 1950s and 1960s (Finnegan and Lavery 2010, 1). Yet the statistics do not indicate that these changes have led to any change in the fortunes of women authors when it comes to winning literary prizes and accruing literary prestige.

This regrettable lack of prestige can be explained by the fact that women authors' success is too often linked to a perceived deterioration in quality in the literary field and the rise of market forces. Institutional consecration and commercial success have long been incompatible for women authors the latter being much more readily available than the former. When she won the Premio FIL in 2010, Mexican author Margo Glantz noted the widespread reluctance to recognize the quality of women's writing: 'Siento que hay todavía una reticencia muy grande para contemplar la escritura femenina como una escritura tan importante como cualquier otra' (I regret that there is still a significant reticence to contemplate women's writing as being as important as any other) (quoted in Velasco and Alejo 2010). In 2013 Mexican newspaper *Excélsior* ran a feature to mark the twentieth anniversary of the Premio Sor Juana which included interviews with former winners Glantz, Tununa Mercado, Lina Meruane and Claudia Piñeiro (Bautista 2013). The consensus among these former winners was that the position of women writers was now better than twenty or thirty years ago but that women authors who were not willing to cater to the demands of the market still struggled in comparison to their male counterparts.

For Spanish American male authors the literary field is no longer polarized around the autonomous and heteronomous poles in the way that Bourdieu described. However, for women authors commercial success is still equated with low prestige. In the Spanish context Laura Freixas has observed that 'las mujeres triunfan en lo commercial y mediático, y fracasan en la calidad y el prestigio' (women triumph in commercial and media terms but fail in terms of quality and prestige) (quoted in Bermúdez 2002, 228). Writing about the Victorian literary field in Britain, Marty Hipsky notes the incompatibility of the two poles meant that women writers could either be 'the woman novelist of genius' with high symbolic capital or the 'scribbling "silly lady novelist" with her low symbolic capital but ever increasing potential for high financial capital – that is massive popular sales, and the very real possibility of the author's economic independence' (2000, 193). Sadly, the situation has not changed for Spanish American women authors today.

The reason for this fundamental incompatibility between success and prestige for women authors, Hipsky suggests, is because 'the wider field of positions made possible by "the distribution of specific properties" – in this case, the degree of institutional consecration and the degree of success in the market – is in the case of the woman writer's works narrowed down dramatically by the possession of yet another "distinctive property", namely the author's gender' (193–4). In other words, a woman's gender is an obstacle to the accumulation of literary prestige, although not to commercial success. The underlying problem, as these findings expose, is that women are only allowed to intervene in the public sphere on certain terms. They can perform the role of 'silly lady novelist' or, in today's terms, literary celebrity; hence, they fair very marginally better in publisher-run prizes, but the roles of a serious writer, public intellectual, as well as that of spokesperson for Spanish America on the world stage are seldom available to them. The role of spokesperson advocating for greater equality and opportunities for women is open, but few are willing to risk being pigeonholed for doing so. The problem is not only the underlying attitudes towards women that these findings expose, but the discrimination women face as a result of these attitudes in many other walks of life.

Evidencing the problem

Women authors are less likely to win a literary prize than male authors. Women are less likely to be the judges of literary prizes. Women are less likely to have literary prizes named after them. What follows is a body of evidence to support these statements and make the scale of the problem apparent. These statistics leave us in no doubt as to the gendered nature of literary prestige which means that women's contributions continue to be undervalued because literary prestige is associated with well-connected male authors. As Emily Hind has hypothesized, 'what creates great literature is as much a performance of power and a network of complicit peers as this nebulous concept of *talent*' (2019, 39). An 'accrediting network of men' keeps women authors out (Hind 2019, 55). Women-only prizes seek to insert women into the male-dominated prize network, but, as will be seen, they have so far had limited success in providing a foothold for women authors in the wider network.

Regardless of whether we look at prizes at a national or international level, regardless of the genre, regardless of whether submissions were done using a pseudonym, whether prizes are for published or unpublished work, whether the prizes are for a single text or for a lifetime of achievements, or whether the prize is awarded by a cultural institution or a publisher, women overwhelmingly lose out to male authors.

The scale of the problem is evident in the following tables. In order to work out the percentage of women winners for a given prize, the total number of women winners was divided by the total number of winners counted from the time an award was established until the latest edition of the prize which in most cases was 2019 or 2020. This number was multiplied by a hundred to give the percentage. Occasions when no award was made were not counted, and years where an award was made to more than one author were counted as multiple winners and added to the totals accordingly.

As much as possible data was gathered from the official websites of the organizations responsible for awarding the prize. This information was supplemented, as required, from other sources most often from newspaper articles reporting the awarding of the prize.

International prizes

When it comes to prizes open to authors of any nationality and writing in any language, Spanish American authors are poorly represented. The few that have received recognition had won previous awards at a national level and/or within the Spanish-speaking world. Since it was first awarded in 1901, only one Spanish American woman, Gabriela Mistral, has received the Nobel Prize for Literature out of a total of six Spanish American laureates. The significance of Mistral's laureateship has been discussed in Chapter 3. We should note, however, that the problem of being under recognized for their work is not the preserve of Spanish American women as only sixteen women have ever won what has been widely considered the top accolade in literature.[2]

---

[2]Information on the fifty-two women to win a Nobel in any field can be found on the website of the Nobel Prize: https://www.nobelprize.org/prizes/lists/nobel-prize-awarded-women/.

In 2006 Nicaraguan Claribel Alegría became the only Spanish American woman to receive the Neustadt Prize. Olga Orozco (1998), Margo Glantz (2010) and Ida Vitale (2018) are the only Spanish American women to have received the Premio FIL de Literatura en Lenguas Romances (FIL Prize for Literature in Romance Languages) awarded annually at the Guadalajara Feria Internacional del Libro (International Book Fair) (FIL). As Table 6.1 shows, the handful of names gathered here are the exception that proves the rule that women are largely excluded from the international prizes network and the literary prestige that they offer.

TABLE 6.1 *Showing Percentages of Women Winners of Major International Literary Prizes*

Name of the Prize	Total Number of Women Winners	Percentage of Women Winners	Number of Spanish American Winners	Number of Spanish American Women Winners
Nobel Prize for Literature (est. 1901)	16	14	6	1
Neustadt International Prize for Literature (est. 1970)	6	23	4	1
International Dublin Literary Award (formerly sponsored by IMPAC) (est. 1994)	4	16	1	0
International Booker Prize (est. 2005)	4	44	0	0
Franz Kafka Prize (est. 2001)	3	15	0	0
Premio Príncipe/Princesa de Asturias de las Letras (est. 1981)	7	16	7	0
Premio FIL de Literatura en Lenguas Romances formerly the Premio Juan Rulfo) (est. 1991)	5	17	18	3
Prix Femina étranger awarded by an all-women jury (est. 1985)	13	36	0	0

Prizes for literature in Spanish

Women authors fare little better when it comes to prizes for authors writing in Spanish regardless of nationality. Table 6.2 shows that there is little sign of change over time as the statistics do not improve following the turn of the new millennium.

TABLE 6.2 *Showing Percentages of Women Winners of Literary Prizes in the Spanish-speaking World for Literature in Spanish*

Name of the Prize	Total Number of Women Winners	Total Number of Women Winners Post 2000	Percentage of Women Winners
Premio Cervantes (est. 1976)	5	3	11
Premio Casa de las Américas (Novels in Spanish) est. 1959)	8	4	19
Premio Casa de las Américas (Short story excluding children's stories) (est. 1959)	5	2	13
Premio Casa de las Américas (Poetry in Spanish) (est. 1959)	7	1	17
Premio Rómulo Gallegos (est. 1964)	3	2	15
Premio Iberoamericano de Poesía Pablo Neruda (est. 2004)	5	5	31
Premio Iberoamericano de Poesía Pellicer para Obra Publicada (est. 1977)	9	5	22
Premio Iberoamericano de Narrativa Manuel Rojas (Chile, est. 2012)	2	2	25
Premio Hispanoamericano de Cuento Gabriel García Márquez (Colombia, est. 2014)	1	1	20
Premio Centroamericano de Literatura Rogelio Sinán (est. 1996)	3	3	13
Premio Reina Sofía de Poesía Iberoamericana (est. 1992)	6	6	21

Even on the rare occasions that women do win these awards, there is a risk of a backlash. When Ángeles Mastretta became the first woman to win the Premio Rómulo Gallegos in 1997, Nuala Finnegan describes the reaction as 'vicious and severe' (2007, 142). She continues: 'As well as the laudatory and, at times, sycophantic reception of the new novel, there were also many reviews that lamented the awarding of the prize to *Mal de amores* denouncing the text and regarding its recognition by the Rómulo Gallegos committee as a debasement of literature' (Finnegan 2007, 142). For many authors winning the Premio Rómulo Gallegos would represent a high point of their career, but Mastretta's win was marred by concerns in the media revolving around the bestseller status of her novel and the perceived problem of the 'feminisation of the market-place' characterized by a growing number of women authors and readers (Finnegan 2007, 146). Ultimately, Finnegan concludes, *Mal de amores* was the victim of 'a disgruntled critical establishment who perceived it as the last straw in a long-running ideological battle with the market-place' (2007, 143). Mastretta's case illustrates how, even when women win major literary prizes, their achievements can be undermined.

It would be ten years before another woman would win the Premio Rómulo Gallegos prize. When Elena Poniatowska won in 2007, the president of the jury pointedly praised her work for its 'densidad temática y estilística' (thematic and stylistic density) (Márquez 2007). There were also political motives which meant that Poniatowska, who was relatively sympathetic to the Chávez regime, and even appeared in a television programme with the president when she went to collect her prize, was seen as a more suitable winner than Mastretta. In this context, the fact that Poniatowska was also a journalist meant that she is also likely to have been seen as better placed to act as a public intellectual. She also had a long-standing and established reputation as a 'serious' author, and she was already the winner of other major awards including the Premio Mazatlán de Literatura (1971 and 1992), the José Fuentes Mares National Prize for Literature (2001), the Premio Alfaguara (2001) and numerous prizes for her journalism. If anything, Poniatowska brought more prestige to the beleaguered prize at this particular juncture. It took a further decade for a third woman to win the Premio Rómulo Gallegos .

Not only are women less likely to win literary prizes open to authors beyond national borders or for their complete works, but there is evidence to suggest that it takes women longer to be recognized than their male counterparts (Table 6.3). Dulce María Loynaz was eighty-nine years old when she won the Premio Cervantes. Poniatowska was eighty-one and Ida Vitale was ninety-four. Yet, the male winners of the Premio Cervantes have been ten years younger if not more. Alejo Carpentier won aged seventy-three, Augusto Roa Bastos aged seventy-two, Sergio Ramírez was seventy-five, Octavio Paz sixty-seven, Carlos Fuentes was just fifty-nine and Mario Vargas Llosa fifty-eight. The same holds true for the winners of the Premio

TABLE 6.3 *Showing Percentages of Women Winners of Awards which Recognize a Lifetime of Work as Opposed to a Single, Named Text*

Name of the Prize	Total Number of Women Winners	Percentage of Women Winners
Premio Iberoamericano de Poesía Pablo Neruda (est. 2004)	5	31
Premio FIL de Literatura en Lenguas Romances (formerly Premio Juan Rulfo) (est. 1991)	5	17
Premio Nacional de Literatura de Chile (est. 1942)	5	9
Premio Pablo Neruda (for authors under 40. est 1987)	8	25
Premio Cervantes (est. 1976)	5	11

FIL. Ida Vitale won aged ninety-five while David Huerta, who won the year after Vitale in 2019, was only seventy. In 2011, the year after eighty-year-old Margo Glantz won, Fernando Vallejo won aged sixty-nine. When Olga Orozco won aged seventy-eight the next winner was Sergio Pitol aged sixty-six. When Glantz won the Premio FIL, she even mused on the fact that women receive prizes so late in life: 'A lo mejor porque ya no vamos a dar lata, o tal vez porque vamos a morir tranquilas' (At best because at this point we won't be a bother any more or perhaps so we can die in peace) (quoted in Hernández 2010). Claribel Alegría was eighty-two when she won the Neustadt Prize compared to Álvaro Mutis, seventy-nine, Octavio Paz, sixty-eight, and Gabriel García Márquez at forty-five. Hind had similar findings when she looked at the age of women winning writing grants at the Centro Mexicano de Escritores noting that women 'seem to take slightly longer than male contemporaries to earn peer recognition' (Hind 2019, 190). Hind suggests that the differing experiences may be down to women's childcare responsibilities and/or the challenges of perfecting the correct writerly performance to be considered eligible (2019, 190). Either way, women writers, like women in other walks of life, have to work longer in order to achieve the same recognition. Indeed, were it not for the fact that women have, on average, longer lifespans than men they may never win these prizes at all!

State-sponsored prizes restricted by nationality

Relatively few writers, either male or female, win awards that operate beyond national and linguistic borders. At a national level, and in the context of the general proliferation of literary prizes and the growing number of women authors and readers, we might expect to see women authors receiving greater recognition. They do not. The percentage of women winners of any given prize in Spanish America is typically 25 per cent or below. Extrapolating this data we might conservatively suggest that three quarters of all literary prizes go to male authors. There is no evidence of improvement post 2000 (Table 6.4).

TABLE 6.4 *Showing Percentages of Women Winners of State-sponsored, National-level Literary Prizes in Spanish American Countries*

Name of the Prize	Country	Total Number of Women Winners	Number of Women Winners Post 2000	Percentage of Women Winners
Premio Nacional de Letras de Argentina up to 2000. Suspended 2000–2011	Argentina	3	n/a	9
Premio Nacional de Letras de Argentina post 2011	Argentina	9	n/a	38
Premio Nacional de Novela (est. 1998)	Bolivia	4	4	19
Premio Nacional de Poesía Yolanda Bedregal (est. 2001)	Bolivia	3	n/a	23
Premio Nacional de Chile (est. 1942)	Chile	5	2	9
Premio Mejores Obras Literarias Publicadas (est. 1993)	Chile	21	16	16
Premio Nacional de Novela (Colombia) (est. 2014)	Colombia	0	0	0
Premio Nacional de Novela Aquileo J. Echeverría (est. 1964)	Costa Rica	14	6	29
Premio Nacional de Poesía Aquileo J. Echeverría (est. 1962)	Costa Rica	18	9	32

(Continued)

TABLE 6.4 (Continued)

Name of the Prize	Country	Total Number of Women Winners	Number of Women Winners Post 2000	Percentage of Women Winners
Premio Nacional de Literatura de Cuba (est. 1983)	Cuba	11	7	27
Premio Nacional de Literatura de La República Dominicana (data since 1990)	Dominican Republic	4	4	12
Premio Eugenio Espejo awards made for literature (est.1975)	Ecuador	1	1	4
Premio Literario Hugo Lindo (est. 2017)	El Salvador	0	0	0
Premio Nacional de Literatura Miguel Ángel Asturias (est. 1988)	Guatemala	6	4	18
Premio Nacional de Literatura Ramón Rosa (est. 1967)	Honduras	5	2	16
Premio Nacional de Ciencias y Artes Rama Literatura (est. 1945)	Mexico	10	10	25
Premio Nacional Rubén Darío (est. 1942)	Nicaragua	Data not available		
Concurso Nacional de Literatura Ricardo Miró (est. 1942)	Panama	See note 6 Chapter 1		
Premio Nacional de Literatura de Paraguay (est. 1990)	Paraguay	4	4	27
Premio Nacional de Literatura del Perú (Novel) (Est. 2017)	Peru	1	1	50
Premio Nacional de Literatura de Uruguay (est.1951. Revised 1986)	Uruguay	Data incomplete.		
Premio Nacional de Literatura de Venezuela (est. 1948)	Venezuela	7	1	10

Prizes by genre

Regardless of genre women authors are less likely to win a literary prize as shown by the following data (Table 6.5) for all of the prizes awarded under the Instituto Nacional de Bellas Artes (National Institute of Fine Arts) in Mexico. Perhaps unsurprisingly women writers come closest to achieving parity in children's theatre and fiction. More interesting is their relative success as critics in the Premio Bellas Artes de Ensayo Literario for literary criticism. It should be noted, however, that this success is not replicated in the other awards for criticism and only two of the eighteen winning entries were written about women authors. The majority wrote about canonical male authors such as Carlos Fuentes, José Revueltas and José Luis Borges. Writing about women authors is unlikely to win prizes for a critic of any gender.

TABLE 6.5 *Showing All Prizes Awarded under the Auspices of the Instituto Nacional de Bellas Artes (INBA), Mexico*

Name of the Prize	Total Number of Women Winners	Total Number of Women Winners Post 2000	Percentage of Women Winners (Rounded to Nearest Whole Number)
Premio Bellas Artes de Cuento Infantil Juan de la Cabada (est. 1977)	20	8	47
Premio Bellas Artes de Cuento Amparo Dávila (formerly de San Luis Potosí) (est. 1974)	7	4	15
Premio Bellas Artes de Ensayo Literario José Revueltas (est. 1976)	18	8	42
Premio Bellas Artes de Ensayo Literario Malcolm Lowry (est. 1986)	3	2	12
Premio Bellas Artes de Narrativa Colima para Obra Publicada (est. 1980)	9	3	23
Premio Bellas Artes de Novela José Rubén Romero (unpublished Works) (est. 1978)	5	2	13

(Continued)

TABLE 6.5 (Continued)

Name of the Prize	Total Number of Women Winners	Total Number of Women Winners Post 2000	Percentage of Women Winners (Rounded to Nearest Whole Number)
Premio Bellas Artes de Obra de Teatro para Niñas, Niños y Jóvenes Perla Szuchmacher (est. 1981)	14	7	44
Premio Bellas Artes de Poesía Aguascalientes (est. 1968)	10	5	19
Premio Bellas Artes de Crónica Literaria Carlos Montemayor (est. 1982)	9	7	24
Premio Juan Rulfo para Primera Novela (est. 1980) (unpublished work)	16	10	42
Premio de Crítica de Arte Luis Cardoza y Aragón (est. 1987)	4	3	20
Premio Bellas Artes Baja California de Dramaturgia Luisa Josefina Hernández (est. 1978)	12	6	29
Premio Iberoamericano Bellas Artes de Poesía Carlos Pellicer para Obra Publicada (est. 1977)	9	5	21
Premio Xavier Villaurrutia de Escritores para Escritores (all categories) (est. 1955)	26	5	23
Premio de Dramaturgia Juan Ruiz de Alarcón (est. 1988)	6	4	19

Source: Statistics are based on information on the INBA website (inba.gob.mx).

Privately run prizes

The statistics for privately run prizes, most of which are organized by publishers, vary little in comparison to state-sponsored prizes. Women are consistently overlooked. This finding is particularly significant given that privately run prizes are thought to be more open to women authors because of their market-oriented priorities. Such is the fear of women authors acquiring visibility in the literary field that even relatively small amounts of success seem to cause overblown claims that they are taking over (Table 6.6).

TABLE 6.6 *Showing Percentages of Women Winners of Privately Run Literary Prizes in the Spanish-speaking World for Literature in Spanish*

Name of the Prize	Country Where Prize Is Based	Total Number of Women Winners	Percentage of Women Winners
Premio Clarín de Novela (est. 1998)	Argentina	9	39
Premio Planeta de Novela (est. 1952)	Spain	16 of which 1 was Spanish American	24
Premio Nacional de Literatura de Colombia (run by the magazine *Libros y Letras* and voted for by readers) (est. 2002)	Colombia	1	10
Premio Biblioteca Breve (est. 1958)	Spain	1	8
Premio Biblioteca Breve (revived 1999)	Spain	9	39
Premio Herralde (est. 1983)	Spain	6 of which 2 were Spanish American	16
Premio Alfaguara de Novela (since 1988)	Spain	5 all Spanish American	23
Premio Mazatlán de Literatura (est. 1965 not awarded 1973–1983)	Mexico	4 including twice to Poniatowska	9
Premio Pablo Neruda (for authors under 40. est 1987)	Chile	8	25
Premio Copé de Novela (est.2007)	Peru	0	0

Women winning prizes for unpublished work submitted using pseudonym

We might expect that anonymized prize submissions whereby the author submits their work using a pseudonym and where judging is done anonymously may go some way to evening out the traditional imbalance in the number of women winning awards. In Fernando Iwasaki's novel *España, aparta de mí estos premios*, discussed in Chapter 4, the instructions for authors submitting works to contests go so far as to suggest that using female pseudonyms will help them to win (2009, 155). Popular perception may be that this strategy would be beneficial, but the statistics say otherwise. Even when pseudonyms are used, women authors are still less likely to win. Using male or gender-neutral pseudonyms also does not help women authors. Entries to the Mexican Premio Bellas Artes de Poesía Aguascalientes (Aguascalientes Poetry Prize) are submitted anonymously. Only 19 per cent of the winners of this prize are women. The pseudonyms, which are announced as part of the official jury declaration, reveal that women authors tend to choose male pseudonyms and male authors choose female ones. Most often the pseudonyms writers use when submitting their works relate to characters from literature or mythology, and many have no discernible gender at all. The overall result is that women are still less likely than men to win awards even when the gender of the author cannot be identified with any certainty by the judges.

The finding that anonymized submissions do not result in more women prizewinners is important. It could suggest that fewer women authors are submitting their texts for consideration in the same way that women have been shown to be less likely to put themselves forward for promotion. Women authors also may not be being put forward by their publishers. If this could be identified as the problem, then strategies could be implemented to address it. It would also be useful to know whether publishers have a greater propensity to submit works by male authors when the award is for published works knowing that women are less likely to win. Again, having this information would help us to find solutions.

Another explanation as to why women authors are less likely to win, even when work is submitted anonymously, is because interpretive strategies, or ways of reading, are gendered as seen in the context of Mexican canon formation in the twentieth century (Bowskill 2011). The result is that certain readings appear more available when it comes to the work of male authors, and it is more likely that their work will be interpreted as conforming to the requirements of a male-dominated literary sphere. Whichever way we look at it, however, the best explanation we have, as to why women do not win literary prizes, comes down to the gendered politics of prestige.

Women on the jury

If male readers tend to favour male authors and female readers tend to favour women authors, then the absence of women on literary prize juries provides another possible explanation as to why women authors are less likely to win.[3] Women are still severely underrepresented on the juries of major prizes around the world and Spanish American prizes are no exception.

Some progress has, however, been made and the percentage of women on juries tends to be higher than the percentage of women winning prizes. The data, however, does not suggest any correlation between women on the jury and women winners. Nor does it suggest that routinely having women on the jury leads to an increase in women winners.

One unlikely explanation is that women's writing really is less deserving of prizes. We must, however, consider that women jurors might feel less able to speak out in support of women's writing perhaps feeling less secure in their positions. Women jurors may find themselves caught in the double bind of being seen to base their support for a text on the gender of the author rather than on literary quality or being seen as less capable critics for favouring supposed lesser quality works. Women jurors may be reluctant to seek to impose their opinion on others and so fail to secure a majority for their view. Finally, women jurors may have adopted and internalized dominant interpretive strategies and prejudices associating women's writing with low quality. All of these possible explanations go some way to accounting for the fact that statistics indicate that at least two women are needed on a jury for a woman author to stand a still limited chance of winning a prize (Table 6.7).

When it comes to juries for international prizes, Spanish American women are rarely invited to participate. The Neustadt Prize has only had 6 Spanish American women jurors and 13 Spanish American jurors out of 266 in its history. The Dublin Literary Award has had similarly few Spanish American jurors, but Luisa Valenzuela, Margo Glantz and Alicia Borinsky all served on the jury in the early years of the prize. In relation to the statistics in Table 6.7, we should also note that prizes such as the Premio FIL and the Premio Casa de las Américas use judges from outside Spanish America. British critic Jean Franco, for example, became only the second woman ever to serve on the jury for the Premio Casa de las Américas prize for a short story in 1969. The participation of Spanish American women in some of the cases cited in Table 6.7 is, therefore, even lower than the statistics suggest.

The Dublin Literary Award seems to be trailblazing in its efforts to include women on juries. It has a five-person jury and alternates between

---

[3]Alison Flood reported these findings based on the website Goodreads (2014).

TABLE 6.7 *Showing Numbers and Percentages of Women on the Juries of a Selection of Literary Prizes*

Name of the Prize	Total Number of Women Jurors	Percentage of Women Jurors
Neustadt Prize (est. 1970)	82	31
Dublin Literary Award (est. 1994)	63	52
International Booker (est. 2005)	17	50
Premio FIL de Literatura (2000–20 only)	57	40
Premio Casa de las Américas (Novel) (est. 1959)	29	14
Premio Casa de las Américas (Short Story) (est. 1959)	28	16
Premio Rómulo Gallegos (est. 1964)	13	14
Premio Iberoamericana de Poesía Pablo Neruda (est. 2004)	27	36
Premio Iberoamericano de Narrativa Manuel Rojas (est. 2012)	13	32.5
Premio Hispanoamericano de Cuento Gabriel García Márquez (est. 2014)	9	38
Premio Bellas Artes de Poesía Aguascalientes (years 1997–2020)	15	23
Premio Clarín de Novela (est. 1998)	20	29
Premio Copé de Novela (est. 2007)	4	11

having three women on the jury in one year and two the next. Few other prizes have made such concerted efforts. Curiously, in the mid-1990s for all of the Casa de las Américas prizes we see majority women juries for a few years. The way this happens across the board suggests a policy initiative, but it quickly ends and the norm returns whereby we see one or no women on panels of five judges. More recently, the Premio FIL also seems to have made a conscious effort to include women judges. The jury of the FIL is typically six or seven people. Between 2000 and 2017 women made up 50 per cent or more of the jury in only five out of the eighteen years. For the last three iterations of the prize, however, four out of six jurors have been women. It is to be hoped that initiatives that boost women's participation on juries continue because, even if they do not lead to more women winners, serving on a prize jury offers women authors opportunities for networking, and public recognition of one's expertise is an important marker of literary prestige in its own right.

A final note of caution is required regarding the composition of juries and women's participation. The same names appear over and over again. This is true for both men and women and speaks to a closed literary field which restricts access to prestige. To some extent, the same names appear as prizewinners for different awards. In terms of women's repeat participation as judges though it means that, while the statistics for women serving on juries may appear to tell a better story than the statistics for women prizewinners, they conceal the fact that only a very small number of individuals really have access to such opportunities. The most likely reason for women to be on the jury is because they previously won the prize. In the case of the Aguascalientes Poetry Prize, Claudia G. Sorais Castañeda found that the judges often served more than once, past winners often become jurors and repeat jurors were significantly more likely to be men.[4] From 1999 to 2002 the jury of the Premio Clarín de Novela consisted of the same three men. For that particular prize, 29 per cent of jurors have been women, but it should be noted that Rosa Montero, Sylvia Iparraguirre, Claudia Piñeiro (former winner) and Liliana Hecker have all judged multiple times. To take just one other example, Margo Glantz has served on the jury of the Dublin Literary Award, the Premio Iberoamericano de Narrativa Manuel Rojas, the Premio Pablo Neruda and the Premio Lowe de Poesía. In the case of the Premio Rómulo Gallegos, no women served on the jury until Elena Poniatowska in 1995. A few years later Ángeles Mastretta was on the jury as she had previously won the prize in 1999 and, as was customary, served on the next jury. Poniatowska later went on to become the second woman to win this prize. In a literary field that is stacked against women's participation these achievements are extraordinary markers of prestige, but they should not be allowed to conceal the fact that far fewer women have access to these opportunities than men.

Prizes named after women

The final nail in the coffin comes when we look at the names of literary prizes. Just as the project 'Gendering Latin American Independence: Women's Political Culture and the Textual Construction of Gender' showed

---

[4]This summary is based on details of the unpublished study described in Hind (2019, 29).

how few public monuments there were to women who had participated in Independence movements, Spanish American women rarely find themselves memorialized when it comes to the naming of literary prizes.[5] Across the world few literary prizes are named after women in part because they lacked access to the private finance necessary to act as benefactors. Hind further suggests that 'the more important the prize, however, the more likely it carries a man's, rather than a woman's, name' (2019, 97). When juries are awarding prizes named after male authors, they are perhaps more likely to recognize other male authors, as Hind speculates that naming a prize after a man 'may affect the probability that the winners are also men' (2019, 96).

In 2018 the Mexican government decided to address the under-representation of women in the names of its national prizes. Three new prizes were established in order to acknowledge women's contributions and achievements. These prizes were only open to women writers and were named after notable Mexican women authors. The new prizes were the Premio Bellas Artes de Trayectoria Literaria Inés Arredondo, the Premio Bellas Artes de Traducción Literaria Margarita Michelena and the Premio Bellas Artes de Cuento Hispanoamericano Nellie Campobello for complete works, literary translation and short stories respectively. In addition, three prizes out of the nineteen then awarded by the Instituto Nacional de Bellas Artes were renamed after women authors. The Premio Bellas Artes de Cuento short story prize would henceforth carry the name Amparo Dávila, the Premio de Dramaturgia for drama would be named after Luisa Josefina Hernández, and the Premio Obra de Teatro para Niñas, Niños y Jóvenes for children's and youth theatre would be named after Perla Szuchmacher. Prior to this intervention no INBA sponsored prize had been named after a woman.

As will be discussed in Chapter 7, 2018 marked another important shift towards state-sponsored prizes promoting identity politics in Mexico. This was also the first year in which all prizes accepted submissions in indigenous languages. Previously, in the late 1970s and due to the work of Víctor Sandoval, the INBA had created and renamed prizes after different states with a view to decentralizing Mexican culture. These more recent name and policy changes reflect new priorities as the state seeks to use prizes to incorporate previously marginalized groups into the imagined community of the nation.

---

[5]On the project led by Catherine Davies and Hilary Owen, see 'Digital Resources; Gender and Latin American Independence', *Oxford Research Encyclopedia of Latin American History* https://oxfordre.com/latinamericanhistory/view/10.1093/acrefore/9780199366439.001.0001/acrefore-9780199366439-e-6.

Are women-only prizes the solution?

The statistics provide ample evidence that the politics of literary prestige are gendered. One solution to address the fact that women authors have been systematically overlooked as both winners and jurors of awards has been to create literary prizes only open to women and/or prizes where all jurors are women. The Premio Sor Juana Inés de la Cruz is the most significant award of this kind for Spanish American authors. Analysing the circumstances around the creation of the Premio Sor Juana and press coverage of the prize provides insight into the effectiveness of women-only prizes as well as their drawbacks.

Awards similar to the Premio Sor Juana are found in other countries where identity politics have taken hold and where there are wider movements which seek greater equality and visibility for women in society. Despite differences in the prize criteria and the makeup of the jury, reading the various mission statements of such prizes reveals that they arose from shared concerns and a sense of injustice. They aim to raise the profile of women writers, celebrate their work and bring it to the attention of readers. Examples include the French Prix Femina (originally the Prix Femina-Vie Heureuse) awarded by an all-female jury to texts written by an author of any gender. This prize was established in 1904 just one year after the Prix Goncourt and in response to the Goncourt committee overlooking the work of Myriam Harry who, of course, went on to become the first winner of the Prix Femina.[6] The Prix Femina aimed to create an audience for the work of women authors as well as for the new women's magazines behind the creation of the prize. The Women's Prize for Fiction (formerly known as the Orange Prize for Fiction and the Baileys Prize) in the UK was likewise established in response to the failings of another prize, this time the Booker Prize, to recognize women's accomplishments on the 1991 shortlist.[7] The Women's Prize for Fiction is awarded to a woman author of any nationality and is judged by an all-women panel. The Australian Stella Prize for fiction or non-fiction by an Australian woman similarly arose out of dissatisfaction that women were not only less likely to win prizes, but their work was also less frequently reviewed in the press than that of men.[8] The questions that remain to be answered in the rest of this chapter, however, are whether these prizes are an effective mechanism for tackling women's marginalization in the literary field, undoing the gendered nature of the politics of prestige and creating new roles and opportunities for women authors in society.

---

[6] On the history of the Prix Femina, see Ducas (2013, 58–60).
[7] Information based on a statement by the Founder Director Kate Mosse on the website of the Women's Prize for Fiction: https://www.womensprizeforfiction.co.uk/about/history.
[8] Information based on 'About the Prize' on the website of the Stella Prize https://thestellaprize.com.au/prize/about-the-prize/.

Established in 1993 the creation of the Premio Sor Juana coincided with a period of commercial success for Spanish American women writers including, most famously, Isabel Allende, Laura Esquivel and Ángeles Mastretta. It was also a period in which the feminist movement was consolidating independently of political parties and within the context of identity politics. The prize was initially for a published novel, written in Spanish by a woman author and arose out of discussions at the IV Symposium Internacional de Crítica Literaria y Escritura de Mujeres de América Latina (IV International Symposium of Literary Criticism and Writing by Women) which was held as part of the FIL book fair in Guadalajara, Mexico.[9] In the first year entries had to have been published in the preceding three years, but the timespan was subsequently reduced to two and then one year reflecting the way in which writing by women was going from strength to strength in terms of quantity if not in terms of having its quality recognized. The Premio Sor Juana sought to redress this imbalance by associating women authors with literary prestige.

The winner of the Premio Sor Juana has always benefitted from the increased visibility resulting from the award being presented at the FIL book fair. However, the Premio FIL de Literatura en Lenguas Romances (FIL Prize for Literature in Romance Languages) (formerly the Premio de Literatura Latinoamericana y del Caribe Juan Rulfo) has been awarded at the festival since 1991. The Premio Sor Juana, therefore, risks being overshadowed by the Premio FIL which is open to all authors writing in a romance language regardless of gender.

When the Premio Sor Juana began, women authors were still experiencing difficulties getting published. In 2004 Laura Niembro, who organized the prizes at the FIL book fair, noted that, although there had been progress, 'ingresar en este ámbito es complicado para las mujeres, debido a que las editoriales aún tienen ciertas reservas respecto de los trabajos escritos por ellas' (breaking into this arena is complicated for women, because publishers still have some reservations when it comes to works written by women) (quoted in Palapa Quijas 2004). Nevertheless, in its early years the Premio Sor Juana opted to recognize published texts and offer the prize of translation into French and, in some years, into English in lieu of prize money. In 1997 the prizewinning author was given the opportunity to have her work published in English by Curbstone Press and again in Spanish by the prestigious Mexican publishing house Fondo de Cultura Económica (FCE), provided the original publisher agreed ('Darán mayor difusión' 1997). In addition, the winning author would be invited to the book fair in Los Angeles organized by the *Los Angeles Times* ('El FCE' 1997). In

---

[9]This goal is stated on the 2021 call for submissions document which can be viewed here: https://www.fil.com.mx/media/convocatorias/fil_sor_juana_21.pdf.

1999 the prize offered translation and publication in French, English and Portuguese, as well as republication with the FCE (Quezada 1999). At the turn of the century, however, the FCE stopped republishing the winning texts and the Universidad Católica de Salta in Argentina stepped in with the offer of publishing a critical edition. This opportunity was perhaps less attractive and less beneficial in terms of securing a wide general readership but held out the potential to help the texts to gain a place on university curricula and is evidence that the prize had an impact beyond Mexico. Complications regarding the translation into English arose when Curbstone went bankrupt. At a roundtable of past winners organized in 2014, there were calls for the prize to once again include the translation of the text into English demonstrating the value they attached to this part of the award (Beauregard 2014).

The original organizers, among them Milagros Palma, the Nicaraguan author and director of the French publishing house Indigo Coté-Femmes, were well placed to provide publishing opportunities abroad. Perhaps it was thought that recognition abroad was the most effective route to bypass national and regional networks of literary prestige that had long proved unfavourable to Spanish American women authors. If, as Pascale Casanova (2004, 146) suggests, the availability of a text in French is key to an author's consecration on the world stage, then the Premio Sor Juana was potentially very valuable for women authors giving them access to the literary field beyond Spanish America. However, the fact that the prize consisted of having the novel translated meant that, in effect, the prize was only open to authors without publishing agreements in those countries. While it would have been rare for women authors in particular to have such contracts, it does mean that the prize was effectively closed to the few more established women authors.

Some prizes offer little or no prize money, perhaps in an attempt to avoid the confusion between symbolic and economic capital to which prizes are prone. The prize money offered can be dwarfed by the amount of money authors and publishers receive from the increased sales that may result from winning a prize. The French Prix Femina, for example, carries no prize money while the Prix Goncourt now offers only 10 euros, although the original bequest was much more generous.[10] The Prix Femina, nevertheless, is estimated to boost sales by an average of 150,000 copies and the Goncourt by 400,000.[11] Even taking into account these precedents, the initial lack of prize money for the Premio Sor Juana may have contributed to a perception that it lacked prestige and limited its effectiveness in enhancing

---

[10] On the history of the Prix Goncourt and the bequest that led to its creation, see Ducas (2013, 40–54).
[11] These estimates are taken from the presentation for LCI by Léa Bons (2018).

the careers of Spanish American women authors. The remarks of reporter Virginia Bautista in 2005 suggest that this was the case. She wrote that 'al principio fue un reconocimiento simbólico' (initially it was a symbolic form of recognition), but the introduction of prize money 'ha significado para sus ganadores prestigio, honor, luz sobre su novela pero, sobre todo, la apertura de puertas en las editoriales de América Latina y la posibilidad de llegar a más lectores' (has meant prestige and honour for the winners, has drawn attention to their novel but, above all, has opened doors to publishers in Latin America and to the possibility of reaching more readers) (Bautista 2013). Prize money of 100,000 pesos was finally introduced for the Premio Sor Juana in 2004, and it was raised to US$10,000 in 2005 marking the twentieth anniversary of the award.

The initial lack of prize money was likely to be all the more damaging because of the substantial prize money offered to the winner of the Premio FIL which was also awarded at the FIL book fair each year. In 1992, on the occasion of the sixth edition of the festival, a document found in the archive of the Centro Nacional de Literatura outlining the prize ceremony for the FIL lists no fewer than twelve sponsors for the Premio FIL including the Consejo Nacional para la Cultura y las Artes (the National Council for Arts and Culture), the publisher FCE, the oil company Petróleos Mexicanos, the National Lottery and no fewer than four major banks.[12] The prize money which Juan José Arreola received that year was US$100,000 and was given in recognition of the author's complete works. In comparison the Sor Juana prize would have seemed tokenistic to say the least!

The amount of prize money offered to the winners of the Premio Sor Juana remains substantially less than that offered for the Premio FIL and other prizes organized by the FIL reflecting once again the gendered nature of pay as well as of the politics of literary prestige. This discrepancy in prize money has not gone unnoticed. Margo Glantz, the only woman to win both the Premio Sor Juana and the Premio FIL, said: 'Si se dan 150 mil dólares por el FIL de Literatura, pues deberían aumentar el Sor Juana. Ahora parece que el coto reservado a las mujeres es un poco menor que el coto reservado a los grandes escritores' (If they give 150,000 dollars for the FIL Literature Prize, then they should increase the money for the Sor Juana prize. Currently it seems that the amount allotted to women is a little less than that put aside for the great (male) authors) (Bautista 2013). Tununa Mercado was similarly perplexed by the disparity: 'No sé por qué un premio con el nombre de Sor Juana tiene que ser más magro que otros' (I do not know why a prize carrying the name of Sor Juana has to be more meagre than others) (Bautista 2013).

---

[12]The eleven-page document is entitled 'Homenaje a Juan José Arreola Ganador del Premio de Literatura Latinoamericana y del Caribe Juan Rulfo 1992 en la VI Feria Internacional del Libro'. CNL Exp. Premio de Literatura Latinoamericana y del Caribe Juan Rulfo.

The result is that women authors whose sales will be boosted to a lesser extent by the Sor Juana prize than the winners of, for example, the Premio FIL are given less prize money, meaning that they are doubly disadvantaged.

The number of entries for the Premio Sor Juana gives some indication of its limited impact. Presumably, no one would submit work for a prize they did not value. Texts can be sent in by authors, their publisher or any educational or cultural institution. In 1994 twenty-three entries were submitted; in 1995 only fifteen entries were received (Matadamas 1994, 1995). In 1997 forty-nine submissions were received (Agencias 1997). Thirty women submitted their work in 1998 ('Obtiene Silvia' 1998). Even in 2004, when prize money was first introduced, there was no significant change as forty-five entries were received. In 2016 eighty entries from nineteen countries competed for the US$10,000 prize money, and in 2020 there were sixty-seven candidates for the prize ('Partida 2016' and 'FIL 2020' 2020). In comparison, the Premio Planeta in 2010 had 509 entries and in 2016 the Premio Bienal de Novela Mario Vargas Llosa, which had been established in 2014 with prize money of US$100,000 for a published novel, received 255 entries ('Los premios literarios aguantan' 2010 and Tova 2016). The Premio Sor Juana thus receives far fewer entries than one would expect suggesting that publishers have not identified it as a significant opportunity and that women authors are either unwilling to put themselves forward or that they attach less prestige to a prize that is only open to women authors. Educational and cultural institutions might also be falling short in their duties.

In 1996 the Premio Sor Juana benefitted from its first scandal involving, perhaps unsurprisingly, one of Mexico's most controversial authors, Elena Garro. The debate revolved around whether or not Garro's text was a novel and therefore whether it qualified for entry under the prize criteria. There were also allegations that Garro was awarded the prize out of cronyism to help with her precarious financial situation ('¿Favores?' 1996). Edward Mack has suggested, with reference to the Akutagawa Prize in Japan, that it was the making of the prize when, early on, a prestigious author made no secret of his desire to win but failed to do so (2010, 197–9). Similarly, having Garro associated with the Sor Juana prize doubtless raised its profile. As Margarita Sierram coordinator of the FIL festival and a member of the prize organizing committee said at the time: 'Hubo contradicciones y qué bueno que las hubo, porque nos ayudará a ir precisando más el desarrollo del premio, porque es todavía un certamen muy chiquitito al que nadie le hacía caso y gracias a esta contradicción maravillosa ahora todo el mundo le pondrá atención' (There were disagreements and what a good job that there were because it will help us to develop the prize which is still a very small contest which no one was paying attention to and now thanks to this wonderful disagreement now everyone will pay attention to it) (quoted in Mendoza 1996). Far from jeopardizing a prize that was still in its infancy, the 1996 scandal seems to have led to an enhanced profile within Mexico and abroad.

In 2013 past winners looked back on the impact the Premio Sor Juana had on their careers. All viewed the prize as effective but largely in terms of sales and visibility more than prestige. Tununa Mercado, winner in 2007, stated: 'En Buenos Aires, la edición estaba en las mesas de saldos a precio vil. Y en la FIL de Guadalajara se agotaron los ejemplares' (In Buenos Aires the book was cut price on the remainders tables while at the FIL in Guadalajara all the copies sold out) (Bautista 2013). Lina Meruane, winner in 2012, similarly noted the increased interest in her work as a whole as a result of the prize: 'El Sor Juana ha permitido dar a conocer mi trabajo, que había circulado por espacios minoritarios, casi de manera secreta y solamente en Chile. La novela ha recibido más atención que sin el premio' (The Sor Juana has made my work known where it had previously circulated at the margins, almost in secret and only in Chile. The novel has received more attention than it would have done without the prize) (Bautista 2013). Claudia Piñeiro, winner in 2010, underscored the role of the prize in enabling circulation within Spanish America: 'Me ha abierto puertas, principalmente, en otros países latinoamericanos, además de por supuesto en México. La circulación transversal de la literatura en Latinoamérica no es fácil. Por eso, la difusión gracias a premios literarios te permite llegar a lectores que no sabían de tu existencia' (It has opened doors for me mainly in other Latin American countries as well as in Mexico, of course. Circulation of literature within Latin America is not easy. That is why dissemination as a result of literary prizes allows you to reach readers who didn't know you existed) (Bautista 2013). Only Margo Glantz, winner in 2003, referred to the prestige of the prize as opposed to its economic benefits and noted the changing status of the prize over time: 'Ahora es un premio de gran importancia. Me da gusto haberlo ganado en medio. Es reconocido, te da prestigio' (Now it is a very important prize. I'm pleased to have won it in the in between stage. It is well known, it gives you prestige) (Bautista 2013).

The jury for the Premio Sor Juana typically consists of two women and one man and often includes past winners. The decision to have a mixed jury may be strategic and designed to protect the prize's prestige. Sylvie Ducas notes with reference to the Prix Femina's all-women jury that there is a double risk attached to the prize because if the prize is seen as being awarded by women jurors to minor works by women authors, then both the status of women as critics and literature by women is stigmatized (2013, 196). In the Mexican context, Hind similarly finds that women supporting or writing about women is taken as an indication of 'lower status' (2019, 98). Such prejudiced attitudes are likely to hinder the effectiveness of women-only prizes.

One possible measure of the effectiveness of the Premio Sor Juana is to consider the profile of the winners when they win the prize and the extent to which it leads to further success in the prize network. The majority of winners had established national, though not international, reputations and had published several novels, but few were able to dedicate themselves to full-time writing. Only Marcela Serrano has won the Premio Sor Juana for her first publication. A few winning authors, including Garro and Giaconda Belli, were so well established that their entry is likely to have had a positive impact on the status of the prize as much as on theirs. Women, especially those who are not journalists, seldom go on to win state-sponsored awards at an international level as the role of spokesperson is stereotypically coded male. Nevertheless, several went on to win publisher-run prizes further evidence that the role of literary celebrity is available to women authors. Marcela Serrano subsequently won the Premio Planeta in 2001, Laura Restrepo went on to win the 2004 Premio Alfaguara de Novela, Cristina Sánchez-Andrade, a decade after winning the Sor Juana prize, was a finalist for the Premio Herralde, Belli won the revived Premio Biblioteca Breve in the same year as the Sor Juana prize. Cristina Rivera Garza, the only woman to win the Premio Sor Juana twice, in 2001 and 2009, bucked the trend as she went on to be a finalist for the IMPAC International Dublin Literary Award and won the Roger Caillois Award for Latin American Literature in 2013. The fact that a few winners of the Premio Sor Juana went on to win publisher-run prizes suggests that the prize has at least some positive impact on the careers of women authors, but the impact of the awards is almost certainly best measured in terms of economic benefits and increased visibility rather than literary prestige. The snowball effect we see in the careers of male authors who seem to go from winning one prize to the next does not happen for women authors. One explanation for this in relation to the Premio Sor Juana is because it is seen as less prestigious because it is only open to women authors. The other explanation is because it is harder for women to perform the role of public intellectual which has long been coded as a masculine domain and so they are less likely to win state-sponsored prizes at national level which provide a better stepping stone into the wider network.

The struggle Spanish American women authors face in accruing symbolic capital is evidenced in the press coverage of the Premio Sor Juana. The prize is regularly covered in the cultural sections of Mexican newspapers such as *La Jornada*, *El Universal* and *Excélsior*. There are broadly two types of articles about the Premio Sor Juana and indeed other prizes. The first, less common type of article announces the launch of the prize and its criteria. The impact of these articles in enhancing the prestige of the prize or of women authors is negligible. The second type, which makes up the majority of articles, are those published on the day after the prize ceremony. For the Premio Sor Juana these articles have become more substantial over time indicating the growing media interest in the prize. Typically, articles consist of biographical details about the author, the names of the judges, the judges' citation, quotations from interviews with the prize winner and details of prize money and other benefits.

The articles do not contain any meaningful discussion of the winning novels even though the prize is for published works. The prize commentary thus prioritizes the visibility of the author over the text and the accrual of literary prestige. In the French context Ducas concludes that the absence of analysis in reports about literary prizes is the result of a move away from aesthetic concerns to a short-term celebrity culture and a focus on the average, as opposed to expert, reader in the context of an industrialized publishing industry (2013, 144). Average readers may read this type of article where they do not read reviews (Ducas 2013, 30). The announcement of the prize winner without discussion of the winning text, therefore, would seem to be favourable in terms of increasing sales. The absence of any meaningful discussion of the texts, however, means that these articles, unlike reviews, do not bolster literary prestige, but there are no negative judgements about the winning novel and so the articles are essentially free publicity.

In contrast to this emphasis on the figure of the author, the comments of the prize jury reported in the press reveal a keen awareness that they are responsible for defending the prize's credentials against the kind of attacks that associate women's writing with the popular and with low quality. The comments from the judges repeatedly refer to literary quality, use of language in the winning text, its universalism and social significance. In other words, the judges' comments associate the winning text with the universal criteria associated with literary prestige. The judges selected Serrano's novel because 'a su calidad literaria suma un contenido social muy importante de conocer' (its literary quality combined with an important social message) (quoted in Matadamas 1994). Judges recognized Tatiana Lobo's *Asalto al paraíso* in 1995 for 'un rico lenguaje' (the richness of its language) (quoted in García Hernández 1995). Elena Garro's 'Busca mi esquela' won 'por su indiscutible calidad literaria y trascendencia humana' (for its indisputable literary quality and human transcendence) (quoted in López 1996). Restrepo's *Dulce compañía* won thanks to its 'personajes entrañables que denuncian problemas específicos de la sociedad colombiana y latinoamericana' (endearing characters who denounce problems that are particular to Colombian and Latin American society) (quoted in Agencias 1997). And, to give one more example, the judges rewarded Cristina Sánchez-Andrade's *Ya no piso la tierra tu rey* 'por su indiscutible calidad y originalidad' (indisputable quality and originality) (quoted in Arriaga 2004). In employing the vocabulary of universal literature as opposed, for example, to emphasizing entertainment and readability, the judges seek to defend the literary prestige of their choice.

As the Sor Juana prize approaches its thirtieth anniversary, its longevity now acts as a marker of its prestige. Some articles list previous winners of the prize thus linking present and past creating a literary genealogy of the kind seen in the speeches of Spanish American winners of the Premio Cervantes and Nobel Prize. Past winners also reference winners in interviews. Ana García Bergua spoke about the value of having her name associated with former winners:

'este premio lo han recibido Elena Garro, Margo Glantz, Angelina Muñiz Huberman, amigas queridas, mujeres admiradas; me siento muy halagada, es como entrar a una compañía admiradísima' (this prize has been won by Elena Garro, Margo Glantz and Angelina Muñiz Huberman, dearly beloved friends, women who are admired; I feel very flattered, it is like joining a much admired company) ('Otorgan' 2013). In the latest official call for submissions on the left-hand side of the page outlining the various rules and regulations is a list of all of the past winners of the prize and at the top of the page twelve black and white smiling photographs of some of the past winners ('Premio de Literatura Sor Juana Inés de la Cruz 2021'). Those considering submitting their work are invited to imagine their names added to the list, or their photograph beaming out at the reader, in coming years. Notably, this promotion of the prize is only based on the name and image of the author as the titles of winning texts are not included. Just as the genealogies imagined by the winners of the Premio Cervantes, discussed in Chapter 3 and Bowskill (2012), present a time without women so too does this poster imagine a literary history without men. This timeline gives prominence to women authors and gives them prestige by association with one another. However, this timeline, like the prize itself, affirms a division between men and women authors which risks perpetuating, at best, the idea that women are equal but different or, at worst, the idea that women cannot compete with male authors.

The prize also seeks to confer prestige by connecting the winners to Sor Juana Inés de la Cruz, one of Spanish America's best known and most highly regarded women authors. Many of the winners comment on the privilege they feel as a result of this association echoing the sentiments of the winners of the Premio Cervantes. Marcela Serrano said: 'quiero reconocer que lo que más me emocionó del premio fue el nombre que lleva y el lugar en donde me lo otorga' (I want to note that what I was most excited about regarding the prize was its name and the place where it is awarded to me) (Chimley 1994). Sylvia Iparraguirre said: 'Que el nombre de tu libro quede asociado al de Sor Juana es lo máximo que le puede pasar a un escritor' (The idea that the name of your book is associated with that of Sor Juana is the greatest thing that can happen to a writer) (Licona 1999). It is worth noting here that Iparraguirre chose the masculine 'escritor' to include male and female authors as opposed to 'escritora' which would be used to only refer to women writers to indicate that any author would be honoured by the association.

In interviews winners acknowledged the opportunities offered by the prize in the form of translation and wider recognition. Marcela Serrano, Cristina Rivera Garza and Clara Usón were among the few who assumed the role of spokesperson and used the platform the prize provided to talk about the issues faced by women authors and women in society. Serrano spoke out about the silencing of women's voices in historical accounts and in literature (Matadamas 1994). Rivera Garza admitted to having reservations about a prize only open to women: 'En un mundo ideal creo que no tendría que haber premios para mujeres. Desgraciadamente no vivimos en un mundo ideal, por eso existen este tipo de premios, pero qué bueno que lo hagan' (In an ideal world I don't think prizes for women would be needed. Unfortunately, we do not live in an ideal world and that is why this kind of prize exists and it's good that they do) (Camacho Olivares 2001). In 2018 Clara Usón similarly wished that a prize for women's writing were no longer necessary 'porque las mujeres hayamos alcanzado la absoluta igualdad en todos los sentidos' (if only women had achieved total equality in all senses of the word) ('Clara Usón' 2018). The apparent reluctance to speak about their marginalization in the literary field points to the reputational risk women authors perceive if they do act as spokespeople for women's rights.

Conclusions

The findings in this chapter confirm beyond doubt that the politics of literary prestige in Spanish America are gendered. Sadly, this conclusion reinforces the findings of others in relation to other periods and contexts. I will, therefore, borrow the words of Silvia Bermúdez, writing about Spain, to sum up the situation faced by Spanish American women authors: 'in the twenty-first century woman writers are still prevented from accumulating symbolic capital' (2002, 212). Spanish American women authors are visible and economically increasingly well compensated by the market but still not to the extent of their male counterparts, and the roles of stateswoman, public intellectual and spokesperson for Spanish America are less readily available to them. The role of spokesperson on behalf of women is available but seems to be unappealing carrying as it does the risk of leading to further marginalization. The statistics, which add to an already depressing picture about the struggles women face in the literary field, should be used to effect change.

Change may be underway. The problem of women's marginalization in the literary field is now occasionally publicly recognized. In 2019 a small group of authors spoke out following the awarding of the Premio Bienal de Novela Mario Vargas Llosa. That year only three women were invited to participate in panel discussions held as part of the award ceremony. From five finalists for the prize there was only one woman and only one woman was on the five-person jury (Europa Press 2019). Rosa Montero, Laura Freixas, Jorge Volpi, Andrés Neuman, Claudia Piñeiro and Samanta Schweblin among others wrote a letter in protest (Europa Press 2019). The letter stated: 'Los abajo firmantes queremos manifestar nuestro hartzago y rechazo ante la disparidad de género que rige en la mayoría de eventos culturales y literarios en América Latina, así como la mentalidad machista subyacente' (The undersigned want to make known that we are fed up with and reject the gender inequality that prevails in the majority of cultural and literary events in Latin America as well as the underlying sexist mentality) (Europa Press 2019). The letter noted that this was not a one-off occurrence: 'Este año no se diferencia mucho a los anteriores, lo que confirma que el criterio discriminador se impone por sistema' (This year is not that much different to previous years which confirms that the discrimination is systemic) (Europa Press 2019). This chapter has shown how widespread the problem really is.

Women-only prizes have been the main approach that has been employed to try to bring about a change in the status of women authors and women in society as they emerged in the context of the wider identity politics agenda. Increasing women's participation in the juries of literary prizes is another approach that is gaining traction. This chapter has taken a much-needed step in reflecting on the effectiveness of these two mechanisms. Few women benefit from the opportunities offered as a result of including more women on juries and their impact on the outcome is uncertain. Women-only prizes, such as the Premio Sor Juana, doubtless have some impact which tends to be bolstered over time provided they can attract appropriate partners and prize money. Failure to do so is likely to do more harm than good compounding the impression that women's writing is less worthy of serious recognition. However, women-only prizes keep women's writing in a separate category, which risks being seen as inferior and unable to compete. Women-only prizes are supposed to give women a foothold, but they rarely have any impact on women's access to the wider prize network. Until effective methods, and we are likely to need several, are identified and implemented then the politics of literary prestige will remain heavily gendered.

7
Prizes for literatures in indigenous languages

The politics of literary prestige is inflected by ethnicity and gender. Spanish American authors writing in indigenous languages, like women authors, have seldom won literary prizes. In stark contrast, literature about indigenous communities by non-indigenous authors has been widely disseminated and lauded. Indeed, there is a long tradition of non-indigenous authors including the Nobel Prize winner Miguel Ángel Asturias, Bolivian Jesús Lara, Mexican Rosario Castellanos and Peruvian José María Arguedas winning prizes and accumulating literary prestige writing about indigenous communities. Prizes for literatures in indigenous languages seek to rectify the historical marginalization of authors writing in indigenous languages by providing them with a voice rather than having others speak on their behalf. These prizes occupy a similar position in the prize network to the Premio Sor Juana in that they are aligned with identity politics and seek to redress the exclusion of a marginalized group. The prizes have the potential to be a gateway which facilitates access to literary prestige, the prize network and the wider literary field. However, as is the case of the Premio Sor Juana, the potential of prizes for literatures in indigenous languages to alter the politics of literary prestige overall may be limited as the prizes keep authors writing in indigenous languages in a separate category from which it is hard to break out. The majority of awards for writing in indigenous languages are state-sponsored and therefore infer a pact whereby the author accepts the prize and the state gains their (tacit) endorsement as it seeks to present the nation as modern and multicultural in a broader context in which identity politics are increasingly important.

This chapter takes Mexico's Premio Nezahualcóyotl awarded for literature written in an indigenous language as a case study. The Premio Nezahualcóyotl is an apt focus because, comparing literatures in indigenous languages in Mexico and Peru, Jean Franco finds that the situation in Mexico is better due to 'a history of patronage of culture' and the power of cultural institutions such as those behind the Premio Nezahualcóyotl (2005, 465). Elsewhere in Spanish America prizes for literature in indigenous languages are rare. In Peru, for example, the Premio Nacional de Literatura en Lenguas Originarias (National Prize for Literature in Original Languages), run by the Ministry of Culture, has been awarded only twice to date in 2018 to Pablo Landeo and in 2020 to Washington Córdova Humán. In Bolivia, Martin Lienhard reports, there is a Premio Nacional de Narrativa en Idioma Originario (National Prize for Narrative in an Original Language) named after Felipe Guamán Poma de Ayala, but, he laments, 'el único resultado tangible de ese concurso es la publicación de una novela en Aymara; *Jach'a tantachawita pachakutiru* (2010)' (the only tangible result from this contest is the publication of a novel in Aymara called *Jach'a tantachawita pachakutiru* (2010) (2014, 89). No Spanish translation was published (Lienhard 2014, 89). The few prizes that do exist beyond Mexico are relatively recent creations indicating the regrettably low prestige previously attached to indigenous languages and cultures within elite institutions in Spanish America. Against this backdrop, understanding the role the Premio Nezahualcóyotl has played in promoting and shaping political and literary agendas in Mexico may be particularly useful in terms of lessons to be learnt elsewhere.

The chapter locates the Premio Nezahualcóyotl in the context of the politics of the Mexican state in relation to indigenous communities and other community-led initiatives. It uses press coverage to reveal how different stakeholders, including authors, and representatives of the awarding institutions understand the prize and how the prize evolved from its inauguration in 1993, when it recognized an author's lifetime achievement, to becoming an award for a single work post 2000. Finally, analysing four prizewinning novels from the second phase of the award enables us to identify shared concerns and show how the prize contributed to the creation of a canon of literature in indigenous languages that departed from earlier traditions. The fact that these novels converge in their interests demonstrates how a prize, through its community of judges and selection of prizewinning texts, can respond to and shape political discourse. The result is that, over time, literary prestige comes to be associated with particular attitudes and perspectives in a self-perpetuating cycle.

The Premio Nezahualcóyotl in context

Mexico's Premio Nezahualcóyotl de Literatura en Lenguas Indígenas (Nezahualcóyotl Prize for Literature in Indigenous Languages), founded in 1993, is the most established prize for literatures in indigenous languages in Spanish America. The prize money for the Premio Nezahualcóyotl is higher than that for the Premio Sor Juana, perhaps in recognition of the fact that there are more limited publishing opportunities for authors writing in indigenous languages and in testament to its importance to the Mexican state. In the first year of the Premio Nezahualcóyotl, the prize money was 30,000 Mexican pesos which was raised to 50,000 pesos in 1996. By 2006 the prize money was raised to 100,000 pesos.

In 2008 the prize was renamed the Premio Nezahualcóyotl de Literatura en Lenguas Mexicanas (Nezahualcóyotl Prize for Literature in Mexican Languages) reflecting the state's desire to use the prize as a means of more visibly including indigenous languages and, by extension, indigenous peoples as part of the imagined community of the nation. The prize is run by the Consejo Nacional para la Cultura y las Artes (National Council for Culture and the Arts) (CONACULTA previously CNCA) under the direction of the Culturas Populares (Popular Cultures) section of the Fondo Nacional para la Cultura y las Artes (National Fund for Culture and the Arts) (FONCA), which is Mexico's main body for awarding grants to authors. These organizations place 'a high premium on cultivating and displaying diversity, accomplished semiotically by emphasizing the array of ethno-linguistic groups supported' (Faudree 2015, 16). The Premio Nezahualcóyotl is in keeping with these goals.

The politics of the Premio Nezahualcóyotl are all the more apparent when we keep in mind that it is institutionally separated from the vast majority of state-sponsored literary prizes in Mexico which are organized under the auspices of the Instituto Nacional de Bellas Artes (Institute for Fine Arts) (INBA). This separation from the INBA is indicative of the way in which indigenous literatures have historically been related to ethnography and language preservation rather than literature per se and means that indigenous literatures are marginalized from the country's main institution responsible for bestowing literary prestige.

This hierarchical division between Mexican literatures in indigenous languages and literature in Spanish was addressed in 2018 when the rules for all INBA prizes for literature were amended to permit authors to submit works in any one of Mexico's officially recognized national languages.[1] In order to implement this policy, the INBA website reports that around a quarter of the jurors now available have expertise in indigenous languages with the remaining three quarters being Spanish speakers ('Premios Bellas Artes de Literatura'). Furthermore, in 2019 the Premio Bellas Artes de Literatura en Lenguas Indígenas (Bellas Artes Prize for Literature in Indigenous Languages) was created. In time, for literatures in indigenous

---

[1] For a list of the INBA prizes see Chapter 6, Table 5.

languages, the literary prestige of the INBA awards may come to overshadow the Premio Nezahualcóyotl despite its established history.

The creation of these new prizes means that we may be witnessing the emergence of a network of prizes for literatures in indigenous languages. Since 2013, in addition to the Premio Nezahualcóyotl and the INBA prize, Mexico is also home to the Premio de Literaturas Indígenas de América (PLIA) (Prize for Indigenous Literatures of America). The PLIA is organized and funded by a group of national and regional institutions including the University of Guadalajara, the Instituto Nacional de Lenguas Indígenas (INALI) (National Institute for Indigenous Languages) and the Culturas Populares, Urbanas e Indígenas (Popular, Urban and Indigenous Cultures) section of the Ministry of Culture. While the Premio Nezahualcóyotl, operating at a national level, has been described as 'basically the Pulitzer for indigenous languages', the PLIA is said to be 'on its way to becoming the "indigenous Nobel" for Latin America' (Ryan Mihaly and David Shook quoted in Gentes 2019, 83–4). To date, all of the winners of the PLIA have been Mexican, which speaks to the relative strength of indigenous literatures in the country. The fact that so many prizes for literatures in indigenous languages are based in Mexico also confirms that the Mexican state is eager to position itself as progressive in its attitude to indigenous literatures and is particularly agile in its use of prizes to further political agenda.

The emergence and evolution of prizes for literatures in indigenous languages in Mexico and elsewhere are connected to changing attitudes towards indigenous populations. Official discourses now recognize 'la alteridad cultural [. . .] no como algo negativo destinado a ser necesariamente reprimido en cuanto amenaza a los discursos unificadores, sino como una parte esencial del encanto de la cultura nacional que permite su comodificación en producto destinado a una audiencia local y global' (cultural otherness [. . .] not as something negative destined to be necessarily repressed when it threatens unifying discourses, but as an essential part of national culture which allows it to be commodified as a product for local and global audiences) (Vich and Jouve-Martín 2013, 6). The Premio Nezahualcóyotl, founded in 1993, was thus an early part of, and reflected, a broader step change in attitudes towards indigenous populations and languages in Mexico, in Spanish America, and internationally. For example, the first reference to indigenous people was included in the 1991 Mexican Constitution. In 1994 the Constitution was amended to proclaim Mexico a pluricultural nation and to include indigenous languages as national languages. 1994 was also the year of the Zapatista uprisings in Chiapas. The creation of the prize also coincided with the quincentenary of the conquest of Spanish America and the awarding of the 1992 Nobel Peace Prize to the Rigoberta Menchú for her work defending the rights of indigenous people in Guatemala. Finally, the United Nations declared 1994–2004 the Decade of Indigenous Peoples. The Premio Nezahualcóyotl thus allows the Mexican state to demonstrate that it is aligned with a wider multicultural agenda.

Later, the new Premio Nezahualcóyotl rules introduced in 2000 coincided with wider changes in attitudes to indigenous languages and literatures. In 2003 the Instituto Nacional Indigenista (National Indigenist Institute) (INI) became the Comisión Nacional para los Pueblos Indígenas (CNDI) (National Commission for Indigenous Peoples) reflecting an official move away from *indigenista* policies. The Ley General de Derechos Lingüísticos de los Pueblos Indígenas (General Law on the Linguistic Rights of Indigenous Peoples) was also passed in 2003 and the National Institute of Indigenous Languages (INALI) was established in 2005. Other steps taken by the Mexican government to preserve indigenous languages included targeted grants via FONCA fellowships and support for book publishing in indigenous languages. As Lienhard cautions, however, this does not necessarily mean that the Mexican government wished to encourage the widespread day to day use of indigenous languages (2014, 91).

Prior to these government initiatives, grassroots work relating to indigenous languages and literatures was well underway, but it had to balance a dual agenda of preservation and prestige. As Paja Faudree points out, indigenous authors struggle to balance the need to promote practical literacy so as to create new audiences for their texts and a desire to achieve literary acclaim (2015, 14). Important earlier initiatives from the 1980s included Carlos Montemayor's Workshop on Mayan Literature and the founding of the Asociación de Escritores Indígenas (Association of Indigenous Writers). In 1991 the second National Congress of Literature in Indigenous Languages was held in Chiapas. Another association, Escritores en Lenguas Indígenas, Asociación Civil (The Civil Association of Writers in Indigenous Languages) (ELIAC), was founded in the same year as the Premio Nezahualcóyotl. Writing about Zapotec literature and the work of author Javier Castellanos, Anna M. Brígido-Corachán noted the significant role played by grassroots initiatives but grudgingly acknowledged that government initiatives also contributed (2016, 175). In an interview with Brígido-Corachán Castellanos was more generous in his assessment as he acknowledged that commercial publishing houses are not interested in literatures in indigenous languages, and so authors rely on government institutions (2016, 177). Eva Gentes concurs that '[p]ublication possibilities for authors in Indigenous languages are rare and virtually non-existent without state support' (84). In this context, the Premio Nezahualcóyotl gains added significance as it provides a route to publication. However, publication and dissemination are not the same things. Print runs sponsored by government institutions are small, and I can attest that these books are not widely stocked. The prizewinning novels discussed later in the chapter had print runs of 2,000 or 3,000 copies and were only available from CONACULTA bookshops.

Stakeholder perspectives

Newspaper coverage of the Premio Nezahualcóyotl contains the views of representatives of state institutions and prizewinning authors and reveals the extent to which their priorities coincide. Comments by representatives of the sponsoring institutions speaking at the prize ceremony focused on the prize as a means of recognizing the cultural diversity of the Mexican nation more than the literary significance of the prizewinning texts and reflecting the way the prize positions indigenous authors as representatives of their communities. At the 1999 prize ceremony, the minister for education said 'que la SEP proporciona todos los apoyos a su alcance, a fin de que los centros institucionales de cultura, creadores y difusores puedan contribuir a la revaloración de nuestras culturas originales, y una muestra de ello es el Premio Nezahualcóyotl' (that the Ministry for Education (SEP) provides all of the support it can so that cultural institutions, creators and disseminators can contribute to the revaluing of our original cultures and the Premio Nezahualcóyotl is evidence of this) ('Gabriel Pacheco Recibió' 1999). In a similar vein, at the prize ceremony in 2000 president of the CNCA, Rafael Tovar, stated: 'Promover y difundir entre los mexicanos el conocimiento de nuestra diversidad lingüística, además de reforzar y ampliar los espacios y medios de expresión y creatividad de nuestras lenguas, son las consecuencias lógicas trae consigo la entrega del Premio Nezahualcóyotl de Literatura Indígena 2000' (Promoting and disseminating among the Mexican people knowledge about our linguistic diversity, as well as strengthening and increasing the spaces and means of expression and creativity in our languages, is the logical outcome of the awarding of the Nezahualcóyotl Prize for Indigenous Literature in the year 2000) ('Premio Nezahualcóyotl a Patricio Parra' 2000). For the state, the political purpose of the prize is paramount.

The remarks of prizewinning authors focus more on the dual literary and social significance of the prize seeking to combine both political agenda and literary prestige. Speaking to the newspaper *Excélsior* when the competition for the first edition of the prize was announced, Tzotzil writer Jacinto Arias, for example, saw the prize as contributing to the development of writing in indigenous languages and as having an impact on indigenous peoples' sense of pride in their identity: 'Fomentar este tipo de símbolos fortalece la imagen que debe tener el indígena de sí mismo' (Fostering this type of symbol strengthens the image that indigenous people should have of themselves) ('Convocan al Premio' 1994). Just as the Spanish American winners of the Nobel and the Premio Cervantes discussed in Chapter 3 used the opportunity afforded to them for winning a prize to speak about political and literary issues, so too do the winners of the Premio Nezahualcóyotl. Unlike the winners of major international prizes, however, their literary prestige is less secure so the risk to their reputations is greater. The strength of their remarks is nevertheless in contrast with those made by the women winners of the Premio Sor Juana who seem to be more reluctant to embrace the identity politics agenda of the prize. Perhaps conscious that to discuss gender politics risks undermining the literary significance of the award the women winners rarely used their interviews or speeches to talk about the marginalization of women in the literary field.

On receiving the first Premio Nezahualcóyotl Zapotec author Víctor de la Cruz spoke about the significance of receiving this award in the same year as the uprising in Chiapas and called on the government to implement 'cambios profundos y comprender las condiciones de marginación y miseria de los pueblos indios' (meaningful changes and to understand the conditions of marginalization and misery of Indian communities) (Martínez Solorzano 1994). He used the opportunity to 'talk back' to power but he balanced his criticism by praising the way that the prize was organized, which meant that he was a candidate in spite of being an outspoken critic of the government and the PRI (Amador 1994). In other words, he endorsed the government's democratic credentials and defended the literary prestige of the prize by suggesting that had literary criteria not been paramount he could not have won.

In 2006 joint winners Mario Molina and Juan Hernández gave the most politically charged acceptance speeches in the history of the prize. Molina called for the withdrawal of troops from Oaxaca and denounced the absence of indigenous cultures in the education system and the closure of the Centro de Lenguas Indígenas de Oaxaca (Centre for Indigenous Languages of Oaxaca) (Jiménez 2006). Hernández, described how he had been sent to another indigenous community with a mission to 'castellanizar' (make [it] more Castilian) but had come to realize 'que aquello que estaba haciendo era exterminar una cultura, matando una lengua que también era la mía' (that what I was doing was exterminating a culture, killing a language that was also mine) (Jiménez 2006). That year, neither officials from the Comisión Nacional para el Desarrollo de los Pueblos Indígenas (National Commission for the Development of Indigenous Peoples) nor the president of CONACULTA attended even though they had been expected to do so (Jiménez 2006). Arturo Jiménez also reported that there was a lack of publicity (2006). The pact was broken. There was also a limit to dissent that the government would tolerate, and so it decided not to draw attention to the award nor the authors' political agenda.

While the Premio Nezahualcóyotl is used by authors and the state to further their political agenda, it is important to all concerned to preserve the literary prestige of the prize. In 2004, the proposed publication of an anthology of works by all of the winners to date marked an important landmark in terms of consolidating the literary credentials of the prize. The collection was to be published in a bilingual edition creating a genealogy of authors who shared a common marker of prestige. This type of publication has significant potential to contribute to canon formation and to the longevity of the authors' prestige and is an example of how, despite the often very prominent political agenda of the prize, it is usually in both parties' interest to maintain the appearance of a balance between politics and literary prestige.

The evolution of the Premio Nezahualcóyotl

The history of the Premio Nezahualcóyotl can be divided into two phases. In the first phase (1993–2000), the prize consolidated the prestige of authors writing in indigenous languages. Later, it sought to steer the direction of indigenous literature in the future. The authors recognized in the first phase were those who, in less favourable times, had contributed to the preservation of indigenous languages. They were author-activists and so were well placed to become spokespeople for their communities. The regulations stipulated that the winner's work had to be 'conocida' (known) ('Convocan al Premio' 1994). In practice this meant the prize went to established authors with an existing body of work who had often been activists. The citation for Juan Gregorio Regino (b.1962) when he won the prize in 1995 reveals the importance of this dual role of author and activist as he was praised for 'la riqueza expresiva de su poesía, así como por su carácter de educador y promotor de la lengua mazateca, que contribuye a la construcción de la nueva literatura mexicana' (the expressive richness of his poetry, as well as for his work as an educator and promoter of the Mazatec language which contributes to the construction of the new Mexican literature) (quoted in Camacho Suárez 1996). That is not to say, however, that the winning authors were well known among the general public or had books published by traditional publishers. The first winner Víctor de la Cruz (1948–2015), for example, had most of his work published in Zapotec newspapers where it could reach other Zapotec speakers (Martínez Solorzano 1994). The prizewinner had to be nominated 'por instituciones culturales o académicas, asociaciones o grupos de personas interesadas en el desarrollo de la literatura indígena contemporánea' (by cultural or academic institutions, associations or groups of people interested in the development of contemporary indigenous literature), a criteria which again favoured those who were well embedded in established networks around indigenous culture and activism ('Convocan al premio' 1994). Jurors were drawn from this same community.

As in the case of other literary prizes in Mexico, the presence of past winners and repeat jurors was common, although it became a little less so after 2002.² This practice was perhaps somewhat inevitable given the relatively small group writing in and/or being able to read any given indigenous language, but it is still a symptom of a closed literary field. The consistent presence of Carlos Montemayor is perhaps particularly notable in terms of bolstering the prize's prestige while it was in its infancy because, as Eva Gentes notes, 'most renowned Indigenous writers have participated in one of the governmental mentoring programs, often led by writer, literary scholar and translator Carlos Montemayor (1947–2010)' (2019, 81).

In the year 2000 the rules of the prize changed significantly as the organizers apparently sought to expand the field by prioritizing new voices providing support and visibility for up-and-coming authors some of whom were younger, had grown up against the backdrop of the government's new policies and had new perspectives. Having shored up the foundations, both of the prize and of indigenous literary history, by recognizing an author's trajectory over decades it was now time to look to the future. From 2000 the prize went to a single text opening it up to less established authors. The official call for submissions stated that entries should be submitted in both the indigenous language and Spanish translation ('Convocatoria Premio Nezahualcóyotl' 2000). The new Premio Nezahualcóyotl was open to poetry, short stories, essays and novels. Entries now had to be unpublished because, in addition to receiving prize money of 50,000 pesos, the winning text would be published in a bilingual edition as part of CONACULTA's Letras Mexicanas collection.

The prize criteria have since evolved further to ensure that they keep up to date with current literary trends. From 2002 essays were no longer accepted (Jiménez 2002). As in the case of Panama's Premio Literario Ricardo Miró discussed in Chapter 1, the exclusion of essays marks a definitive shift to connecting the prize to a specifically literary prestige. A further shift came in 2014 when the new category of graphic narrative was introduced as the prize sought to recognize the importance of the visual in prehispanic indigenous texts ('Convocatoria' 2014). The Mazatec poet and director of Intercultural

---

²In the first edition of the prize in 1994, the jury was formed by Miguel León Portillo, Carlos Montemayor, Eraclio Zepeda, Luis Reyes and Jacinto Arias. In 1996 the jury included the 1994 winner Víctor de la Cruz, Miguel León Portillo and Carlos Montemayor. In 1997 Carlos Montemayor was again on the jury alongside Ireneo Rojas Hernández, Román Güemes and Víctor Hernández López. In 2002 the jury was Elisa Ramírez, Enrique Pérez, Briceida Cuevas, Juan Bañuelos and Carlos España. In 2006 María Esther Hernández Palacios, Jesús Morales Bermúdez, Ramón Bolívar, Carlos España and Auldarico Hernández Jerónimo were on the jury. In 2008 Mario Molina and Juan Hernández Ramírez (both winners of the 2006 prize) were accompanied by the author Teresa Day and academic Patrick Johansson. In 2012 the jury consisted of Wildernain Villegas, Ámbar Past, Mardonio Carballo, Mario Bellatín and Luz María Lepe and, in 2014, Benito Taibo, Javier Castellanos, Patrick Johansson. Details of jury members are taken from articles in the CNL archive. Expediente PRE0033.

Development in the Popular Cultures section of CONACULTA, Juan Gregorio Regino, explained that the new category is a way to recuperate 'toda esta tradición que ha habido entre los pueblos indígenas: la escritura pictográfica' (the complete tradition that has existed among indigenous peoples: pictographic writing) (Martínez Torrijos 2014). The following creators would also now be eligible to submit work: 'tejedores, bordadores, dibujantes, ilustradores, entintadores, grabadores y coloristas' (weavers, embroiderers, artists, illustrators, printers, engravers and colorists), and the work may be individual or by a group (Flores 2014). To date, no graphic narrative has won the prize. Nevertheless, different genres have come to be recognized on a rotating basis as a means to showcase the diversity of contemporary writing in indigenous languages and challenge established hierarchies of literary prestige.

The creation of the new novel in indigenous languages expressing the shared concerns of a new generation

The Premio Nezahualcóyotl has recognized a variety of genres, but it is noteworthy that the history of the Premio Nezahualcóyotl has been coterminous with that of the emergence of the novel in indigenous languages in Mexico as Javier Catellanos's *Wila che be se lhao/ Cantares de los vientos primerizos* (1994), the first novel in an indigenous language in Mexico, was published just one year after the Premio Nezahualcóyotl was established. The emergence of novels in indigenous languages is all the more significant when we recall that novels were banned for the first 300 years of colonial rule, and from 1543 a decree was introduced specifically aimed at restricting indigenous peoples' access to works of fiction. The challenges faced by novelists writing in indigenous languages today remain particularly acute. Poetry and short stories can be published in literary magazines, but this is not the case for novels (unless published in serialized form).

Post 2000, winners of the Premio Nezahualcóyotl were typically, although not exclusively, younger authors who had already won some recognition at a local level. Among them were four novelists. In 2002 the Premio Nezahualcóyotl went to the Zapotec author Javier Castellanos (b. 1951) for *Gaa ka chhaka ki /Relación de hazañas del hijo del Relámpago*.[3] Castellanos was an established writer who has been credited as being the author of the first novel written in an indigenous language in Mexico. It was

---

[3]For a biography of Castellanos, see the *Enciclopedia de la literatura en México*: http://www.elem.mx/autor/datos/4790.

perhaps fitting, therefore, that his work should be among that recognized following the changes to the award in the year 2000. In 2013 he won the first Premio de Literatura Indígenas de América.

In 2006 Mario Molina Cruz's novel *Xtille Zikw Belé, Ihén bene nhálhje ke Yu'Bza'o/ Pancho Culebro y los naguales de Tierra Azul* won. Molina Cruz (1955–2012) was already one of the most established writers in indigenous languages in Mexico. This was to be his only novel, but he also wrote poetry and short stories.[4] He had previously won the Premio Nacional de Cuentos, Mito y Leyenda Indígena Andrés Henestrosa (Andrés Henestrosa Prize for Short Stories, Myths and Indigenous Legends) in 2002.

The 2010 winner of the prize was Isaac Esau Carrillo Can (1983–2017) for *U yóok'otilo'ob áak'ab/Danzas de la noche*.[5] As well as being an author Carillo Can was also a musician and artist who had his work exhibited in the United States. Prior to winning the Premio Nezahualcóyotl Carillo Can had won the Premio Nacional de Literatura Maya Waldemar Noh Tzec for a collection of short stories. He was subsequently awarded a FONCA Jóvenes Creadores (Young Creators) grant in 2016–17.

In 2014 Marisol Ceh Moo (b.1968) received the prize for *Chen tumeen x ch' úupen /Sólo por ser mujer*. She thus became the second woman to win the award after Natalia Toledo did so in 2004. She had a strong publication trajectory and became the first indigenous woman novelist when she published *X-Teya, u puksi' ik'al ko'olel /Teya, un corazón de mujer* (Teya, A Woman's Heart) (2008).[6] She had won numerous awards including three FONCA scholarships. Ceh Moo began writing in Spanish, but Arturo Arias reports that when she heard about 'a government sponsored contest aimed at young writers of short stories written in indigenous languages' she started writing in Maya (2017, 129). Ceh Moo's experience shows how prizes can be effective in stimulating a literary culture and in encouraging young indigenous people to think differently about indigenous languages.

The remainder of this chapter focuses on the common issues addressed in the novels which have won the Premio Nezahualcóyotl drawing attention to this relatively recent significant development in literatures in indigenous languages and prioritizing novels because it is the novel that 'is becoming an important genre for autonomous political projects' (Chacón 2018, 125). As

---

[4] A biography of Molina Cruz and details of his published works can be found via the online Encyclopedia de la literatura en México: 'Mario Molina Cruz' http://www.elem.mx/autor/datos/108801.

[5] A biography of Carillo Can and a translation of a segment of *Danzas* can be found in *Latin American Literature Today* http://www.latinamericanliteraturetoday.org/en/2018/may/u-y%C3%B3ok%E2%80%99otilo%E2%80%99ob-%C3%A1ak%E2%80%99ab-danzas-de-la-noche-isaac-esau-carrillo-can. Audio of his poems can be found via the online Encyclopedia de la literatura en México http://www.elem.mx/autor/datos/119403.

[6] For Ceh Moo's biography, see the online *Encyclopedia de la literatura en México* http://www.elem.mx/autor/datos/110472 and Chacón (2018, 143–4).

the genre least associated with literature in indigenous languages, the choice to write a novel in an indigenous language can be understood as a marker of the intent of these authors to produce a different kind of literature. Ida Kozlowska-Day makes a point with reference to Mario Molina Cruz and *Pancho Culebro* that is equally relevant to other novels studied here: 'Al escoger la novela – un género tradicionalmente considerado occidental – el autor desafió la atribución de ciertos géneros a ciertas culturas y amplió el canon de las literaturas indígenas, dominado por la poesía y el drama' (By choosing the novel – a genre that is generally considered to be Western – the author challenged the attribution of certain genres to certain cultures and expanded the canon of indigenous literatures that is dominated by poetry and drama) (2014, 413). The analysis is based on the Spanish-language texts which are usually self-translations by the authors.[7]

Identifying the common issues addressed in the prizewinning novels provides an insight into the politics of the new indigenous novels that have acquired literary prestige through the Premio Nezahualcóyotl. These texts are written in diverse languages from different cultural perspectives, but they share in common their consecration via this prize. Through the prize, the judges, as privileged readers, establish an association between certain themes and forms of writing and literary prestige which creates an impetus for other novels with similar themes to be produced in the future. The way in which prizes and awards can come to shape cultural production and audience taste has been observed with reference to film festivals and film funding. Tamara L. Falicov (2013), R. Halle (2010), Cindy Wong (2011), Miriam Ross (2009 and 2011), Deborah Shaw (2015) and Michael Purvis (2017) have observed that there is a particular kind of film, referred to as the 'festival film', that is consistently financed by European funding agencies, and shown and recognized with awards at film festivals. Writing about the French Goncourt prize for literature Diana Holmes (2016) has likewise proposed that the prize consistently goes to what she terms middle brow fiction. The Premio Nezahualcóyotl, the Premio Biblioteca Breve discussed in Chapter 5, and other awards also develop their own aesthetics and set a social or political agenda in what can become a self-perpetuating cycle.

The novelists who win the Premio Nezahualcóyotl represent a distinctive tradition. They sit between the second and third trends in indigenous

---

[7]Regrettably, I am unable to read any of the indigenous languages in which the novels are written. Given that an indigenous author, particularly one wishing to have their work considered for a literary prize, is frequently required to translate their work into Spanish Paja Faudree argues that they produce their texts with this in mind so that 'The meaning of the text lies not in one version of the other but rather in both as they work in concert' (2015, 231). On issues surrounding self-translation and the relationship between Spanish and indigenous language text whereby the relationship may be more complex than simple translation, see Faudree (2015, 19).

literatures identified by Luz María Lepe Lira (2010). Lepe Lira proposes that the initial trend towards transcribing collective memory persists alongside second and third categories of indigenous literature. The second category is rooted in the oral tradition but often presents alternative representations of women's roles. The third category is a 'literatura indígena híbrida' (hybrid indigenous literature) which 'no se refiere directamente a la vida en la comunidad o a las tradiciones ancestrales, se enfoca en el registro de las nuevas identidades y de las configuraciones de lenguaje y estética de los indígenas inmigrantes en las grandes ciudades o en los nuevos territorios ocupados por todos los *otros* habitantes de la marginalidad' (does not make direct reference to community life or ancestral traditions, it focuses on the new identities and configurations of language and aesthetics of indigenous immigrants to major cities or in the new territories occupied by all of the *other* inhabitants of the margins) (Lepe Lira 2010, 54–5).

The Premio Nezahualcóyotl prizewinning novels all demonstrate formal innovation in their use of narrative voice. Carillo Can's *Danzas* employs a female protagonist-narrator, Flor, who looks back on her younger self's lack of knowledge and laughs at her own naivety. The father-in-law narrator in *Relación* also provides a distinctive voice to tell Guzio's life story. Lienhard describes *Relación* as 'una novela hablada' (a spoken novel) (2014, 95). He suggests that the narrator draws on different oral and local traditions making the novel 'como un tejido de fragmentos de una memoria colectiva' (like a weaving together of the fragments of a collective memory) (2014, 95).

Ceh Moo's *Sólo por ser mujer* employs multiple narrators to provide different perspectives. The majority of the novel is narrated by the indigenous female protagonist Honorina who progresses from being a silent victim of domestic abuse to finally being able to speak for herself. Honorina's account is supplemented by those of another female narrator, Honorina's friend Doña Tiva, and that of the municipal president, and a third-person narrator. Doña Tiva's story demonstrates that sadly Honorina's experience of abuse is not unique. The municipal president and the third-person narrator describe the flawed legal procedures which led to Honorina being imprisoned based on a falsified statement and eventually released thanks to the efforts of her lawyer, Delia, Delia's mother and her well-connected friends. This final shift in narrative perspective serves verisimilitude.

All of the prizewinning novels are interested in the recent experiences of indigenous communities. They retell familiar national narratives as a means to write indigenous communities into national history and address contemporary issues, including environmental issues, migration, racial and gender equality and domestic abuse, from an indigenous perspective. Through Guzio's story, for example, *Relación* recounts large parts of the history of the Sierra Madre region of Oaxaca showing how its experience was both separate from and intersected with 'national' history. Much of the novel is taken up with Guzio's experiences of the Mexican Revolution. The novel of the Mexican Revolution is the cornerstone of the Mexican national canon, but indigenous people rarely feature in it. Such is the prominence of the revolution in *Relación* that a case could be made for it to be considered part of that tradition even though it adopts a new Zapotec perspective and 'often mocks the heroic accents of the "novels of the Revolution"' (Peña 2019, 339). For this reason, Lienhard terms it 'una contrahistoria "india" de la Revolución mexicana' (an 'Indian' counterhistory of the Mexican Revolution) (2014, 96).

Molina Cruz's *Pancho Culebro* tackles more recent history as it begins in the 1960s and explores the changes in Tierra Azul brought about as a result of government programmes to modernize Mexico. The start of the novel coincides with the presidencies of Adolfo López Mateos (1958–64) and Gustavo Díaz Ordaz (1964–70) when indigenous populations were seen as incompatible with the Mexican nation and measures to tackle illiteracy and promote 'la industrialización, la urbanización y el intercambio de bienes de consumo mayores' (industrialization, urban growth and the exchange of consumer goods) were introduced (Maldonado 2018, 180). The consequences of industrial development for the environment are a source of particular concern for the community in the novel. Environmental challenges caused by industrialization face the whole of Mexican society. The novel suggests that the solution for all would be to adopt a way of life that is more akin to that of the Zapotec community.

Pancho Culebro also explores the theme of migration and the related problems of people trafficking and narcotrafficking. Migration creates inequality as those who leave and later return use the money they have earned while away to lead privileged lives apart from the rest of the community. Few returning migrants use their newfound wealth to support community events. Returning migrants, represented by the *mestizo* Mund Dách and his associates, are seen as particularly damaged and become damaging to the community. Mund Dách uses his role as a *coyote* to lead people into prostitution and narcotrafficking. Dách also brings pornography, gambling, drink and drugs into Tierra Azul leading to women being raped in the streets and an increase in domestic violence.

Ceh Moo's *Sólo por ser mujer* explores issues of gender equality and domestic violence from the perspective of an indigenous woman. Honorina is sold by her father to her husband, Florencio. Florencio verbally and physically abuses her, forces her into prostitution, kills a co-worker and steals. Through Honorina, the novel exposes the dangers to which indigenous women are exposed as a result of the practice of selling daughters as wives. Even Honorina's mother considers the custom 'cosa de salvajes' (a thing of savages) suggesting that, even though they disagree with it, women may be powerless to affect change within the community (Ceh Moo 2015, 222). The narrator's comments leave the reader in no doubt that Honorina's upbringing keeps her in this abusive relationship because 'no se atrevía a actuar en contra de los designios de su cultura' (she did not dare to act against the wishes of her culture) (Ceh Moo 2015, 217). *Sólo por ser mujer* thus points to the ways in which women are let down by their own communities as well as by public institutions and a justice system which only paid attention to Honorina after she had murdered her husband. Upon release from prison Honorina's liberation is signified by the fact that she can articulate that racism and sexism were the cause of her suffering.

Danzas de la noche also has a female protagonist and advocates for women's self-determination. By making Flor the protagonist and the narrator of her own coming-of-age story, Carillo Can gives an indigenous female character a voice and highlights her road to independence and fulfilment. As Lepe Lira has noted, this contribution is significant because 'la descripción de lo femenino en el mundo indígena' (the portrayal of the feminine in the indigenous world) is a perspective which has long been silenced (2011, 16). The radical potential of putting a girl at the centre of a coming-of-age story is further underscored with reference to the female *bildungsroman*. As Esther Kleinbord Labovitz notes, this genre did not exist in the nineteenth-century European novel because it 'was made possible only when *Bildung* became a reality for women, in general, and for the fictional heroine, in particular. When cultural and social structures appeared to support women's struggle for independence, to go out in the world, engage in careers, in self-discovery and fulfilment, the heroine in fiction began to reflect these changes' (1988, 6–7). In the same way, the existence of *Danzas* as a female bildungsroman with an indigenous protagonist reflects, and advocates for, the changing place of indigenous women in society.

In their interest in contemporary issues all four prizewinning novels represent a shift away from the documentary or anthropological bent that has been identified in earlier indigenous literature. Yet they still feature insights into indigenous beliefs and practices. The novels are thus in keeping with the new trend in literatures in indigenous languages that first emerged in the 1990s which 'aborda la "recuperación" de los conocimientos tradicionales en el contexto de la globalización' (approaches the 'recuperation' of traditional knowledge in the context of globalization) (Kozlowska-Day 2014, 412). Recuperation is not the main focus of the prizewinning novels, but this knowledge is used in them to suggest that we can still learn from these traditions.

Relación invites the reader to consider different political systems. We learn that in Zapotec communities, people are chosen to occupy positions of responsibility for one year as an act of service to the community, but the characters do not crave high office because it means that they have less time to work and earn money to support themselves. The community leaders are portrayed in stark contrast to the ambitious politicians in the city who use their office to protect and further their own interests. Community politics are generally presented as more democratic, but there is also a recognition that communities and individuals can be misled by outsiders if they lack knowledge and experience beyond their villages. Through Guzio's character it is suggested that the solution is to preserve the community system of government but also to gain greater knowledge and experience of the world beyond.

Indigenous history, legends and beliefs feature prominently in *Pancho Culebro*. Pancho is the latest in a long line of *naguales* who are able to cure people of sickness, predict the fortunes of newborns, have supernatural powers and can turn into animals or natural phenomena. In the battle against the dam builders, we are introduced to other supernatural figures including *chaneques*, who are dead children returned to earth as dwarves and who are knowledgeable about nature, and Yelhellích, the woman who kills rapists. Pancho and these characters are pivotal in saving the community and so suggest the importance of preserving indigenous knowledge and beliefs.

Danzas incorporates some indigenous beliefs and practices. For example, through Doña Makin we learn about the customs surrounding birth. As the title suggests, dance is important in the novel, and it includes descriptions of the dances performed in the village noting that their significance goes beyond entertainment: 'Aquella danza no era una danza para entretenerse, era una danza que estaba llena de enseñanzas por la vida y para nuestra raza' (That dance was not a dance for entertainment, it was a dance that was full of instructions about life and for our race) (Carillo Can 2011, 123). *Danzas* and other prizewinning novels may not focus on indigenous beliefs and practices to the extent that earlier literatures in indigenous languages did, but they do not overlook them or their value.

The prizewinning novels all share a common interest in education and bilingualism. In *Relación* bilingualism is essential because for Guzio Spanish is the 'herramienta que le permite participar de manera privilegiada en sucesos históricos de su pueblo, de Oaxaca y de México en general' (tool that enables him to participate in a privileged way in the historic events in his village in Oaxaca and in Mexico as a whole) (Maldonado 2018, 173). The equal importance of Zapotec is underscored when Guzio returns from years away fighting because his inability to speak Zapotec signifies that he has lost a vital part of himself.

In *Pancho Culebro* formal education comes with the risk that indigenous perspectives will be lost. Education is portrayed as an instrument for alienating children from the community and a way of preparing them for migration. Equally, a lack of widespread education leaves the community vulnerable to being manipulated. Eleazar, however, represents the 'good' teacher, a typical figure found in much literature about indigenous communities including, for example, in *El indio* by Gregorio López y Fuentes which won the first Mexican Premio Nacional de Literatura (National Prize for Literature) in 1935.[8] Unlike his counterparts in the novels of the 1930s, however, Eleazar

---

[8] On this award, see Bowskill (2011, chapter 1).

rejects socialist education as part of 'la teoría de la asimilación que promueve la gradual desaparición del indio' (assimilation theory which promotes the gradual disappearance of the Indian) (Molina Cruz 2007, 340). Only by abandoning his connections to the outside world and learning Zapotec can Eleazar gain acceptance.

Danzas emphasizes the importance of informal education. It places a high value on women learning from other women as Noche instructs Flor about puberty and who can and cannot be trusted. Learning customs is also valued as exemplified by the importance attached to dance in the novel.

Sólo por ser mujer is critical of the failure of the justice system to cater for speakers of indigenous languages. When Honorina was arrested she spoke little Spanish, but officials were unable to identify the language she spoke and so, when she did not respond to questioning, her witness statement was fabricated. Education is part of the solution because learning Spanish in prison enables Honorina to go from being the victim of domestic violence not heard by those in authority to speaking out in public with a full understanding of the ways in which she has been oppressed.

Although there are subtle differences, all of the prizewinning novels end with the protagonists settling within indigenous communities with limited contact with the outside world. In *Relación* the main benefit of Guzio's time away is that he can use the knowledge he has gained to protect his community. Building intercommunity relationships with *mestizo* communities is not deemed worthwhile but improving relations between Zapotec communities is a high priority.

Pancho Culebro presents an even more isolationist view which suggests that indigenous communities are better off separating themselves from an outside world characterized by widespread corruption. Change is to be resisted as it threatens community cohesion. Women and the natural environment, around which community life is built, are both particularly vulnerable and should be shielded from outsiders. The community's lack of experience of the outside world leaves them vulnerable to those like Mund Dách who seek to take advantage of them, but ultimately, the novel suggests, they will be protected if they preserve their traditional beliefs and practices.

Sólo por ser mujer presents the most optimistic portrayal of relationships with non-indigenous communities as the novel highlights the impact of alliances of women working across ethnic and class boundaries. Women, including Doña Tiva and her lawyer, help Honorina to free herself from her husband. Upon release from prison, Honorina works as a personal assistant for her *mestizo* lawyer's mother. The novel narrowly avoids falling into a cliché whereby the middle-class *mestizo* save the indigenous woman as Honorina ultimately asserts her independence and returns to her village with her children. The closing image of the novel is one which reinforces the network of female support that has helped Honorina to regain her independence as she is waved off at the train station by Doña Tiva, Delia and her mother.

Whereas the other prizewinning texts endorse a return to the indigenous community, *Danzas* introduces a note of caution that such communities can become isolated and isolating in ways that are especially harmful to women. Flor's stepparents' household is patriarchal and does not value women or indigenous knowledge and medicine. They exploit Flor for her labour, and she is at risk of becoming the victim of sexual abuse at the hands of her stepfather. In the end, though, Flor is integrated into a community that values indigenous culture.

The prizewinning novels engage with contemporary issues, portraying indigenous protagonists assuming agency and still valuing tradition. However, some still rely on stereotypical representations of female characters. In *Relación* Guzio's mother is presented as being overprotective to the point of being emasculating as well as superstitious. The novel recognizes the strength of women in surviving and even thriving alone, but there is surprisingly little judgement implied for Guzio's when he leaves his wife for his sister-in-law. In this way, the novel fails to recognize the underlying problems which lead to some women being forced to be resilient. Similarly, when the women of one village are left alone because the men are taken away by the authorities, they become 'presidente-mujer, síndico-mujer, topil-mujer' (Madam President, Madam Official Receiver, Madam Constable) and manage in this way for over a year (2003, 346). There is no sense, however, that this should lead to a rethinking of gender roles in the community. In *Pancho Culebro* female characters appear equally fleetingly and fall into established stereotypes of the wife/mother, the victim or the vengeful temptress. Women are closely associated with nature, the domestic sphere and the continuance of community traditions.

Sólo por ser mujer and *Danzas de la noche* foreground the potential of women supporting other women. Noche and Doña Makin are instrumental in helping Flor on her journey to find her father which is also a journey of self-discovery. Nevertheless, and despite the significance of having a female protagonist and narrator, it could be argued that the novel presents a rather conservative view of women's roles. Flor becomes a skilled dancer, but this ability is presented as being more innate than learnt. Otherwise, her 'education' is concerned with teaching her about avoiding untrustworthy people and what she needs to know to be a good wife and mother. Her story ends with the clichéd happy ending to which all girls are supposed to aspire as she meets a husband and is pregnant. Indeed, the presence of the stepparents who mistreat her and the happy ending is reminiscent of a fairy tale. There is, of course, a risk of interpreting these novels according to Western feminist attitudes and standards, but it is worth registering that, while Flor's ambitions satisfy her, they are modest and so represent only a small broadening of horizons.

Despite some differences, particularly in the representation of women, the prizewinning novels share their choice of genre and at least four major areas in common. To acquire the literary prestige associated with the

Premio Nezahualcóyotl novels need to be formally innovative and portray empowered indigenous protagonists who are able to stand up for themselves and their communities and are not willing to give up their language, traditions or customs. The prizewinning novels incorporated myths and traditions within broader narratives addressing contemporary issues. They represent a clear shift away from writing by earlier indigenous authors which portrayed indigenous people as victims and/or aimed to preserve traditions and retell community myths and in which the author is a kind of scribe documenting shared narratives.

Conclusions

The Premio Nezahualcóyotl has contributed to the consolidation of the novel in indigenous languages and has used the literary prestige it can offer to bolster a political agenda which can be identified by looking at the shared values in the novels as well as the comments of stakeholders in the press. From the authors' perspective, this new political agenda and the novels, like the revamped Premio Nezahualcóyotl, are forward looking. They engage with contemporary issues and challenges while being attentive to the lessons that indigenous and non-indigenous communities alike can learn from indigenous practices and perspectives. There is also evidence of increasing awareness of the need to reflect on the position of women. The novels are confident in the future of indigenous communities able to assume agency and strongly advocate for an education that is rooted in indigenous languages and perspectives while not being fully isolationist. Finally, the novels embed strategies of resistance within their narratives to prevent easy assimilation by outside readers. The fact that the political agenda set and embraced by the novels is not as integrationist as that espoused by the Mexican state is, on the one hand, testament to the independence of the judges. On the other, it shows that the content of prizewinning novels is not so important to awarding bodies so long as they can be seen to be promoting identity politics and secure the tacit endorsement of authors writing in indigenous languages.

The winners of the Premio Nezahualcóyotl have not gone on to win other prizes beyond Mexico or even, as yet, INBA prizes unless specifically for literatures in indigenous languages. There is evidence, however, of the emergence of a prize network around indigenous literature in which these authors are circulating. In terms of acting as a gateway prize, the most we can say is that Javier Castellanos and Sol Ceh Moo subsequently won the PLIA. Conversely, Esteban Ríos Cruz, winner of the PLIA in 2014, subsequently won the Premio Nezahualcóyotl in 2018. The only winner of the INBA prize to date is Kalu Tatyisvai who is also the only author to win the Premio Nezahualcóyotl twice.

While not yet facilitating access to the wider prizes network the Premio Nezahualcóyotl has succeeded in connecting authors to the wider literary field in other ways. The Premio Nezahualcóyotl has helped to raise the profile of authors writing in indigenous languages nationally and even internationally. Gentes notes that authors writing in indigenous languages have limited profiles on the international stage but those who do 'are often writers who have gained visibility through the Premio Nezahualcóyotl de Literatura en Lenguas Mexicanas' (2019, 92). Natalia Toldeo Paz's prizewinning poetry collection, for example, when translated into English went on to be shortlisted for the National Translation Award, and many other winners of the Premio Nezahualcóyotl have had their works translated into other languages (Gentes 2019, 92). These are important steps towards gaining a foothold in the wider prize network.

The prizewinning texts may not be widely read, and the prize may do little to increase access to the texts for speakers in indigenous communities, but the Premio Nezahualcóyotl is bestowed by privileged readers, many of whom are from indigenous communities, and they are endorsed by state institutions in their capacity as awarding bodies. The readers, such as they are, are also likely to be drawn from privileged groups of critics, academics, educators, translators and activists in positions of influence in terms of providing pathways to further literary prestige and political agenda. The Premio Nezahualcóyotl has, therefore, greater potential impact than the print run may suggest. Moreover, its very existence is a marker of how attitudes have evolved since indigenous languages were seen as an obstacle to national progress.

The Premio Nezahualcóyotl was an important early step in consolidating the canon of authors writing in indigenous languages securing for them literary prestige as well as recognition for their activism in ensuring the survival of indigenous languages. The prize contributed to the preservation of Mexico's indigenous languages and subsequently to the promotion of a new kind of indigenous literature and the incentivization of the next generation of authors.

Since the 1990s, when the Premio Nezahualcóyotl was established, Norma Klahn suggests that 'se evidencia una acrecentada producción expresiva de literaturas indígenas en México' (we can see an increase in the production of indigenous literatures in Mexico) (2011/12, 171). The Premio Nezahualcóyotl, alongside other government and grassroots initiatives outlined earlier, doubtless contributed to this growth and is part of a wider shift in attitudes and thinking about the country's indigenous populations and their languages. Even if the prize gives the government a cover to tokenistically recognize indigenous authors and claim to promote multiculturalism and preserve indigenous languages, it seems the authors and judges have seized it as an opportunity to affect real change. One testament to the success of these policies is the fact that the winner of the Premio Nezahualcóyotl in 2018, Esteban Ríos Cruz, said that indigenous languages were flourishing ('Florece' 2018). The prize and texts are tools which amplify the voices and political agenda of authors writing in indigenous languages even when they do not perfectly align with official policies. The prize may have started out as 'window dressing' for the state's image, but it seems that members of the literary field connected to indigenous literatures from authors to judges and journalists have seized the opportunity it offered to construct a forward-looking agenda with its own politics and priorities.

Despite, or perhaps because of, these achievements, there are signs that the Premio Nezahualcóyotl is being superseded. Yasanya Elena Aguilar Gil's proposal to overcome the marginalization and devaluation of literatures in indigenous languages by making sure that 'the spaces, the systems that support literary creation, the anthologies, and the prizes for Mexican literature were also multilingual' is being implemented (2016, 158). Dedicated FONCA grants and the prestigious Young Creators grants are now available for authors writing in indigenous languages. All of the INBA awards are open to authors writing in indigenous languages, and there is a new INBA prize for indigenous literatures bringing indigenous literature under the auspices of the principal institution in Mexico responsible for consecration and nation-building through literature. Texts in indigenous languages can now compete for national prizes alongside those in Spanish. These prizes may be more attractive than the Premio Nezahualcóyotl for authors seeking literary prestige and may, in time, have greater potential to connect these authors to the wider prize network.

8

The never-ending network?

Even as I worked on this manuscript, at least two new prizes were created. The Premio Primera Novela in Mexico was established in March 2021 and the Premio Fundación Medifé Filba de Novela launched in Argentina in 2020. The prize network is constantly evolving to enable new positions in the fields of literature and politics. As Bourdieu contends, between the field of cultural production and the field of power there is 'an almost perfect homology between two chiastic structures' (1993, 45). The literary field is the field of politics in reverse, and so it stands to reason that as new positions emerge in one, they are reflected in the other. Here, I will briefly outline the politics of literary prestige of two of the most recent trends when it comes to prizes for Spanish American literature before considering the successes and limitations of the strategies employed by authors who have tried to negotiate a position beyond the prize network. Few viable alternatives to the prize network exist, and when they emerge, they tend to be rapidly co-opted. For the foreseeable future it seems the prize network will be never ending.

The first trend is for prizes that are funded through public–private partnerships reflecting the neoliberal turn in Spanish America since the 1980s. Neoliberalism, as Sánchez Prado has observed, does not necessarily mean a weakening of the state (*Pierre Bourdieu* 2018, 189). It does, however, favour a reduced or more 'hands-off' role for the state, and increased privatization. These changes allow the author to appear increasingly independent from the state. This illusion of independence may be beneficial to both parties concealing the process of capital intraconversion. The downside to such prizes is that the role of the author is diminished in comparison to traditional, state-sponsored awards. For states seeking to marginalize potentially influential voices of dissent, changing prize criteria, regulations and funding to change their relationship with authors and thence change the author's role in society is a way to achieve this goal. The effectiveness of this strategy was seen in Chapter 1 with reference to the changes in the Premio

Rómulo Gallegos. In March 2021 the Mexican government announced a partnership with Amazon to create the Premio Primera Novela (Zamarrón 2021). The prize for the published work of a first-time Mexican novelist offers prize money from Amazon of 250,000 pesos for the winner and 3 runners up prizes of 35,000 pesos as well as the chance to have their work promoted by Amazon throughout Spanish America. This type of partnership is not without precedent. In Peru, for example, the Premio Nacional de Literatura (National Prize for Literature) has been sponsored for the last five years by the mining company AngloAmerican and the state-owned fuel company Petroperú has sponsored the Premio Copé since 1979. At the end of Chapter 1 we noted similar events in Bolivia. The websites of both organizations proudly announced the latest prizes for 2021. These prizes represent a coming together of the politics of nation-building and the politics of neoliberalism and globalization in a way that is in keeping with the broader political trends in Spanish America. It would not be surprising to see more and more of this new type of prize in the near future.

The second trend is for city-sponsored prizes. Cities are using prizes, as nations did before them, to associate themselves with literary prestige. Cities and regional state authorities have been involved in this type of activity for some time as we saw in Chapter 1 in relation to the creation of the Premio Nacional in Panama, and as happened when Mexico underwent a process of decentralizing culture beginning in the late 1970s. The extent of the phenomenon is, however, increasingly significant in the prize network. Dunja Fehimović and Rebecca Ogden refer to 'nation branding' to describe the way in which nations have been involved in 'polishing their pitches in order to highlight their own advantages and define their specificities – in other words, to *brand* and successfully *sell* their countries' (2018, 1). In creating prizes named after places cities participate in a similar process we might call city branding.

The goal of city-sponsored prizes is to create an association between place and culture, which will promote tourism and the economy through creative industries. In this regard, they are part of a broader process in which cities are using literature and its associated prestige to drive their economy. The Hay Festival has been a leader in expanding its events from a small town on the Welsh borders to cities across the Spanish-speaking world including Cartagena in Colombia, previously Xalapa in Mexico, and now Querétaro, Arequipa in Peru and Segovia in Spain. As seen in Chapter 2, the Hay Festival, with its origins in the UK, has been instrumental in shaping Spanish American literature through the Bogotá 39 lists of up-and-coming writers under forty who are increasingly the recipients of publisher-run prizes. Other initiatives which have sought to help cities to capitalize on literary prestige include UNESCO's City of Literature and World Book City programmes. Marcy Schwartz describes the experiences of Bogotá and Buenos Aires of being World Book Cities noting that these campaigns are examples of 'cultural management (gestión cultural), that has emerged in the neoliberal period' (2018, 42). The City of Literature designation likewise aims to 'treat a city's literary heritage and present book industry as an occasion to develop cultural tourism and creative economy sectors' (Brouillette 2019, 103). This program also requires cities to 'have demonstrated that they have "public and private infrastructure dedicated to the preservation, promotion and dissemination" of the culture in question' (Brouillette 2019, 102). The public–private collaboration at the heart of these programmes is common to many Spanish American city-sponsored prizes just as it is increasingly seen in the aforementioned prize collaborations between the state and private enterprise. Both of these recent prize trends, therefore, are aligned with neoliberal politics which instrumentalize culture for profit and deprive the author of the role of public intellectual.

Perhaps the best-known example of a city-sponsored prize, which began as a partnership between the city council and a US productivity company, is the Dublin Literary Award, formerly the International IMPAC Dublin Literary Award. In Spanish America examples include a suite of Premios Municipales (Municipal Prizes) for poetry, essays, short stories and novels established in Buenos Aires in 2006. Another interesting example for the manner in which it combines neoliberal politics and city branding is the Premio Spiwak Ciudad de Cali a la Novela del Pacífico Americano en español (Spiwak Prize for the City of Cali for a Novel in Spanish from the American Pacific) established in 2016. The prize was the result of a partnership between an NGO set up by the hospitality company Spiwak and the publisher Siglo XXI which undertook to publish the winning text. An award of $50,000 was to be made every two years. To date Miguel Botero García is the only recipient. The prize sought to promote the city of Cali, which had so long been linked to narcotrafficking and corruption, as a tourist destination. The glossy brochure announcing the prize referred to 'los inmensos problemas de orden social que vive esta zona del hemisferio' (the immense social problems experienced by this part of the hemisphere) and called on the academic community and its research to propose 'soluciones creativas y respetuosas de nuestra diversidad social y cultural, enriquece la proyección estratégica de la región' (creative solutions that are respectful of our social and cultural diversity and enrich the strategic external image of the region) (Fundación Spiwak 2016, 2). The potential economic benefits for the prize sponsors and the winning author are clear. Judges and winning authors lend their prestige to support development initiatives driven by industry tacitly endorsing the withdrawal of the state.

As the prize network colonizes more and more positions in the literary and political fields, there remain few options for authors wishing to remain beyond the network. Authors may refuse permission for their work to be entered. Alternatively, they can refuse prizes. Such a move today risks appearing 'self-consciously dated and curmudgeonly' and 'can no longer be counted upon to reinforce one's artistic legitimacy' (English 2005, 221). Even so, some Spanish American authors have pulled it off. After he won the Nobel Prize for Literature Gabriel García Márquez declined all prizes including the Premio Cervantes. *El País* reported the response of the director of the Academia Española de la Lengua who described it as 'una decisión respetable' (a respectable decision) ('García Márquez Rechaza' 1997). As described in Chapter 1, some authors are currently boycotting the Premio Rómulo Gallegos for political reasons. They have, somewhat naively, been accused of politicizing the prize as if it were not already politicized, but their position has legitimacy and precedent exemplified when Elena Poniatowska refused the Premio Xavier Villaurrutia in 1970 for *La noche de Tlatelolco* following the massacre in the Plaza de las Tres Culturas in Mexico City reportedly asking '¿Quién va a premiar a los muertos?' (Who is going to give a prize to the dead?) (Montaño Garfias 2015). Refusal of a prize on political grounds is still a legitimate choice in Spanish America.

For some, strategies of condescension, as defined by Bourdieu (1991, 124), may provide a route to occupy an in-between space. Eli Neira's positioning of herself as an occupier of a 'zona peligrosa' (danger zone) is an example of such an approach (Bowskill and Lavery 2020, 20). Neira worked as a journalist, receiving funding from the Chilean government's funding body, the Fondo Nacional para el Desarrollo Cultural y las Artes (National Fund for the Cultural Development and the Arts) (FONDART), and spoke at universities and poetry workshops with consecrated poets. She subsequently became an outspoken critic of FONDART publishing witty open letters in which she 'criticized the iniquitous mechanisms FONDART uses to select potential award holders' (Bowskill and Lavery 2020, 107). She has not completely shunned established agents of legitimation though. Rather, where possible she operates 'in an in-between space reserving the right to criticize even when partaking in the benefits of cultural consecration' (Bowskill and Lavery 2020, 109).

Cartonera (cardboard book) and other alternative publishing formats, such as those coming out of the Taller Letañeros (Letañeros Workshop) where books are made out of plants, offer another way to bypass the prize network and the large publishing conglomerates.[1] In many cases the format of these books means that they would not meet the criteria to be eligible to enter prizes. The politics of the *cartonera* movement are in marked contrast to those of commercial publishers. As Schwartz writes: 'Cartonera publishing dramatizes the move toward collective rather than individual initiatives to confront the consequences of neoliberal economic politics, particularly in the publishing industries' (2018, 153). Their endeavours

---

[1] On the Chiapas-based workshop, see http://www.tallerlenateros.com/. For an overview of cartoneras, see Bilbika and Carbajal (2009).

are based on cooperation, engagement with the communities in which they work and concern for the environment (Schwartz 2018, 154). I would not be surprised, however, if the prize network did not seek to colonize this space with awards for books published in alternative formats.

Self-publishing and online publishing also present an increasingly viable alternative for authors to resist the prize network. These ventures have their roots in initiatives seen in the context of the Chilean dictatorship when the Colectivo de Acciones de Arte (CADA) (Art Actions Collective) (1979–85) and other groups of authors and artists sought spaces outside the cultural hegemony of the dictatorship. CADA pursued independent publishing ventures, but, Sebastián Vidal argues, it was not until the advent of the internet that things radically changed: '[p]asamos de una editorialidad de arte limitada y de resistencia a una múltiple y de código abierto; ahí sin duda hay un cambio radical' (we went from the publication of restricted art and art of resistance to multiple editors and open code; there without doubt is a radical change) (quoted in Barria Bignotti 2013). Today, we can look to independent publishing projects such as the publisher Tumbona Ediciones in Mexico which is involved in the creation of 'una "literatura mundial" desde abajo a contrapelo de la literatura mundial construida desde arriba a través de circuitos hegemónicos de circulación transnacional' (a 'world literature' from below that runs contrary to world literature from above which operates through hegemomic transnational circuits of circulation) and operates on a copyleft policy (Sánchez Prado 2020, 268). In these cases, the creators and publishers have tried to assert greater independence, but CADA members, including Diamela Eltit winner of Chile's Premio Nacional de Literatura in 2018 and of the Premio FIL in 2021, have become consecrated authors and artists illustrating how positions in the literary field constantly shift. This evolution means that today's alternative initiatives and outliers may not remain beyond the prize network in the long term.

Caution must also be exercised when proclaiming the freedoms of publishing online as this space is increasingly colonized by corporations using our data for profit. As Mejias (2013) suggests, we might think twice about what resistance via social media means in this context. Access is neither free nor equal. Computers and broadband cost money. Visibility depends on algorithms and users actively searching for the content. Nevertheless, online does provide exciting opportunities for writers to explore the possibilities of multimedia literature and disrupt the hierarchy of values when it comes to different genres and artforms.[2] Spanish American women authors in

---

[2] On the growing use of multimedia by Spanish American women authors, see Sarah Bowskill and Jane Lavery eds. *The Multimedia Works of Contemporary Latin American Women Artists and Writers* (Forthcoming). This book includes a chapter by Bowskill with further analysis of the work of Mónica Nepote and Rocío Cerón and chapters by Jane Lavery on Ana Clavel, Emily Hind looking at the work of Carla Faesler, Carolina Gainza on Prado Bassi, Thea Pitman

particular are making use of this space to bypass networks, including the prize network, from which they have traditionally been excluded. Bencomo discusses the case of Cristina Rivera Garza's blog (2006, 23). The websites of Karen Villeda, Ana Clavel, Rocío Cerón, Eugenia Prado Bassi, Jacalyn Lopez Garcia, Lucia Grossberger Morales, Belén Gache and Marina Zerbarini, as well as Cerón's 'La observante' project on Instagram, and Carla Faesler's YouTube channel, are fascinating examples of how women authors are bypassing or supplementing traditional 'agents of legitimation' with the authority to consecrate through, for example, literary prizes (Bourdieu 1993, 121).[3] That is not to say that they avoid them completely though. Rather, these online environments are providing an alternative form of visibility to that offered by prizes that may be effective in reaching new or different audiences. As visibility and literary prestige connect other options offering greater freedom from the demands of states and publishers may also open up for authors who wish to participate in alternative circuits of value and define their own, new role in society. In the meantime, it is incumbent on us to continue to recognize the politics of literary prestige when it comes to prizes for Spanish American literature even when they are concealed.

---

on Jacalyn Lopez Garcia and Lucia Grossberger Morales, Debra Ann Castillo on Karen Villeda and Claire Taylor on Belén Gache.
[3]See http://poetronica.net/home.html, https://anaclavel.com/, https://www.rocioceron.com, https://eugeniapradobassi.cl, http://artelunasol.com/GHstatement.html, https://luciagrossbergermorales.com/, http://belengache.net/, https://www.marina-zerbarini.com.ar/WordPress/ and https://www.youtube.com/user/motinpoetacanal.

REFERENCES

Carlos Barral Archive, Biblioteca de Catalunya, Barcelona

'Agreements taken on the meeting of September 18th 1962 in the Hotel Hessicher Höf in Frankfurt', Caixa 2.8 Formentor. Sub File Formentor 1962. Sub Sub File Jaime Salinas. Fons Barral Fons Barral. CII/Z-8.

'Nota sobre *El Ojo Exiliado*', no date. Fons Barral. Corresp. Editor. Carmen Balcells – captea. No date.

'¿Existe o no una nueva novela Española?', Barral Editores 2.3. Barral Editores. Fons Barral.

José María Espinas, 'El coloquio internacional de novela, en Formentor, Mallorca', article in CII Doc. Professional. Caixa 2.8 Formentor. Sub file. Formentor 1959. Conversaciones Formentor (1959). Sub sub file Conversaciones Poéticas Formentor (Cart. prensa época). Fons Barral.

Text sense titol, incl, 'Los años 1959 y 1960', Prix Formentor 1962. Caixa 2.8 Formentor. CII Doc. Professional. Fons Barral.

Text sense titol, incl: 'Michel Mohrt y, François Erval…', Prix Formentor 1962. Fons Barral. CII/Z-8.

'La experiencia que un editor literario', Caixa 2.8 Formentor. Sub File Prix Formentor 1962. Text sense titol. C.II 2.8. Fons Barral.

Doc. 41.1.11, 'Protesta Intelectuales, Valescure Telegrama de Protesta, Valescure', Prix Formentor 1965. Z.5. Fons Barral.

Legal Documents

Argentina

Argentina. Congreso de la Nación. Senado de la Nación (1935), *Diario de Sesiones* 1913, 1095–98.

Chile

Decree 681 Decreto Ley-681 10-OCT-1974 MINISTERIO DE EDUCACIÓN PÚBLICA - Ley Chile - Biblioteca del Congreso Nacional (bcn.cl).

Ley-19169 26-SEP-1992 MINISTERIO DE EDUCACIÓN PÚBLICA – Ley Chile – Biblioteca del Congreso Nacional (bcn.cl).
Ley 17595 8th January 1972 https://www.bcn.cl/leychile/Navegar?idNorma=29135.

Panama

Decreto No. 332 del 15/10/70. Reglamentación del 'Premio Literario Ricardo Miro'. On UNESCO site. List of National Cultural Heritage Laws | UNESCO.
Gaceta Oficial, Lunes 19 de octubre de 1970. No. 16.717 p.2 DECRETO DE GABINETE No.332 DE 15-10-1970 (332) POR EL CUAL SE ADOPTAN MEDIDAS RELATIVAS AL CONCURSO LITERARIO RICARDO MIRO. (justia.com).
Gaceta Oficial. No. 8779. Thursday 16th April 1942 p.9 Ordenanza Número 4 (de 20 de Marzo de 1942)8779 –1942 - 76 - 1408 - 1423 (procuraduria-admon.gob.pa).
Ley 27 1946. https://en.unesco.org/sites/default/files/pa_ley27_1946_spaorof.pdf.

Paraguay

Paraguay Ley No 97/90 por el cual se instituyen premios nacionales de literatura y ciencia. para_ley9790_spaorof.pdf (unesco.org) and Ley por la cual se instituye Premios Nacionales de Literatura y Ciencia. No. 97/90|Ko Léi he'i oñembojopóitaha Ñe'arcolegal/ley-por-la-cual-se-ino. 97/90 | Secretaría Nacional de Cultura.

Venezuela

Venezuelan Constitution Articles 100 and 101 1999 Constitution. (anonymous) (constituteproject.org). The text in Spanish www.minci.gob.ve/wp-content/uploads/2011/04/CONSTITUCION.pdf.
Ley Orgánica de Cultura. Article 3.18 Ley-orgánica-de-cultura.pdf (minci.gob.ve).
'República Bolivariana de Venezuela', Ministerio del Poder Popular Para la Cultura. Informe de Gestión de los Organos Desconcentrados y Entes Descentralizados de la Memoria y Cuenta 2014. Published 2015 memoria-2014-cultura.pdf (transparencia.org.ve).

Nobel Prize Documents

'Alfred Nobel's Will', Available online: www.nobelprize.org/alfred-nobel-alfred-nobels-will/ (accessed 19 March 2021).
'Nomination and Selection of Literature Laureates', *NobelPrize.org. Nobel Media AB 2021. Sun*, 13 June 2021. Available online: https://www.nobelprize.org/nomination/literature/.

REFERENCES

Mistral, Gabriela, 'Nobel Lecture', Available online: http://www.memoriachilena.gob.cl/602/w3-article-132057.html.
Gabriela Mistral Nobel Prize Citation, 'The Nobel Prize in Literature 1945', *NobelPrize.org. Nobel Media AB 2021. Sun*, 13 June 2021. Available online: https://www.nobelprize.org/prizes/literature/1945/summary/.
Asturias, Miguel Ángel (1967), 'Nobel Lecture', *NobelPrize.org. Nobel Media AB 2021*, Tue. 16 March 2021. Available online: https://www.nobelprize.org/prizes/literature/1967/asturias/lecture/.
Miguel Ángel Asturias, 'Nobel Prize Citation. The Nobel Prize in Literature 1967', *NobelPrize.org. Nobel Media AB 2021*, Sun. 13 June 2021. Available online: https://www.nobelprize.org/prizes/literature/1967/summary/.
Österling, Anders, 'Miguel Ángel Asturias Award Ceremony Speech', *NobelPrize.org. Nobel Media AB 2021*, Sat. 20 March 2021. Available online: https://www.nobelprize.org/prizes/literature/1967/ceremony-speech/.
Pablo Neruda Citation The Nobel Prize in Literature (1971), *NobelPrize.org. Nobel Media AB 2021*, Fri. 19 March 2021. Available online: https://www.nobelprize.org/prizes/literature/1971/summary/.
Neruda, Pablo (1971), 'Nobel Lecture', *NobelPrize.org. Nobel Media AB 2021*, Sat. 12 June 2021. Available online: https://www.nobelprize.org/prizes/literature/1971/neruda/lecture/. Award ceremony speech.
Karl Ragnar Gierow, 'Pablo Neruda. Award Ceremony Speech', *NobelPrize.org. Nobel Media AB 2021*, Sun. 13 Jun 2021. Available online: https://www.nobelprize.org/prizes/literature/1971/ceremony-speech/.
Gabriel García Márquez Citation The Nobel Prize in Literature (1982), *NobelPrize.org. Nobel Media AB 2021*, Fri. 19 March 2021. Available online: https://www.nobelprize.org/prizes/literature/1982/summary/.
Gyllensten, Lars. Gabriel García Márquez (1982), 'Award Ceremony Speech', *NobelPrize.org. Nobel Media AB 2021*, Thu. 18 March 2021. Available online: https://www.nobelprize.org/prizes/literature/1982/ceremony-speech/.
García Márquez, Gabriel, 'Nobel Lecture', *NobelPrize.org. Nobel Media AB 2021*, Sun. 13 June 2021. Available online: https://www.nobelprize.org/prizes/literature/1982/marquez/lecture/.
Paz, Octavio (1990), 'Nobel Lecture', *NobelPrize.org. Nobel Media AB 2021*, Mon. 15 March 2021. Available online: https://www.nobelprize.org/prizes/literature/1990/paz/lecture/.
Espmark, Kjell (1990), 'Award Ceremony Speech', *NobelPrize.org. Nobel Media AB 2021*, Sat. 20 March 2021. Available online: https://www.nobelprize.org/prizes/literature/1990/ceremony-speech/.
Octavio Paz Citation, 'The Nobel Prize in Literature 1990', *NobelPrize.org. Nobel Media AB 2021*, Mon. 14 June 2021. Available online: https://www.nobelprize.org/prizes/literature/1990/summary/.
Vargas Llosa, Mario (2010), 'Nobel Lecture', *NobelPrize.org. Nobel Media AB 2021*, Mon. 15 March 2021. Available online: https://www.nobelprize.org/prizes/literature/2010/vargas_llosa/25162-mario-vargas-llosa-nobel-lecture-2010/.
Wästberg, Per (2010), 'Mario Vargas Llosa Award Ceremony Speech', *Award Ceremony Speech. NobelPrize.org. Nobel Media AB 2021*, Sun. 13 June 2021. Available online: https://www.nobelprize.org/prizes/literature/2010/ceremony-speech/.

Mario Vargas Llosa Citation, 'The Nobel Prize in Literature 2010', *NobelPrize.org. Nobel Media AB 2021*, Sun. 13 June 2021. Available online: https://www.nobelprize.org/prizes/literature/2010/summary/.

Premio Cervantes Speeches

del Paso, Fernando (2015), 'Ceremonia de entrega del Premio Cervantes 2015. Discurso de Fernando del Paso', Thurs. 2 December 2021. Available online: https://www.culturaydeporte.gob.es/premiado/downloadBlob.do?idDocumento=3256

Edwards, Jorge (1999), 'Ceremonia de entrega del Premio Cervantes 1999. Discurso de Jorge Edwards', Thurs. 2 December 2021. Available online: https://www.culturaydeporte.gob.es/premiado/downloadBlob.do?idDocumento=2494

Gelman, Juan (2007), 'Ceremonia de entrega del Pemio Cervantes 2007. Discurso de Juan Gelman', Thurs. 2 December 2021. Available online: https://www.culturaydeporte.gob.es/premiado/downloadBlob.do?idDocumento=1947

Gobierno de España. Ministerio de Cultura y Deporte, 'Presentación. Premio de Literatura en Lengua Castellana Miguel de Cervantes', Available online: http://www.culturaydeporte.gob.es/cultura/libro/premios/listado-de-premios/cervantes/presentacion.html (accessed 19 March 2021).

Pacheco, José Emilio (2009), 'Ceremonia de entrega del Premio Cervantes 2009. Discurso de José Emilio Pacheco', Thurs. 2 December 2021. Available online: https://www.culturaydeporte.gob.es/premiado/downloadBlob.do?idDocumento=1945

Poniatowska, Elena (2013), 'Ceremonia de entrega del Premio Cervantes 2013. Discurso de Elena Poniatowska', Thurs. 2 December 2021. Available online: https://www.culturaydeporte.gob.es/premiado/downloadBlob.do?idDocumento=3389

Ramírez, Sergio (2017), 'Viaje de ida y Vuelta. Discurso de Sergio Ramírez al recibir el Premio Cervantes 2017', Thurs. 2 December 2021. Available online: https://www.culturaydeporte.gob.es/premiado/downloadBlob.do?idDocumento=3406

Roa Bastos, Augusto (1989), 'Ceremonia de entrega del Premio Cervantes 1989. Discurso de Augusto Roa Bastos', Thurs. 2 December. Available online: https://www.culturaydeporte.gob.es/premiado/downloadBlob.do?idDocumento=2527&prev_layout=premioMiguelCervantesLibro&layout=premioMiguelCervantesLibro&language=es

Sábato, Ernesto (1984), 'Ceremonia de entrega del Premio Cervantes 1984. Discurso de Ernesto Sábato', Thurs. 2 December 2021. Available online: https://www.culturaydeporte.gob.es/premiado/downloadBlob.do?idDocumento=1704

Vargas Llosa, Mario (1994), 'Ceremonia de entrega del Premio Cervantes 1994. Discurso de Mario Vargas Llosa', Thurs. 2 December 2021. Available online: https://www.culturaydeporte.gob.es/premiado/downloadBlob.do?idDocumento=3474

Websites and Online Documents

Casa de las Américas www.casadelasamericas.org.
CELARG. Premio Rómulo Gallegos. Available online: https://web.archive.org/web/20120207112559/ http:/www.celarg.org.ve/Ingles/Premio%20Romulo%20 Gallegos.htm.
Editorial Anagrama (2020), 'Presentación conjunta de las obras ganadora y finalista del Premio Herralde de Novela', 18 December 2020. Available online: https://www.youtube.com/watch?v=xYj6dNm_HaA&t=306s (accessed 11 June 2021).
Fundación Premio Spiwak de Cali, 'Premio a la Novela del Pacífico Americano en español 2016', Available online: www.premiospiwak.org (accessed 14 June 2021).
Gijón (N.d.), 'Premio Café Gijon', Available online: https://www.gijon.es/es/eventos/premio-cafe-gijon (accessed 28 April 2021).
Gobierno de Venezuela/ Ministerio del Poder Popular para la Cultura/ Venezuela (1982), 'Premio Internacional de Novela Rómulo Gallegos Vol 2', CNL Exp PRE0708.
Literatura.us, 'Herberto Padilla (1932–s2000)', 'Declaración de la UNEA' 1968 https://www.literatura.us/padilla/uneac.html (accessed 14 June 2021).
Mexico Gobierno Federal, *Catálogo de las Lenguas Nacionales Indígenas*, Gobierno Federal, SEP. 2009. Available online: https://site.inali.gob.mx/pdf/catalogo_lenguas_indigenas.pdf (accessed 21 July 2020).
Mexico Secretaría de Cultura. Instituto Nacional de Bellas Artes, 'Premios Bellas Artes de Literatura', Available online: https://literatura.inba.gob.mx/premios-bellas-artes.html (accessed 26 September 2019).
Mueso Gabriela Mistral de Vicuña, 'Hitos de la vida de Gabriela Mistral', Available online: https://www.mgmistral.gob.cl/634/w3-article-30305.html?_noredirect=1 (accessed 18 March 2021).
Penguin España (2021), 'Premio Alfaguara de novela 2021', 21 January 2021. Available online: https://www.youtube.com/watch?v=zC_s6wcQ_8s (accessed 11 June 2021).
Petroperú, 'Petroperú inicia convocatoria al Premio Copé 2021', Available online: https://mineriaenergia.com/petroperu-inicia-convocatoria-al-premio-cope-2021/.
Petroperú, 'Premio Copé', Available online: https://www.petroperu.com.pe/gestioncultural/premio-cope/presentacion/.
Planeta, 'Premio Biblioteca Breve', Available online: https://www.planetadelibros.com/premios/premio-biblioteca-breve/5 (accessed 21 August 2019).
'Premio de Literatura Sor Juana Inés de la Cruz 2021', Available online: https://udg.mx/es/convocatorias/premio-de-literatura-sor-juana-ines-de-la-cruz-2021 (accessed 14 June 2021).
'Premio Nacional de Literatura - Memoria Chilena, Biblioteca Nacional de Chile', Available online: http://www.memoriachilena.gob.cl/602/w3-article-3399.html.
República Bolivariana de Venezuela, 'Ministerio de Poder Popular Para La Cultura. Informe de gestion de los órganoos desconcentradoos y entes descentralizados de la memoria y cuenta 2014', Available online: memoria-2014-cultura.pdf (transparencia.org.ve).

'Taller Letañeros', Available online: http://www.tallerlenateros.com/.
Women's Prize for Fiction, 'History', Available online: www.womensprizeforfiction.co.uk/about/history

Articles from the Centro Nacional de Literatura CNL Archive, Mexico City

'30 de junio, plazo para entrega de trabajos. Premio Sor Juan, difusión de autoras en español', *El Nacional*, 25 de junio 1998, p.40 CNL. Exp. Premio Sor Juana.
'620 obras compiten', 2014. CNL. Exp. PRE0704.
Abelleyra, Angélica (1997), 'Lanzan Premio Internacional Alfaguara de Novela', *La Jornada*, 23 April 1997. Premio Alfaguara de Novela (Editorial Alfaguara/ España) (1997–) Exp PRE0704.
Agencias (1997), 'Laura Restrepo, premio Sor Juana Inés 1997', *La Jornada. Secc. Cultura*, 21 noviembre 1997, p.25. CNL. Exp. Premio Sor Juana.
Aguilar Sosa, Yanet (2009), 'Boullosa recrea "pleito" de escritores vivos y Muertos', *El Universal*, 14 de abril 2009, p.F4. CNL. Exp. Carmen Boullosa.
Alvarado, Nicolás (2009), 'Cirugía mayor', *Milenio*, 31 de marzo 2009, p.53. CNL. Exp. Carmen Boullosa.
Amador, Judith (1994), 'Gana Víctor de la Cruz Premio Nezahualcóyotl', *Reforma*, 14 de octubre 1994, CNL Exp PRE0033.
Anabitarte, Ana (1998), 'Premio Alfaguara. Alta calidad en las obras finalistas: Fuentes', *El Universal*, 18 de febrero 1998 Premio Alfaguara de Novela (Editorial Alfaguara/ España) (1997–) Exp PRE0704.
Arriaga, Erika (2004), 'El premio Sor Juana a una novela que satiriza a la Iglesia católica', *La Jornada*, 2 diciembre 2004 p2a. CNL. Exp. Premio Sor Juana.
Bautista, Virginia (2011), 'Premio apoya ensayo y novela', *Excélsior*, 9 febrero 2011, CNL Exp 0038 Expediente – Concurso Internacional de Ensayo y Narrativa (UNAM/UAS/El Colegio de Sinaloa/Siglo XXI Editores). PRE0038.
Bautista, Virginia (2013), 'Premio de Literatura Sor Juana Inés de la Cruz. Veinte años de abrir puertas a mujeres', *Excélsior*, 26 enero, 2013, p.11 CNL. Exp. Premio Sor Juana
Beauregard, Luis Pablo (2014), '"Las juanas" de Guadalajara, contra el machismo literario', *El País*, 6 diciembre 2014, p.30 CNL. Exp. Premio Sor Juana.
'Boullosa gana premio Café Gijón', *El Economista*, 19 September 2008, p.7. CNL. EXP. Carmen Boullosa.
Camacho Olivares, Alfredo (2001), 'Cristina Rivera Recibió el Premio Sor Juana Inés', *Excélsior,* 30 noviembre 2001, p.1 and 2C CNL. Exp. Premio Sor Juana.
Camacho Suárez, Eduardo (1996), 'Canasta Cultural', *Excélsior*, 28 noviembre 1996, CNL Exp PRE0033.
'Carlos Fuentes anunciará al ganador del Premio Alfaguara de Novela', *Crónica*, 12 de febrero 1998 Premio Alfaguara de Novela (Editorial Alfaguara/ España) (1997–) Exp PRE0704.
Chimely, Eduardo (1994), 'Marcela Serrano ganó el II Premio Sor Juana Inés', *Excélsior*, p.2C, 30 noviembre 1994. CNL. Exp. Premio Sor Juana.

'Clara Usón, ganadora del Premio Sor Juana', *El Universal*, 30 octubre 2018, p.E9, CNL. Exp. Premio Sor Juana.
'Convocan al Premio Nezahualcóyotl de Literatura', *Excélsior*, 13 enero 1994, CNL Exp PRE0033.
'Convocatoria. Premio Nezahualcóyotl 2000 Literatura en Letras Indígenas', *Sábado supl. de Uno más uno*, 18 marzo 2000, CNL Exp PRE0033.
'Convocatoria', *La Jornada*, 21 febrero 2014, CNL Exp PRE0033.
'Darán mayor difusión al premio Sor Juana Inés de la Cruz', *El Nacional sec. Cultura*, 4 de julio de 1997, p.40. CNL Exp. Premio Sor Juana.
Domínguez Michael, Christopher (2005), 'El fin de un premio literario', *Reforma. Supl. El Angel*, 31 de julio 2005, CNL Exp PRE0708.
'El FCE y *Los Angeles Times* apoyarán el Premio Sor Juana Inés de la Cruz', *Unomásuno secc. Cultura*, 4 de julio de 1997, p.26 CNL. Exp. Premio Sor Juana.
Europa Press (2019), 'Firman manifiesto contra la bienal Vargas Llosa por la falta de mujeres', *La Jornada*, 28 mayo, 2019, p.5ª, CNL Exp 0801 Premios Extranjeros de Narrativa sin Expediente.
'¿Favores? Premio Sor Juana para Elena Garro', *El Financiero*, 5 de diciembre 1996, p.72 CNL. Exp Premio Sor Juana.
Figueroa, Adrián (2014), 'Ganan cubano y español el XI Concurso Internacional de Ensayo y Narrativa', *La Crónica de Hoy*, 12 febrero 2014, CNL Exp 0038 Expediente – Concurso Internacional de Ensayo y Narrativa (UNAM/UAS/El Colegio de Sinaloa/Siglo XXI Editores). PRE0038.
Flores, Alejandro (2009), 'Libros para quedarse en casa. Todo un complot literario', *El Economista*, 4 de mayo 2009, p.55. CNL Exp Carmen Boullosa.
Flores, Alondra (2014), 'Lanzan convocatoria del premio Nezahualcóyotl', *La Jornada*, 22 febrero 2014, CNL Exp PRE0033.
'Florece lengua indígena', *Excélsior*, 20 agosto 2018, CNL Exp PRE0033.
'Gabriel Pacheco Recibió el Premio Nezahualcóyotl', *Excélsior*, 27 febero 1999, CNL Exp PRE0033.
García Hernández, Arturo (1995), 'La Feria. Tatiana Lobo, premio Sor Juana', *La Jornada*, 1 de diciembre 1995. CNL. Exp. Premio Sor Juana.
Hernández, Edgar A. (2003), 'Crean premio literario', *El Reforma*, 17 julio 2003, CNL Exp 0038 Expediente – Concurso Internacional de Ensayo y Narrativa (UNAM/UAS/El Colegio de Sinaloa/Siglo XXI Editores). PRE0038.
Hernández, Juan (2010), [title unknonwn]. *El Universal*, 28 noviembre 2010. CNL archive. Exp. FIL.
'Homenaje a Juan José Arreola Ganador del Premio de Literatura Latinoamericana y del Caribe Juan Rulfo 1992 en la VI Feria Internacional del Libro', CNL Exp. Premio de Literatura Latinoamericana y del Caribe Juan Rulfo.
Jiménez, Arturo (2002), 'En agosto se cierra el Premio Nezahualcóyotl', *La Jornada*, 22 abril 2002, CNL Exp PRE0033.
Jiménez, Arturo (2006), 'La cultura indígena, "ausente en aulas"', *La Jornada*, 10 noviembre 2006, CNL Exp PRE0033.
Licona, Sandra (1999), 'La tierra del fuego, de Sylvia Iparraguirre, recibió en Guadalajara el Premio Sor Juana Inés de la Cruz', *Crónica*, 2 diciembre 1999, p.14b CNL. Exp. Premio Sor Juana.

López, María Luisa (1996), 'Recibe Elena Garro el Premio Sor Juana', *Reforma*, 24 de noviembre de 1996 p.2c CNL. Exp. Premio Sor Juana.
'Mañana se da a conocer al ganador del II Premio Alfaguara de Novela', *Unomasuno*, 1 marzo de 1999 Premio Alfaguara de Novela (Editorial Alfaguara/ España) (1997-) Exp PRE0704.
Márquez, José (2007), 'Recibió Poniatowska el Premio Rómulo Gallegos', *Milenio*, 3 de agosto 2007, p.39 CNL Exp. Elena Poniatowska vol. 8.
Martínez Solorzano, Adolfo (1994),'Víctor de la Cruz: crear el Premio Nezahualcóyotl, una muestra de la apertura al diálogo', *El Universal*, 15 octubre 1994 CNL Exp PRE0033.
Martínez Torrijos, Reyes (2014), 'Por primera vez, el Premio Nezahualcóyotl incluye narrativa gráfica', *La Jornada*, 16 febrero 2014, CNL Exp PRE0033.
Matadamas, Ma Elena (1994), 'El Premio Sor Juana para la chilena Marcela Serrano', *El Universal secc. Cultural*, 29 de noviembre de 1994. CNL. Exp. Premio Sor Juana.
Matadamas, Ma Elena (1995), 'Tatiana Lobo, una escritora "no professional", recibirá el Premio Sor Juana', *El Universal secc. Cultura*, 1 de diciembre 1995. CNL. Exp. Premio Sor Juana.
Mendoza, Arturo (1996), 'La polémica es la sombra que persigue incasable a Elena Garro y su obra', *Reforma*, 5 de diciembre 1996. CNL Exp. Premio Sor Juana.
'Obtiene Silvia Molina el Premio "Sor Juana" por su novela "El amor que me juraste".' *El Universal*, 22 octubre, 1998, p.2 CNL. Exp. Premio Sor Juana.
'Otorgan a Ana García Bergua el Premio Sor Juana Inés de la Cruz', *La Crónica de Hoy*, 5 noviembre 2013, p.21 CNL Exp. Premio Sor Juana.
Palacios Goya, Cynthia (1997), 'Premio Alfaguara. Lengua española, patria única de los escritores', *El Nacional*, 23 de abril 1997, p.41 secc cultural. Premio Alfaguara de Novela (Editorial Alfaguara/ España) (1997-) Exp PRE0704.
Palapa Quijas, Fabiola (2004), 'La literatura de mujeres crece porque trasciende el género: Laura Niembro', *La Jornada*, 26 mayo 2004, p.6ª. CNL. Exp. Premio Sor Juana.
'Participan 604 trabajos en el Premio Internacional Alfraguara.' *El Universal*, 9 de febrero 1998 Premio Alfaguara de Novela (Editorial Alfaguara/ España) (1997-) Exp PRE0704.
Partida, Juan Carlos G. (2016), 'Premian a autora española con el Sor Juana Inés la Cruz', *La Jornada, Secc. Cultura*, 1 noviembre 2016, p. 6ª CNL. Exp. Premio Sor Juana.
'Premian ensayo y narrativa.' *Excélsior*, 30 enero 2008, CNL Exp 0038.
'Premio Nezahualcóyotl a Patricio Parra y Carlos España', *Excélsior*, 7 octubre 2000, CNL Exp PRE0033.
Quezada, Isela Carolina (1999), 'Premio "Sor Juana" Convocatoria de la FIL de Guadalajara', *El Universal*, 25 enero, 1999, p.3 CNL. Exp. Premio Sor Juana.
Ramos, Jacqueline (1997), 'Premio Alfaguara de Novela con 175 mil Dls', *Excélsior*, 23 de abril 1997, p10B secc. Cultural Premio Alfaguara de Novela (Editorial Alfaguara/ España) (1997-) Exp PRE0704.
'Retrasan pago del Premio Rómulo Gallegos', *Excélsior*, 16 de julio 2001, CNL Exp PRE0708.

Rosales y Zamora, Patricia (1996), 'Ahora está muy triste por los golpes que le ha dado la vida: su hija), 'Elena Garro, entre los tres mejores escritores mexicanos'", *Excélsior*, sec. B, 5 de diciembre 1996, p.3B. CNL. Exp. Premio Sor Juana.

Tova, Raúl (2016), 'El español en cinco libros', *El País*, 21 abril 2016 p28, CNL Exp 0801 Premios Extranjeros de Narrativa sin Expediente.

Vales, José (2004), 'Andrés Sebastián gana una batalla a la burocracia editorial', *El Universal*, 22 enero 2004, CNL Exp 0038. Expediente – Concurso Internacional de Ensayo y Narrativa (UNAM/UAS/El Colegio de Sinaloa/Siglo XXI Editores). PRE0038.

Velasco, Édgar and Jesús Alejo (2010), 'El Premio FIL es, para mí, el Juan Rulfo: Margo Glantz', *Milenio*, 31 agosto 2010, 42. CNL Exp Margo Glantz Exp. 3.

Velazquez Yebra, Patricia and Ana Anabitarte (1997), 'Nace el Premio Internacional Alfaguara de Novela', *El Universal*, 23 de abril 1997 Secc Cultural p2. Premio Alfaguara de Novela (Editorial Alfaguara/ España) (1997–) Exp PRE0704.

General references

Abreu Arcia, A. (2007), *Los juegos de la escritura o la (re)escritura de la historia*, Havana: Casa de las Américas.

Agence France Presse (2021), '"El viaje vertical" del español Vila-Matas gana Premio Rómulo Gallegos', 6 July 2001. Nexis UK.

Aguilar Gil, Yasnaya Elena (2016), '(Is There) An Indigenous Literature?', Translated by Gloria E. Chacón, *Diálogo*, 19 (1, Spring): 157–9. DOI: 10.1353/dlg.2016.0024

Aguirre, Carlos (2018), 'Los sesenta años del Premio Biblioteca Breve', *La ciudad y los perros. Biografía de una novela*, 20 October 2018. Available online: https://blogs.uoregon.edu/lcylp/2018/10/20/los-sesenta-anos-del-premio-biblioteca-breve/.

Aguirre, Carlos (2017), 'Cuando el boom llegó a Casa de las Américas', *La ciudad y los perros. Biografía de una novela*, 13 May 2017. Available online: https://blogs.uoregon.edu/lcylp/2017/05/13/cuando-el-boom-llego-a-casa-de-las-americas/

Amell, Samuel (1985), 'Los premios literarios y la novela de la postguerra', *Revista del Instituto de Lengua y Cultura Españolas*, 1 (2): 189–98.

Anderson, Benedict (1991), *Imagined Communities. Reflections on the Origin and Spread of Nationalism*, London: Verso.

Anderson, Danny J. (1996), 'Creating Cultural Prestige: Editorial Joaquin Mortiz', *Latin American Research Review*, 31 (2): 3–41.

Anderson, Mark (2003), 'A Reappraisal of the "Total" Novel: Totality and Communicative Systems in Carlos Fuentes's Terra Nostra', *Symposium: A Quarterly Journal in Modern Literatures*, 57 (2): 59–79. DOI: 10.1080/00397700309598551.

AngloAmerican, 'Seguimos Apoyando la cultura: Patrocinamos el Premio Nacional de Literatura 2021', Available online: https://peru.angloamerican.com/es-es/moquegua/mejor-educacion/premio-nacional-de-literatura-2020

Arce, Carlos de (1972), *Grandeza y servidumbre de veinte Premios Planeta*, Barcelona: Picazo.

Arias, Arturo (2017), *Recovering Lost Footprints. Vol 2. Contemporary Maya Narratives*, New York: SUNY.

Asiain, Aurelio (2015), 'Octavio Paz, diplomático en Japón', *Letras Libres*, 7 October 2015. Available online: https://www.letraslibres.com/mexico-espana/octavio-paz-diplomatico-en-japon

Attree, L. (2013), 'The Caine Prize and Contemporary African Writing', *Research in African Literatures*, 44 (2): 35–47.

Bagué Quílez, Luis (2010), '"Yo soy Arturo Belano": voces y ecos autobiográficos en la narrativa de Roberto Bolaño', *Bulletin of Spanish Studies*, 87 (6): 829–47.

Bakhtin, Mikhail (1994), 'Carnival and the Carnivalesque', in John Storey (ed.), *Cultural Theory and Popular Culture. A Reader*, 2nd edn., 250–9, London: Prentice Hall.

Barrera, Víctor (2002), 'Entradas y salidas del fenómeno literario actual o la 'alfaguarización' de la literatura hispanoamericana', *Sincronía*, 1. Available online: http://sincronia.cucsh.udg.mx/alfaguar.htm

Barria Bignotti, Cristóbal Fabrizzio (2013), 'Sebastián Vidal: En el principo', 17 April 2013, *Artishock Revista*, n.p. Available online: http://artishockrevista.com/2013/04/17/sebastian-vidal-en-el-principio/ (accessed 27 March 2019).

Beasley-Murray, (2003), 'Latin American Studies and the Global System', in Philip Swanson (ed.), *The Companion to Latin American Studies*, 222–38, London: Hodder Education.

Beerman, Hans (1962), 'Review. Ana Mairena. Los extraordinarios. Barcelona. Seix Barral. 1961. 178 pages', *Books Abroad*, 36 (1, Winter): 61.

Belmonte Serrano, José (2001), 'Los premios literarios: la sombra de una duda', in José Manuel López de Abiada, Hans-Jörg Neuschäfer and Augusta López Bernasocchi (eds), *Entre el ocio y el negocio: industria editorial y literatura en la España de los 90*, 43–53, Madrid: Verbum.

Bell-Villada, Gene H. (2010), 'Gabriel García Márquez: Life and Times', in Philip Swanson (ed.), *The Cambridge Companion to Gabriel García Márquez*, 7–24, Cambridge: Cambridge University Press.

Bermúdez, Silvia (2002), 'Let's Talk About Sex?: From Almudena Grandes to Lucía Extebarria, the Volatile Values of the Spanish Literary Market', in Ofelia Ferrán and Kathleen M. Glenn (eds), *Women's Narrative and Film in Twentieth-Century Spain: A World of Difference(s)*, 223–37, Oxford: Routledge.

Bencomo, Anadeli (2006), 'El premio Rómulo Gallegos: Avatares de una trayectoria', in Carlos Pacheco, Luis Barrera Linares and Beatriz González Stephan (eds), *Nación y literatura: itinerarios de la palabra escrita en la cultura venezolana*, 763–80, Caracas: Equinoccio/ Fundación Bigott.

Bencomo, Anadeli (2007), 'La lógica de los premios literarios: políticas culturales, prestigios literarios, y disciplinas de lectura en la época de la literatura transnacional', *Estudios*, 14 (28): 13–29.

REFERENCES

Benisz, Carla Daniela (2020), 'Literatura en transición – Del binarismo entre lo "culto" y lo popular a la vanguardia en guaraní', *Nuevo Mundo Mundos Nuevos* [En ligne], Débats, mis en ligne le 24 février 2020, consulté le 25 mars 2021. Available online: http://journals.openedition.org/nuevomundo/79742. DOI: 10.4000/nuevomundo.79742

Bilbika, Ksenija and Paloma Celis Carbajal, ed. (2009), *Akademia Cartonera: A Primer of Latin American Cartonera Publishing*, Madison: Parallel Press.

Bolaño, Roberto (1997), *Llamadas telefónicas*, Barcelona: Anagrama.

Bons, Léa. (2018), 'Qui gagne quoi? La saison des prix littéraires s'ouvre ce lundi avec la remise du prix Femina, avant le Médicis mardi puis le Goncourt et le Renaudot mercredi. Mais que rapportent-ils à leurs lauréats?'. 5 November 2018. Available online: https://www.lci.fr/sorties/video-femina-goncourt-medicis-renaudot-combien-gagnent-les-laureats-des-prix-litteraires-2069800.html

Boullosa, Carmen (2009), *El complot de los románticos*, Madrid: Siruela.

Bourdieu, Pierre (1993), *The Field of Cultural Production*, ed. Randal Johnson, Cambridge: Polity Press.

Bourdieu, Pierre (1991), *Language and Symbolic Power*, ed. and Introduction John B. Thompson, trans. Gino Raymond and Matthew Adamson, Cambridge, MA: Harvard University Press.

Bourdieu, Pierre (1996), *The Rules of Art. Genesis and Structure of the Literary Field*, trans. Susan Emanuel, California: Stanford University Press.

Bourdieu, Pierre (2012), *Outline of a Theory of Practice*, trans. Richard Nice, Cambridge: Cambridge University Press 1977. 27th printing 2012.

Bowskill, Sarah (2011), *Gender, Nation and the Formation of the Twentieth-Century Mexican Literary Canon*, Oxford: Legenda.

Bowskill, Sarah E. L. (2012), 'Politics and Literary Prizes: A Case Study of Spanish America and the Premio Cervantes', *Hispanic Review*, 80 (2): 289–311.

Bowskill, Sarah E.L. and Jane Lavery (2020), 'Eli Neira: Pursuing Community and Interconnectedness against the Commodification and Institutionalization of Culture in Chile', *Bulletin of Spanish Visual Studies*, 4 (1): 93–124. DOI: 10.1080/24741604.2020.1726066

Bowskill, Sarah and Jane Lavery, eds. *The Multimedia Works of Contemporary Latin American Women Artists and Writers* (Forthcoming).

Braun, Rebecca (2011), 'Fetishizing Intellectual Achievement: The Nobel Prize and European Literary Celebrity', *Celebrity Studies*, 2 (3): 320–34.

Braun, Rebecca (2014), 'Prize Germans?: Changing Notions of Germanness and the Role of the Award-Winning Author into the Twenty-First Century', *Oxford German Studies*, 43 (1): 37–54.

Brígido-Corachán, Anna M. (2016), 'Una aproximación a la obra de Javier Castellanos Martínez en el marco de la literatura zapoteca contemporánea: Reflexiones, inquietudes y pláticas', *Diálogo*, 19 (1, Spring): 175–83.

Brouillette, Sarah (2007), *Postcolonial Writers in the Global Literary Marketplace*, Basingstoke and New York: Palgrave Macmillan.

Brouillette, Sarah (2019), *Unesco and the Fate of the Literary*, California: Stanford University Press.

Brown, Katie (2019), '"There Can Be No Revolution without Culture": Reading and Writing in the Bolivarian Revolution', *Bulletin of Latin American Research*, 38 (4): 438–52.

Brushwood, John (1962), 'The Hispanic World', *Hispania*, 45 (1, March): 123–57.
Brushwood, John (1983), 'La novela mexicana (1967–1982): los que siguieron narrando', *Symposium*, 37 (2, Summer): 91.
Buell, Frederick (1994), *National Culture and the New Global System*, Baltimore and London: Johns Hopkins University Press.
Buxton, Julia (2011), 'Foreword', in David Smilde and Daniel Hellinger (eds), *Venezuela's Bolivarian Democracy. Participation, Politics, and Culture under Chávez*, ix–xxii. Durham: Duke University Press.
Caballero, Erol E. (2003), 'Dos premios desiertos en el "Ricardo Miró"'. *Panamá América*, 6 October 2003. Available online: https://www.panamaamerica.com.pa/nacion/dos-premios-desiertos-en-el-ricardo-miro-134067 (accessed 14 June 2021).
Caballero Excorcia, Boris, ed. (2011), *Utopías en movimiento. Premio Internacional de Novela Rómulo Gallegos. Discursos de los gandores (1967–2011)*, Caracas: Monte Ávila Editores.
Carrasco, Francisco Antonio (2010), 'Fernando Iwasaki, Escritor, 'El humor en la literatura no es algo que entusiasme mucho a la crítica', *Diario Córdoba*, 24 de febrero 2010. Nexis UK.
Carillo Can, Isaac (2011), *U yóok'otilo'ob áak'ab/Danzas de la noche*, Mexico: Conaculta.
Casanova, Pascale (2004), *The World Republic of Letters*, trans. M. B. Debevoise, Cambridge MA and London: Harvard University Press.
Castilla, Amelia and Rosa Mora (1998), 'La entrega del Premio Alfaguara se convirtió en la gran fiesta de las letras latinoamericanas', *El País*. Available online: https://elpais.com/diario/1998/05/27/cultura/896220001_850215.html (accessed 26 May 1998).
Castany Prado, Bernat (2016), 'El mito del "soldado desconocido" en la literatura hispanoamericana', *Mitología Hoy*, 13. DOI: 10.5565/rev/mitologias.290
Castellanos, Javier (2003), *Gaa ka chhaka ki/Relación de hazañas del hijo del Relámpago*, Mexico: Conculta.
Castillo, Debra (1998), *Easy Women: Sex and Gender in Modern Mexican Fiction*, Minneapolis: University of Minneapolis Press.
Ceh Moo, Sol (2015), *Chen tumeen chu'upen/ Sólo por ser mujer*, Mexico: Conaculta.
Chacón, Gloria Elizabeth (2018), *Indigenous Cosmoletics*, Chapel Hill: University of North Carolina Press.
Damrosch, David (2003), *What is World Literature?*, Princeton, NJ: Princeton University Press.
Davies, Catherine (1997), *A Place in the Sun?: Women Writers in Twentieth-Century Cuba*, London: Zed Books.
Davies, Catherine (2017), 'Digital Resources: Gender and Latin American Independence', 26 October 2017. Available online: https://oxfordre.com/latinamericanhistory/view/10.1093/acrefore/9780199366439.001.0001/acrefore-9780199366439-e-6. DOI: 10.1093/acrefore/9780199366439.013.6
Delprat, François (2005), 'Les prix littéraires, un modèle répandu', *América: Cahiers de CRICCAL*. No. 33: 227–34.
Dennison, Stephanie (2013), 'National, Transnational and Post-National: Issues in Contemporary Film-making in the Hispanic World', in Stephanie Dennison (ed.),

Contemporary Hispanic Cinema: Interrogating the Transnational in Spanish and Latin American Film, 1–24, Woodbridge, Suffolk and Rochester, NY: Tamesis.

'Denuncian campana contra participantes del Premio Rómulo Gallegos', *Ultimas Noticias*, 25 July 2020. https://ultimasnoticias.com.ve/noticias/chevere/denuncian-campana-contra-participantes-del-premio-romulo-gallegos/?fbclid=IwAR35_ksL49Td6xP3pfx-g-936PDuYUdtIx3jHQLv_PmYLdhu3oTRjKVXjJU.

de Valck, M. (2006), 'Film Festivals: History and Theory of a European Phenomenon that Became a Global Network', PhD Diss. Amsterdam ASCA.

Díaz, Antonio (2018), 'Anuncia Siglo XXI Editores ganadores de sus premios de ensayo y narrativa', *La Crónica de Hoy*, 14 febrero 2018, CNL Exp 0038 Expediente – Concurso Internacional de Ensayo y Narrativa (UNAM/UAS/El Colegio de Sinaloa/Siglo XXI Editores). PRE0038.

Díaz Arciniega, Víctor (1991), *Premio Nacional de Ciencias y Artes, 1945–1990*, Mexico: Secretaría de Educación Pública and Fondo de Cultura Económica.

Díaz Arciniega, Víctor (1993), 'En la casa de los espejos: el Premio Nacional de Ciencias y Artes', *Estudios de historia moderna y contemporánea de México*, 16: 153–91.

Díaz-Vega, María (2012), 'Ni Castro ni Boom: denuncia, resistencia y confesión en *Espero la noche para soñarte, Revolución*', in María Hernández-Ojeda (ed.), *Canarias, Cuba y Francia: Los exilios literarios de Nivaria Tejera*, 47–58, Madrid: Torremozas.

DPA Caracas (2017), 'Un año sin el Rómulo Gallegos', *El Mundo*, 2 August 2017. Nexis UK.

Ducas, Sylvie (2013), *La littérature à quel(s) prix? Histoire des prix littéraires*, Paris: Éditionas La Découverte.

Dumas, Jean-Louis (1969), 'Asturias en Francia', *Revista Iberoamericana*, 35 (67, January–April): 117–25.

EFE Newswire (2020), 'Rodrigo Blanco: "escritores negocian con narcoterroristas" al participar en el Rómulo Gallegos', *PanAm Post*, 10 August 2020.

English, James (2005), *The Economy of Prestige: Prizes, Awards, and the Circulation of Cultural Value*, Cambridge, MA: Harvard University Press.

'Enrique Vila-Matas defiende la rebellion de la novela. El escritor español recogió en Caracas el Premio de Novela Rómulo Gallegos', *El País*, 4 August 2001. Nexis UK.

'Enrique Vila-Matas gana el Premio Rómulo Gallegos con "El viaje vertical". El Jurado del galardón latinoamericano destaca el estilo transparente y eficaz del escritor', *El País*, 7 July 2001. Nexis UK.

'Entrevista al autor argentino Ricardo Piglia. Escritores del antichavismo 'actúan como los estalinistas', *Correo del Orinoco*. Entrevista al autor argentino Ricardo Piglia|Escritores del antichavismo 'actúan como los estalinistas' | (correodelorinoco.gob.ve).

Espmark, Kjell (1986), *Le Prix Nobel. Histoire intérieure d'une consécration littéraire*, trans. Philippe Bouquet, Paris: Editions Balland.

Espósito, Fabio (2009), 'Seix Barral y el boom de la nueva narrativa hispanoamericana: Las mediaciones culturales de la edición española', *Orbis Tertius*, 14 (15). Available online: http://www.orbistertius.unlp.edu.ar

Falicov, T. (2013), 'Cine en construcción (Films in progress): How Spanish and Latin American filmmakers negotiate the construction of a globalized art house aesthetic', *Transnational Cinemas*, 4 (2): 253–71.

Faudree, Paja (2015), 'What is an Indigenous Author?: Minority Authorship and the Politics of Voice in Mexico', *Anthropological Quarterly*, 88 (1, Winter): 5–35.

Faúndez Morán, Pablo (2016), 'El Premio Nacional de Literatura en Chile: De la Construcción de una Importancia', PhD diss, Humboldt University.

Fehimović, Dunja and Rebecca Ogden (2018), 'Introduction. Context and Contestation', in Dunja Fehimović and Rebecca Ogden (eds), *Branding Latin America. Strategies, Aims, Resistance*, 1–33. Lanham, Boulder, New York, London: Lexington Books.

Feldman, Burton (2000), *The Nobel Prize: A History of Genius, Controversy, and Prestige*, New York: Arcade Publishing.

Fell, Claude and Rutes Sébastien (2013), 'Avant le crime politique: discours sur le crime dans le roman policier mexicain antérieur au neopolicial (Usigli, Bermúdez, Lenero, Bernal)', *América: Cahiers du CRICCAL*, 43: 39–55; Available online: https://www.persee.fr/doc/ameri_0982-9237_2013_num_43_1_1973

Fiddian, Robbin W. (1989), 'James Joyce and Spanish American Fiction: A Study of the Origins and Transmission of Literary Influence', *Bulletin of Hispanic Studies*, 66: 23–39.

'FIL 2020 Camila Sosa Villada recibe el Premio de Literatura Sor Juana Inés de la Cruz', *El Informador*, 3 diciembre, 2020. Available online: https://www.informador.mx/cultura/FIL-2020-Camila-Sosa-Villada-recibe-el-Premio-de-Literatura-Sor-Juana-Ines-de-la-Cruz-20201203-0018.html

Finnegan, Nuala (2000), 'Light Women/Light Literature: Women and Popular Fiction in Mexico since 1980', *Donaire*, 15: 18–23.

Finnegan, Nuala (2007), *Ambivalence, Modernity, Power: Women and Writing in Mexico since 1980*, Oxford: Peter Lang.

Finnegan, Nuala and Jane Lavery (2010), 'Introduction. The Boom Femenino in Mexico: Reading Contemporary Women's Writing', in Nuala Finnegan and Jane Lavery (eds), *The Boom Femenino in Mexico. Reading Contemporary Women's Writing*, 1–24. Newcastle Upon Tyne: Cambridge Scholars Publishing.

Fong, A. and Carlos, E. (2004), 'Valoración crítica de los premios Ricardo Miró de la Sección Cuento en la década de los 80', *Revista Cultural Lotería*, 457: 114–20.

Franco, Jean (1999), *Critical Passions*, ed. and introduction by Mary Louise Pratt and Kathleen Newman, London: Verso.

Franco, Jean (2002), *The Decline and Fall of the Lettered City. Latin America in the Cold War*, Cambridge, MA and London: Harvard University Press.

Franco, Jean (2005), 'Some Reflections on Contemporary Writing in the Indigenous Languages of America', *Comparative American Studies An International Journal*, 3 (4): 455–69. DOI: 10.1177/1477570005058961.

Freudenthal Juan, R. (1985), 'Chile. Libraries and Information Centers in', in Adam Kent (ed.), *Encyclopedia of Library and Information Science*, vol. 38, Supplement 3, 72–129. Taylor and Francis.

Flood, Alison (2014), 'Readers Prefer Authors of their Own Sex, Survey Finds', *The Guardian*, 25 November 2014. Available online: https://www.theguardian.com/books/2014/nov/25/readers-prefer-authors-own-sex-goodreads-survey

Foucault, Michel (1998), *History of Sexuality vol. 1 The Will to Knowledge*, trans. Robert Hurley, London: Penguin.

Freixas, Laura (2000), *Literatura y mujeres*, Barcelona: Destino.

Fuentes, Carlos (1962), *La muerte de Artemio Cruz*, Madrid: Cátedra. First published 1962.

Fuentes, Carlos (1999), *La región más transparente*, Madrid: Cátedra. First published 1958.

Fuentes, Víctor (1962), 'Review', *Revista Hispánica Moderna*, 28 (2/4, Apr.–Oct.): 344–5.

Fuster García, Francisco, (2016), 'La edición iberoamericana (México y Argentina, siglo XX)', *Cuardernos Hispanoamericanos*, 1 Dec 2016. Available online: https://cuadernoshispanoamericanos.com/la-edicion-iberoamericana-mexico-y-argentina-siglo-xx/4/

Gabilondo, Joseba (2001), 'The Hispanic Atlantic', *Arizona Journal of Hispanic Cultural Studies*, 5: 91–113.

Gallego Cuiñas, Ana (2018), 'La Alfaguarización de la literatura latinoamericana: mercado editorial y figura de autor en *Sudor* de Alberto Fuguet', in Pablo Brescia and Oswaldo Estrada (eds), *McCrack: McCondo, El Crack y los Destinos de la literatura latinoamericana*, 235–52. Valencia: Albatros.

García Canclini, Nestor (2005), *Hybrid Cultures. Strategies for Entering and Leaving Modernity*, trans. Christopher L. Chiappar and Silvia L. López. Minneapolis. University of Minnesota Press.

García-García, José Manuel (2002), '20th Century Prose Fiction. Mexico', *Handbook of Latin American Studies*, 58: 513.

'García Márquez rechaza ser candidato al Cervantes', *El País*, 8 December 1997. Available online: https://elpais.com/diario/1997/12/09/cultura/881622002_850215.html.

'González Delvalle: "Este gobierno humilla a la literatura y al guaraní"', *Ciencia del Sur*, 18 February 2018. Available online: https://cienciasdelsur.com/2018/02/18/gonzalez-delvalle-gobierno-humilla-literatura-guarani/ (accessed 14 June 2021).

Gentes, Eva (2019), 'Self-Translation in Contemporary Indigenous Literatures in Mexico', in L. Bujaldslation in Contemporary Indigeno (eds), *Literary Self-Translation in Hispanophone Contexts – La autotraducción literaria en contextos de habla hispana*, 75–102. New York: Palgrave. DOI: 10.1007/98-3-030-23625-0_3.

Gigena, María Martha (2009), 'El lector intratable. Vidas de artistas y vanguardia en Roberto Bolaño', *Actas del II Congreso Internacional 'Cuestiones Críticas'*. Rosario 2009. Available online: http://www.celarg.org/int/arch_publi/gigena,_mar_a_martha.pdf.

Godoy Gallardo, Eduardo (1970), 'Índice críticobibliográfico del Premio Nadal, 1944–1968', *Mapocho*, 22: 109–36.

Gómez Bravo, Andrés (2005), *El club de la pelea: los Premios Nacionales de Literatura*, Santiago de Chile: Epicentro Aguilar.

González-Ariza, Fernando (2004), 'Literatura y Sociedad: El Premio Planeta', PhD diss. Universidad Complutense de Madrid.

González Ruiz, Sergio (1953), *Veintiseis leyendas panameñas presentadas al concurso Ricardo Miró 1949-50*, Panamá: Imprenta Nacional.
González-Stephan, Beatriz (2002), *Fundaciones: canon, historia y cultura nacional. La historiografía literaria del liberalismo hispanoamericano del siglo XIX*, Madrid: Iberoamericana.
Gortschacher, W., H. Klein and C. Squires, eds. (2006), *Fiction and Literary Prizes in Great Britain*, Vienna: Praesense Verlaf.
Grupp, W. J. (1956), 'The Influence of the Premio Nadal in Spanish Letters', *Kentucky Foreign Languages Quaterly*, 3: 162-8.
Guardián, Reymundo (1994), *Concurso Ricardo Miró. Historia, obras y autores premiados, 1942-1993*, Panamá: Instituto Nacional de Cultura.
Guerrero, Gustavo (2005), 'Requiem por un galardón', *El País*, 15 July 2005. Secc. Cultura p.30. Nexis UK.
Gutiérrez, Diana (2018), 'Ana Mairena más allá de la nota roja', *Letras Libres*, 1 Nov. 2018. Available online: https://www.letraslibres.com/mexico/revista/ana-mairena-mas-alla-la-nota-roja
Halle, R. (2010), 'Offering Tales They Want to Hear: Transnational European Film Funding as Neo-Orientalism', in R. Galt and K. Schoonover (eds), *Global Art Cinema*, 303-19. Oxford: Oxford University Press.
Harris, Mark D. (2009), 'Existence, Nothingness, and the Quest for Being: Sartrean Existentialism and Julio Cortázar's Early Short Fiction', *Latin American Literary Review*, 37 (74): 5-25. Available online: http://www.jstor.org/stable/41478041.
Heinich, Nathalie (1999), *L'épreuve de la grandeur. Prix littéraires et reconnaissance*, Paris: Éditions la Decouverte.
Henseler, Christine (2013), *Contemporary Spanish Women's Narrative and the Publishing Industry*, Urbana and Chicago: University of Illinois Press.
Herralde, Jorge (2005), *Para Roberto Bolaño*, Bogotá: Villegas Asociados.
Hernández-Ojeda, María (2009), *Insularidad narrativa en la obra de Nivaria Tejera: Un archipiélago transatlántico*, Madrid: Editorial Verbum.
Hernández, Tulio (2016), 'Odiar a los civiles', *El Nacional*, 19 June 2016. Nexis UK.
Herrero-Olaizola, Alejandro (2007), *The Censorship Files. Latin American Writers and Franco's Spain*, Albany: State University of New York Press.
Hind, Emily (2019), *Dude Lit. Mexican Men Writing and Performing Competence, 1955-2012*, Tucson: University of Arizona Press.
Hipsky, Marty (2000), 'Romancing Bourdieu: A Case Study in Gender Politics in the Literary Field', in Imre Szeman and Nicholas Brown (eds), *Pierre Bourdieu: Fieldwork in Culture*, 186-206. London: Rowman and Littlefield.
Holmes, Diana (2016), 'Literary Prizes, Women and the Middlebrow', *Contemporary French Civilization*, 41 (3/4): 437-48. DOI:10.3828/cfc.2016.29
Huggan, Graham (2001), *The Post-Colonial Exotic: Marketing the Margins*, New York: Routledge.
Huiskamp, Gerard (2000), 'Identity Politics and Democratic Transitions in Latin America: (Re)organizing Women's Strategic Interests through Community Activism', *Theory and Society*, 29 (3, June): 385-424.
Iber, Patrick (2015), 'The Cold War Politics of Literature and the Centro Mexicano de Escritores', *Journal of Latin American Studies*, 48 (2): 247-72. DOI 10.1017/S0022216X15001492

Illerhaus, Judith (2020), 'Premio porteros. La función del Premio Biblioteca Breve con base en números', in *Literatura latinoamericana mundial*. Berlin: De Gruyter. DOI: 10.1515/9783110673678-003

Isaza Calderón, Baltasar (1957), *Estudios Literarios*, Panamá: Ediciones Cultural Panama.

Iwasaki, Fernando (2009), *España, aparta de mi estos premios*, Madrid: Páginas de espuma.

Jaggi, Maya (2000), 'Scourge of the New Spain', *The Guardian*, 12 August, 2000. Available online: https://www.theguardian.com/books/2000/aug/12/internationalwriting.books

Kiguru, Doseline (2016), 'Literary Prizes, Writers' Organisations and Canon Formation in Africa', *African Studies*, 75 (2): 202-14.

Klahn, Norma (2011/2012), 'El indigenismo desde la indigeneidad', *Nuevo Texto Crítico*, 24-25 (47-48): 165-86. DOI: 10.1353/ntc.2011.0020

Kleinbord Labovitz, Esther (1988), *The Myth of the Heroine. The Female Bildungsroman in the Twentieth Century*, 2nd edn, New York: Peter Lang.

Klengel, Susanne (2018), 'El derecho a la literatura (mundial y traducida). Sobre el sueño translatológico de la UNESCO', in Gesine Müller, Jorge J. Locane and Benjamin Loy (eds), *Remapping World Literature. Writing, Book Markets and Epistemologies Between Latin America and the Global South*, 132-55, Berlin: De Gruyter.

Kozak Rovero, Gisela (2019), 'Cultural Policies and the Bolivarian Revolution in the Socialist Venezuela of Hugo Chávez (1999-2013)', in Lisa Blackmore, Rebecca Jarman and Penélope Plaza (eds), *The Politics of Culture in the Chávez Era*, 20-37, Oxford: Wiley.

Kozlowska-Day, Ida (2014), 'Un zapoteco frente al reto: la globalización y la desmitificación del indigenismo en *Pancho Culebro y los Naguales de Tierra Azul* de Mario Molina Cruz', *Revista de Crítica Literaria Latinoamericana*, 40 (80): 411-27.

Krugman, Paul (2003), 'Everything is Political', *New York Times*, 5 August 2003. Available online: https://www.nytimes.com/2003/08/05/opinion/everything-is-political.html

Kumaraswami, Parvathi and Antoni Kapcia (2012), *Literary Culture in Cuba. Revolution, nation-building and the book*, Manchester: Manchester University Press.

'La edición iberoamericana (México y Argentina, siglo XX)', *Cuadernos Hispanoamericanos*, 1 December 2016. Available online: https://cuadernoshispanoamericanos.com/la-edicion-iberoamericana-mexico-y-argentina-siglo-xx/6/.

'La escritora argentina que ganó un premio en Venezuela y su postura sobre los Derechos Humanos allí: "Nunca dije que me resbala nada"', *Clarín*, 20 November 2020. Nexis UK.

'La literatura de humor tiene que divertir y también hace pensar. El escritor Fernando Iwasaki presenta esta tarde su nuevo libro "España, aparta de mí estos premios" en el foro de la librería Santos Ochoa', *La Rioja*, 14 October 2009. Nexis UK.

Larraz, Fernando (2016), 'Guillermo de Torre y el catálogo de la editorial Losada'. *Kamchatka*, June 2016. 59-71.

Leñero, Vicente (1992), *Asesinato. El doble crimen de los Flores Muñoz*, México: Plaza y Valdés.
Lepe Lira, Luz María (2010), *Lluvia y viento, puentes de sonido. Literatura indígena y crítica literaria*. Monterrey, NL, México: Universidad Autónoma de Nuevo León / Consejo para la Cultura y las Artes de Nuevo León.
Lepe Lira, Luz María (2011), 'Prólogo. Movimiento, danza y voz en la literatura maya contemporánea', in I. E. Carrillo Can *Danzas de la noche. U yóok'otilo'ob áak'ab*, 7–17. Mexico: Conaculta.
Lewis, Egbert (2014), 'No es apropiado premiar los trabajos menos malos', *Panamá América*, 7 December 2014. Available online: https://www.panamaamerica.com.pa/dia-d/no-es-apropiado-premiar-los-trabajos-menos-malos-955479 (accessed 14 June 2021).
Lezcano, Margarita (1992), *Las novelas ganadoras del Premio Nadal (1970-1979)*, Madrid: Pliegos.
Lienhard, Martin (2014), '¿Cuál es el lugar de las lenguas amerindias en la producción literaria escrita de América Latina?" *Revista de Literaturas Populares*, 14 (1): 79–100.
Link, Daniel (2018), 'Rubén Darío: la sutura de los mundos', in Gesine Müller, Jorge J. Locane and Benjamin Loy (eds), *Remapping World Literature. Writing, Book Markets and Epistemologies Between Latin America and the Global South*, 81–91, Berlin: De Gruyter.
'Los premios literarios aguantan', *Hoy*, 16 October 2010. Nexis UK.
Locane, Jorge L. (2017), 'El Premio Herralde de Novela: literatura latinoamericana para el mundo y desterritorialización del prestigio'. *INTI: Revista de literatura hispánica Spring-Autumn*, 85/86: 100–12. http://www.jstor.org/stable/45129661.
López Calvo, Ignacio (2013), *The Affinity of the Eye*, Tuscon: University of Arizona Press.
López-Calvo, Ignacio (2018), 'Worlding and decolonizing the literary world-system: Asian and Latin American literature as an alternative type of *Weltliteratur*', in Gesine Müller, Jorge J. Locane and Benjamin Loy (eds), *Remapping World Literature. Writing, Book Markets and Epistemologies Between Latin America and the Global South*, 15–31, Berlin: De Gruyter
López de Abiada, José Manuel (2001), 'Caballeros de industria y de fortuna. Crónicas del mundo editorial, político y cultural en *El Premio*, de Vázquez Montalbán', in José Manuel López de Abiada, Hans-Jörg Neuschäfer and Augusta López Bernasocchi (eds), *Entre el ocio y el negocio: Industria editorial y literatura en la España de los 90*, 125–55, Madrid: Editorial Verbum.
López de Abiada, José Manuel, Hans-Jörg Neuschäfer and Augusta López Bernasocchi, eds.(2001), *Entre el ocio y el negocio: Industria editorial y literatura en la España de los 90*, Madrid: Editorial Verbum.
López y Fuentes, Gregorio (1972), *El indio*, 5th edn, Mexico: Editorial Porrúa. First pub. 1935.
Lovell, Julia (2006), *The Politics of Cultural Capital: China's quest for a Nobel Prize in literature*, Honolulu: University of Hawaii Press.
Mack, Edward (2010), *Manufacturing Modern Japanese Literature. Publishing, Prizes, and the Ascription of Literary Value*, Durham: Duke University Press.
Mairena, Ana (1961), *Los extraordinarios*, Barcelona: Seix Barral.

Maldonado, Ezequiel (2018), 'Dos novelas zapotecas, desafío a la Ciudad Letrada', *Tema y variaciones de literatura*, 50 (Sem 1): 165–84. UAM-Azcapotzalco.
Maldonado de Maraya, Nancy, ed. (2013), *Premio Nacional de Literatura 'Miguel Ángel Asturias': semblanzas de los galardonados 1988-2012*, Guatemala: Universidad de San Carlos de Guatemala.
Marling, William (2016), *Gatekeepers. The Emergence of World Literature and the 1960s*, Oxford: Oxford University Press.
Martin, Gerald (1984), 'Boom, Yes; "New" Novel, No: Further Reflections on the Optical Illusions of the 1960s in Latin America', *Bulletin of Latin American Research*, 3 (2): 53–63.
Martínez, José Luis (1995), 'Ana Mairena [Asunción Izquierdo Albiñana de Flores Muñoz', in *Enciclopedia de la literatura en México*. Last modified 31 August 2018. Available online: http://www.elem.mx/autor/datos/2400
Mattio, Javier (2020), 'Páginas doradas: la función de los premios literarios', *La Voz del Interior*, 23 de febrero 2020. Nexis UK.
McClintock, Anne (1995), *Imperial Leather: Race, Gender and Sexuality in the Colonial Contest*, London: Routledge.
McDowell Carlsen, Lila (2014), 'Absurdity and Utopia in Roberto Bolaño's *Estrella distante* and "Sensini" Confluencia', *Revista Hispánica de Cultura y Literatura*, 30 (1): 138–51.
Mejias, Ulises (2013), *Off the Network. Disrupting the Digital World*, Minneapolis: University of Minnesota Press.
Menton, Seymour (1969), 'Asturias, Carpentier y Yáñez: Paralelismos y Divergencias', *Revista Iberoamericana*, 35 (67, January–April): 31–52.
Miller, Nicola (1999), *In the Shadow of the State. Intellectuals and the Quest for National Identity in Twentieth-Century Spanish America*, London and New York: Verso.
Molina Cruz, Mario (2007), *Xtille Zikw Belé, Ihén bene nhálhje ke Yu'Bza'o/ Pancho Culebro y los naguales de Tierra Azul*, Mexico: Conaculta.
Montaño Garfias, Ericka (2015), 'Elena Poniatowska, una obra de rabia y amor revela una vida dedicada a elevar la voz', *La Jornada*, 18 May 2015. Available online: https://www.jornada.com.mx/2015/05/18/cultura/a09n1cul
Mora, Rosa (2003), 'Con el Rómulo Gallegos llega el escandalo', *El País*, 1 August 2003. Nexis UK.
Moran, Dominic (2009), *Pablo Neruda*, London: Reaktion Books.
Morris, Andrea E. (2012), 'Caminando por la Habana: la fragmentación del ser y del espacio en *Sonámbulo del sol*', in María Hernández-Ojeda (ed.), *Canarias, Cuba y Francia: Los exilios literarios de Nivaria Tejera*, 85–95, Madrid: Torremozas.
Moure Rojas, Edmundo (2020), 'Premio Nacional de Literatura 2020: Todo comenzó en 1974, con Sandy Zañartu (y Jorge Teillier)', *Cine y Literatura*, 24 June 2020. Available online: https://www.cineyliteratura.cl/premio-nacional-de-literatura-2020-todo-comenzo-en-1974-con-sady-zanartu-y-jorge-teillier/
Moure Rojas, Edmundo (2020), 'Premio Nacional De Literatura 2020. Eduardo Anguita, un poeta de verdad, y su Victoria en el año del Plebiscito', *Cine y literatura*, 3 June 2020. Available online: https://www.cineyliteratura.cl/premio-nacional-de-literatura-2020-eduardo-anguita-un-poeta-de-verdad-y-su-victoria-en-el-ano-del-plebiscito/ (accessed 4 March 2021).

Moure Rojas, Edmundo (2020), 'Premio Nacional de Literatura 2020. En 1976 casi lo gana un general inspector de Carabineros', *Cine y literatura*, 25 June 2020. Available online: https://www.cineyliteratura.cl/premio-nacional-de-literatura-2020-en-1976-casi-lo-gana-un-general-inspector-de-carabineros/ (accessed 24 March 2021).

Moure Rojas, Edmundo (2020), 'Premio Nacional de Literatura 2020. Braulio Arenas, el reaccionario por conveniencia, que ganó en 1984', *Cine y literatura*, 30 June 2020. Available online: https://www.cineyliteratura.cl/premio-nacional-de-literatura-2020-braulio-arenas-el-reaccionario-por-conveniencia-que-gano-en-1984/ (accessed 24 March 2021).

Müller, Gesine (2018), 'Remapping World Literature from Macondo', in Gesine Müller, Jorge J. Locane and Benjamin Loy (eds), *Remapping World Literature. Writing, Book Markets and Epistemologies Between Latin America and the Global South*, 157–73, Berlin: De Gruyter.

Müller, Gesine, Jorge J. Locane and Benjamin Loy (2018), 'Introduction', in Gesine Müller, Jorge J. Locane and Benjamin Loy (eds), *Remapping World Literature. Writing, Book Markets and Epistemologies Between Latin America and the Global South*, 1–12, Berlin: De Gruyter.

'Nielsen: el juicio "fue una cuestión de honor"', *El Nacional*, 2 de marzo 2005. Available online: https://www.lanacion.com.ar/cultura/nielsen-el-juicio-fue-una-cuestion-de-honor-nid684003/

'Ni impaciente ni bravo', *El Correo*, 39 January 2016. Nexis UK.

Nye, Joseph (2004), *Soft Power. The Means to Success in World Politics*, New York: Public Affairs.

Ohayon, Stephen (1983), '"Camus" "The Stranger": The Sun-Metaphor and Patricidal Conflict', *American Imago*, 40 (2, Summer): 189–205.

Peña, Leopoldo (2019), 'Calling on Difference in Javier Castellanos Martínez Dxiokze xha…bene walhall/Gente del mismo corazón', *The Latin Americanist*, 63 (3): 343–53. Available online: muse.jhu.edu/article/736355

Pohl, Burkhard (2001), '¿Un nuevo *boom*? Editoriales españolas y literatura latinoamericana en los años 90', in José Manuel López de Abiada, Hans-Jörg Neuschäfer and Augusta López Bernasocchi (eds), *Entre el ocio y el negocio: industria editorial y literatura en la españa de los 90*, 261–92. Madrid: Verbum.

Pratt, Mary Louise (1991), 'Arts of the Contact Zone', *Profession*: 33–40. Available online: https://www.jstor.org/stable/25595469

'Premio Biblioteca Breve 40 años después (1958–1998)', 1999. *Especulo*, 11. Available online: https://webs.ucm.es/info/especulo/numero11/b_breve.html (accessed 11 October 2019).

Pucherová, D. (2011), 'A continent learns to tell its story at last: notes on the Caine Prize', *Journal of Postcolonial Writing*, 48 (1): 13–25.

Purvis, Michael (2017), 'Moving Images: The Contemporary Distribution and Canonisation of Latin American Cinema', PhD Diss., Queen's University Belfast.

Quintín (2009), 'The Festival Galaxy', Translated by Dennis West and Joan M. West. In Richard Porton (ed.), *Dekalog3: On Film Festivals*. Vol. 3, 38–52. London: Wallflower Press.

Rama, Ángel (1981), 'El "Boom" en perspectiva', in David Viñas (ed.), *Más allá del Boom: Literatura y Mercado*, 51–110. Mexico: Marcha Editores.

Rama, Ángel (1996), *The Lettered City*, trans. and ed. John Charles Chasteen, Durham and London: Duke University Press.
Rama, Ángel (2012), *Writing Across Cultures: Narrative Transculturation in Latin America. Transculturación narrativa en América Latina*, Durham: Duke University Press. First published in Spanish in 1982.
Ríos Baeza, Felipe A. (2013), *Roberto Bolaño. Una narrativa en el margen. Desestablilizaciones en el canon y la cultura*, Valencia: Tirant Humanidades.
Rivero, Raúl (2009), 'Chávez toma el Rómulo Gallegos; los escritores huyen; El premio literario más prestigioso de Venezuela ha perdido varios candidatos que han denunciado la politización y la parcialidad del jurado', *El Mundo*, 18 Abril 2009. Cultura. P50. Nexis UK.
Roche Rodríguez, Michelle (2009), 'El Premio Rómulo Gallegos y las controversiales ediciones del último lustro', *El Nacional*, 31 May 2009. Nexis UK.
Roche Rodríguez, Michelle (2013), 'El Rómulo Gallegos fue para una obra que visibiliza el Caribe', *El Nacional*, 7 June 2013. Nexis UK.
Ross, Miriam (2009), 'Film Festivals and the Ibero-American Sphere', in Dina Iordonova and Ruby Cheung (eds), *Film Festival Yearbook 2: Film Festivals and Imagined Communities*, 171–87, St Andrews: St Andrews Film Studies / College Gate Press.
Ross, Miriam (2011), 'The film festival as producer: Latin American films and Rotterdam's Hubert Bals Fund', *Screen*, 52 (2): 261–7.
Rubio, Carlos (2009), 'Denuncia Iwasaki frivolización social', *Reforma*, 21 September 2009. Cultura p.27. Nexis UK.
Salas Oliva, Francisco (2018), 'Videncia y esfera poética en prosa del otoño en Gerona. Desfiguración, Migrancia y Duelo en al poesía de Roberto Bolaño', *Acta Literaria*, 57: 119–34. DOI: 10.4067/S0717-68482018000200119.
Sánchez, Pablo (2008), '¿Otra vez la metrópoli? La tribuna de *El País* y la literatura hispanoamericana actual', *Caravelle*, 90 (June): 121–33. Available online: https://www.jstor.org/stable/40854402
Sánchez Prado, Ignacio (2018), *Strategic Occidentalism. On Mexican Fiction, the Neoliberal Book Market and the Question of World Literature*, Evanston, IL: Northwestern University Press.
Sánchez Prado, Ignacio (2018), 'Introduction', in Igancio Sánchez Prado (ed.), *Pierre Bourdieu in Hispanic Literature and Culture*, 1–13, London: Palgrave Macmillan.
Sánchez Prado, Ignacio, ed. (2018), *Pierre Bourdieu in Hispanic Literature and Culture*, London: Palgrave Macmillan.
Sánchez Prado, Ignacio (2018), 'África en la imaginación literaria mexicana. Exotismo, desconexión y los límites materiales de la "epistemología del Sur"', in Gesine Müller, Jorge J. Locane and Benjamin Loy (eds), *Remapping World Literature. Writing, Book Markets and Epistemologies Between Latin America and the Global South*, 61–79, Berlin: De Gruyter.
Sánchez Prado, Ignacio (2018), *Mexican Literature in Theory*, New York: Bloomsbury.
Sánchez Prado, Ignacio (2020), 'Cosmopolitanismo copyleft. Tumbona Ediciones, autonomía y localidad', in Gustavo Guerrero, Jorge J. Locane, Benjamin Loy

and Gesine Müller (eds), *Literatura latinoamericana mundial*, Berlin: De Gruyter. DOI: 10.1515/9783110673678-015

Santana, Mario (2000), *Foreigners in the Homeland. The Spanish American New Novel in Spain, 1962-1974*, Lewisburg: Bucknell University Press.

Sapiro, Gisèle (2016), 'The World Market of Translations in the Globalization Era. Symbolic Capital and Cultural Diversity in the Publishing Field', in Laurie Hanquinet and Mike Savage (eds), *Routledge International Handbook of the Sociology of Art and Culture*, 262–76, London: Routledge.

Saval, José-Vicente (2005), 'Carlos Barral's Publishing Adventure: The Cultural Opposition to Francoism and the Creation of the Latin-American Boom', *Bulletin of Hispanic Studies*, 79 (2): 205–11.

Schwartz, Marcy (2018), *Public Pages. Reading along the Latin American Streetscape*, Austin: University of Texas Press.

Shaw, Deborah (2015), 'European Co-production Funds and Latin American Cinema: Processes of Othering and Bourgeois Cinephilia in Claudia Llosa's La teta asustada', *Diogenes*, 62 (1): 88–99.

Shaw, Donald (1981), *Nueva narrativa hispanoamericana*, Madrid: Ediciones Cátedra.

Shaw, Donald (1998), *The Post-Boom in Spanish American Fiction*, New York: SUNY.

Simpson, Amalia S. (1990), *Detective Fiction from Latin America*, London: Associated University Presses.

Smith, Neil (2005), '"Political Element" to Pinter Prize', *BBC News*, 13 October 2005. Available online: http://news.bbc.co.uk/1/hi/entertainment/4339096.stm

Smorkaloff, Pamela Maria (1997), *Readers and Writers in Cuba. A Social History of Print Culture, 1830s-1990s*, New York and London: Garland Publishing.

Sommer, Doris (1991), *Foundational Fictions. The National Romances of Latin America*, Berkeley: University of California Press.

Sottorrío, Regina (2009), 'Cómo ganar siete premios con un relato. Iwasaki construye en su ultimo libro una historia que se adapta a las bases "delirantes" de diferentes certámenes literarios', *Sur*, September 30 2009. Nexis UK.

Squires, Claire (2006), 'Literary Prizes, Literary Categories and Children's Literature in the 1990s–2000s', in V. Guignery and F. Gallix (eds), *Pre- and Post-Publication Itineraries of the Contemporary Novel in English*, 277–90. Paris: Editions Publibook Université.

Squires, Claire (2007), 'Book Marketing and the Booker Prize', in N. Matthews and N. Moody (eds), *Judging a Book by its Cover: Fans, Publishers, Designers, and the Marketing of Fiction*, 71–82. London: Ashgate.

Stavans, Ilan (1997), *Antiheroes: Mexico and Its Detective Novel*, trans. Jesse H. Lytle and Jennifer A Mattson, London: Associated University Presses.

Swanson, Philip (2005), *Latin American Fiction. A Short Introduction*, Oxford: Blackwell.

Swanson, Philip (2012), 'Havana Noir: Time, Place and the Appropriation of Cuba in Crime Fiction', in J. Anderson and B. Pezzotti and C. Miranda (eds), *The Foreign in International Crime Fiction*, 35–46. New York: Bloomsbury Academic.

Swanson, Philip (2020), 'Where is Latin America?: Imaginary Geographies and Cultures of Production and Consumption', in Rory O'Bryen and Catherine Davies (eds), *Transnational Hispanic Studies*, 181–94. Liverpool: Liverpool University Press.

Szmentan, Ricardo (1989), 'Los albañiles, de Vicente Leñero, Dentro de las novelas de detectives', *Confluencia*, 4 (2, Spring): 67–71.
Tejera, Nivaria (1972), *Sonámbulo del sol*, Barcelona: Seix Barral
Thompson, John B. (2010), *Merchants of Culture. The Publishing Business in the Twenty-First Century*, Cambridge and Malden: Polity.
Todd, Richard (1996), *Consuming Fictions: The Booker Prize and Fiction in Britain Today*, London: Bloomsbury.
'Tras la tenue pista de Roberto Bolaño; El Centro de Cultura Contemporánea de Barcelona le dedica una exposición en el décimo aniversario de su muerte El escritor chileno ganó en los noventa dos premios en Gipuzkoa pero apenas dejó huella', *Diario Vasco*, 6 April 2013. Nexis UK.
Ullerhaus, Judith (2020), 'Premio porteros. La función del Premio Biblioteca Breve con base en números', in Gustavo Guerrero, Jorge J. Locane, Benjamin Loy and Gesine Müller (eds), *Literatura latinoamericana mundial: Dispositivos y disidencias*, 33–48. Berlin, Boston: De Gruyter. DOI: 10.1515/9783110673678-003
Uribe, Sarah, ed. (2007), *25 años Premio Nacional de Literatura Efraín Huerta*, Tale: Tampico.
Vargas Llosa, Mario (1986), 'La Literatura es fuego', *Contra viento y marea (1962-1982)*: 132–7. Barcelona. Seix Barral.
'Venezuela-Literatura Polémica sobre continuidad y editorials rodea el Rómulo Gallegos', *EFE Newswire Services*, 6 July 2001. Nexis UK.
Vich, Víctor and José Ramón Jouve-Martín (2013), 'Prefacio de los Editores. Políticas y mercados culturales en América Latina', *Latin American Research Review Special Issues. Políticas y mercados culturales en América Latina*, 48: 3–11.
Vila-Matas, Enrique (2017), 'Ednodio Quinero, Venezuela', *El País*, 25 July 2017. Nexis UK.
Weinberg, Liliana (2004), 'Literatura latinoamericana: entre la forma de la moral y la moral de la forma', in Leopoldo Zea (eds), *El cambio del Viejo Mundo empieza en el Nuevo Mundo. Seis lecturas sobre la América Latina Contemporánea*, 110–30. Mexico: UNAM.
Weiss, Jason (1999), 'Descifrar al exilio. Entrevista a Nivaria Tejera'. *Quimera*, 183: 8–13.
Weiss, Judith A. (1977), *Casa de las Américas: An Intellectual Review in the Cuban Revolution*, Chapel Hill, NC: Estudios de Hispanófila. Editorial Castalia.
Williams, Raymond Leslie (2014), *Mario Vargas Llosa: A Life of Writing*, Austin: University of Texas Press.
Winegarten, Renee (1994), 'The Nobel Prize for Literature', *The American Scholar*, 63 (1, Winter): 63–75.
Wires, Richard (2008), *The Politics of the Nobel Prize in Literature: How the Laureates Were Selected, 1901-2007*, Lampeter: Edwin Mellen.
Witt, Nicole (2001), 'Premios literarios entre cultura, negocio y política', in José Manuel López de Abiada, Hans-Jörg Neuschäfer and Augusta López Bernasocchi (eds), *Entre el ocio y el negocio: industria editorial y literatura en la españa de los 90*, 305–16, Madrid: Verbum.
Wong, Cindy (2011), *Film Festivals: Culture, People, and Power on the Global Screen*, New Jersey: Rutgers University Press.

Wynne, Frank (2016), 'Posh Bingo! Prizes, Translation and the Gatekeepers to Literary Celebrity', *Celebrity Studies*, 7 (4): 591–4.

Zabalgoitia Herrera, Mauricio (2012), 'Enunciación de estereotipos de la mexicanidad en *El laberinto de la soledad* y su relectura en la obra de Carmen Boullosa', *Hispanófila*, 165: 101–15.

Zamarrón, Israel (2021), 'Se buscan nuevas plumas: lanzan Premio Primera Novela 2021', *Forbes Mexico*, 17 March 2021. Available online: https://www.forbes.com.mx/se-buscan-nuevas-plumas-lanzan-premio-primera-novela-2021/

INDEX OF PRIZES

The following is a list of prizes referenced in the text of the book. Prizes which are only referred to in the tables in Chapter 6 which provide statistics about women winners and jurors are not included here.

Akutagawa Prize   21, 147

Booker Prize   28, 74, 77, 143

International Dublin Literary Award/IMPAC Dublin Literary Award   129, 139–41, 149, 179
Neustadt International Prize for Literature   129, 132, 139, 140
Nobel Peace Prize   158
Nobel Prize for Literature   2–4, 8–10, 14, 21, 23, 36, 37, 41, 71–82, 84–91, 93, 128, 129, 155, 180

Premio Nacional de Cuentos, Mito y Leyenda Indígena Andrés Henestrosa   165
Premio Alfaguara/Premio Alfaguara de Novela   2, 15, 23, 51, 57, 59–65, 67, 69, 131, 137, 149
Premio Anagrama de Ensayo   59
Premio Barral de Novela   54
Premio Bellas Artes de Cuento Amparo Dávila   135, 142
Premio Bellas Artes de Cuento Hispanoamericano Nellie Campobello   142
Premio Bellas Artes de Dramaturgia Luisa Josefina Hernández   136, 142
Premio Bellas Artes de Literatura en Lenguas Indígenas   157
Premio Bellas Artes de Poesía Aguascalientes   19, 138, 140, 141

Premio Bellas Artes de Traducción Literaria Margarita Michelena   142
Premio Bellas Artes de Trayectoria Literaria Inés Arredondo   142
Premio Biblioteca Breve/Premio de Novela Biblioteca Breve   2, 20, 23, 24, 40, 52, 54, 57–9, 61–3, 66–7, 74, 111–18, 120–1, 123, 137, 149, 166
Premio Bienal de Novela Mario Vargas Llosa   147, 152
Premio Café Gijón   93, 97
Premio Casa de las Américas (all genres)   2, 18, 25, 39–42, 130, 139, 140
Premio Cervantes   2, 3, 14, 18, 71–7, 79–81, 83–90, 93, 130–2, 150, 151, 160, 180
Premio Ciudad San Sebastián/Premio de Narración Ciudad de San Sebastián   95, 97, 98, 101
Premio Clarín/ Premio Clarín de Novela   15, 61, 137, 140, 141
Premio de Literaturas Indígenas de América (PLIA)   158, 173
Premio Emecé   23, 51, 52, 58
Premio Eugenio Espejo   26, 134
Premio FIL/Premio FIL de Literatura en Lenguas Romances/Premio Juan Rulfo/Premio de Literatura Latinoamericana y del Caribe Juan Rulfo   126, 129, 132, 140, 144, 146, 147, 181

Premio Herralde   2, 10, 18, 23, 51,
   59–66, 68, 69, 98, 137, 149
Premio Internacional de Narrativa
   Siglo XXI-UNAM   23, 52, 64–5
Premio Internacional de Novela Monte
   Ávila Editores   44
Premio Internacional de Poesía Víctor
   Valera Mora   44
Premio Julián del Casal   39
Premio Lanz Duret   61
Premio Literario Internacional de
   Novela *Novedades*-Diana   58, 61
Premio Losada de Novela   23, 51–3
Premio Mazatlán de
   Literatura   131, 137
Premio Nacional (Bolivia)   69–
   70, 133
Premio Nacional de Literatura
   (Chile)   17, 33–7, 132, 181
Premio Nacional de Literatura
   (Mexico)   13, 21, 31, 170
Premio Nacional de Literatura
   (Uruguay)   38, 134
Premio Nacional de Literatura en
   Lenguas Originarias   156
Premio Nacional de Literatura Maya
   Waldemar Noh Tzec   165
Premio Nacional de Literatura
   Miguel Ángel Asturias
   (Guatemala)   38, 134
Premio Nacional de Narrativa en
   Idioma Originario   156
Premio Nacional del Libro de
   Venezuela   43
Premio Nadal   19, 57
Premio Nezahualcóyotl de Literatura
   en Lenguas Indígenas/Premio
   Nezahualcóyotl de Literatura en
   Lenguas Mexicanas   24, 155–
   67, 173–5
Premio Obra de Teatro para
   Niñas, Niños y Jóvenes Perla
   Szuchmacher   136, 142
Premio Planeta   15, 19–20, 23, 45, 51,
   57–9, 65, 67, 137, 147, 149
Premio Planeta-Joaquín Mortiz   58
Premio Ricardo Miró/Premio Annual
   de Literatura Ricardo Miró/Premio
   Literario Ricardo Miró/Concurso
   Nacional de Literatura Ricardo
   Miró   26, 28–33, 134
Premio Rómulo Gallegos/ Premio
   Internacional de Novela
   Rómulo Gallegos   2, 14, 18, 19,
   25, 40–8, 98, 130, 131, 140, 141,
   178, 180
Premio Rubén Darío   26, 134
Premio Sor Juana Inés de la Cruz   10,
   15, 24, 125, 126, 143–53, 157, 161
Premio Xavier Villaurrutia   88,
   136, 180
Prix Femina/Prix Femina Vie-
   Heureuse   142, 145, 148
Prix Formentor   54–6
Prix Goncourt   20, 21, 143, 145, 166
Prix International des Éditeurs   54–6
Pulitzer Prize   28

Roger Caillois Award for Latin
   American Literature   149

Stella Prize   143

Women's Prize for Fiction/Orange Prize
   for Fiction/Bailey's Prize   143

GENERAL INDEX

Alatriste, Selatiel 62, 66
Alduante Phillips, Arturo 35
alfaguarización 60
Allende, Isabel 144
Allende, Salvador 33, 78, 81
ambassador. *See* diplomatic service
Anderson, Benedict 27
   imagined community 26, 142, 157
Anguita, Eduardo 35
Arenas, Braulio 35
Arguedas, José María 155
Asturias, Miguel Ángel 36, 74, 78, 80, 81, 85, 88, 122, 155
aura 9, 11, 101, 106, 109
author
   as celebrity 3, 11, 16, 17, 52, 65–8, 127, 149, 150
   as defender of democracy 23, 72, 76, 80–4
   as public intellectual 3, 4, 11, 12, 14, 16, 27–8, 38, 45, 47, 49, 52, 61, 65, 70, 73, 76–9, 81, 84, 91, 93, 127, 131, 149, 152, 179
   as (cultural) representatives 11, 14–16, 68, 73, 75, 76, 79–80, 84, 160
   as spokesperson or interpreter or translator 3, 4, 11, 12, 14–16, 23, 51, 52, 61, 65–71, 73, 76, 77, 79–82, 84, 91, 127, 149, 151, 152, 162
   as statesperson/stateman/states(wo)man 3, 4, 12, 14–16, 26, 28, 73, 77–9

Bakhtin, Mikhail
   and the carnivalesque 108–9

Barral, Carlos 20, 23, 42, 52–7, 63, 66, 111–13, 115–17
   and Barral Editores 54
Belli, Giaconda 149
Bogotá 39 60, 61, 67, 178
Bolaño, Roberto 23, 93–8, 101–2, 109–10
   Los detectives salvajes 98
   Monsieur Pain 101, 102
   'Sensini' 23, 93–5, 97–104, 106, 109, 110
book fair/literary festival 3, 60, 65, 96, 97, 101, 129, 144, 146, 147, 178
   Feria Internacional del Libro (FIL) Guadalajara 96, 129, 144, 148
   Hay Festival 60, 178
book tour 3, 17, 52, 67, 96
Boom 2, 16, 20, 24, 39, 40, 42, 52, 53, 57, 58, 60, 66, 78, 111–23
boom femenino 98
Boom novel
   existentialism in 119
   male quest for identity in 119, 120, 123
   non-linear narrative 118, 121
   and the nouveau roman 121
   and the *novela del dictador* 122
   rejection of realism in 121, 122
   Shaw's characterization of 117, 118, 121, 123
   social awareness/commentary in 112, 121, 123
   solitude in 121
   technical innovation in 112, 117, 120, 121
   and the total novel 123

Borges, Jorge Luis 54, 73, 87, 135
Borinsky, Alicia 139
Botero García, Miguel 179
Boullosa, Carmen 23, 93, 95–9, 109–10
   El complot de los románticos 23, 93–6, 98, 105–10
Bourdieu, Pierre 3–5, 9, 12, 47, 72–3, 99, 100, 127, 177, 182
   agents of legitimation 180, 182
   autonomous and heteronomous poles 13, 127
   capital (cultural, symbolic, political, economic) 3–4, 10–11, 48, 71–3, 91, 101, 127, 145, 149, 152
   disavowal (of capital) 4, 5, 48, 72
   literary field (*see separate entry*)
   prestige (*see separate entry*)
   Rules of Art 12
   strategies of condescension 95, 97, 98, 180
Buell, Frederick 5–7, 63, 87

Cabrera Infante, Guillermo 87, 113, 116, 121
Cabutí, Nuria 62
Campos Menéndez, Enrique 36
canon 2, 8, 19, 21, 24, 47, 86, 88, 89, 110, 115, 138, 156, 162, 166, 168, 174
Carillo Can, Isaac Esau 165, 167, 169
   U yóok'otilo'ob áak'ab/Danzas de la noche 165, 167, 169–72
Carpentier, Alejo 80, 123, 131
Casa de las Américas 39–41. *See also* Index of Prizes for prizes awarded by the Casa de las Américas
Casanova, Pascale 7, 12, 100, 107, 115, 145
   world republic of letters 7, 73, 107
Castellanos, Javier 159, 164, 173
   Gaa ka chhaka ki/Relación de hazañas del hijo del Relámpago 164, 167–72

Wila che be se lhao/ Cantares de los vientos primerizos 164
Castellanos, Rosario 90, 107, 155
Ceh Moo, Marisol 165, 167, 173
   Chen tumeen chu'upen/ Sólo por ser mujer 165, 167–9, 171–2
   X-Teya, u puksi' ik'al ko'olel/Teya, un corazón de mujer 165
censorship 53–6, 116, 121
Centro de Estudios Latinoamericanos 'Rómulo Gallegos' (CELARG) 41, 43, 45, 46, 48
Chávez, Hugo 25, 43–6, 131
Chávez, Ignacio 14
commercial/commercial success/ commercialization 5, 18, 23, 51–4, 56, 59, 63, 66, 67, 98, 126, 127, 144, 159, 180
communism 2, 22, 39, 40, 44, 55, 78, 81, 116
consecration 5, 7, 12, 40, 42, 46, 58, 62, 63, 65, 69, 75, 86, 91, 103, 115, 124, 126, 127, 145, 166, 175, 180–2
constellation 8
consul. *See* diplomatic service
controversy. *See* scandal
Córdova Humán, Washington 156
Cortázar, Julio 16, 39, 42, 87, 112, 115, 116, 119
crack generation 58
Cruz, Juan 60–1
Cuban Revolution 39, 40, 42, 78, 115, 116, 120

De la Cruz, Víctor 161, 162
Delgado, Susy 38
Del Paso, Fernando 79, 83
democracy 2, 3, 14, 22, 23, 27, 37, 38, 40, 41, 43, 47–9, 54, 56, 72, 75, 77, 80–5, 161, 169
   Spain transition to 75, 82, 83
dictator, dictatorship 2, 11, 14, 17, 34, 35, 37, 38, 41, 47, 78, 79, 81–4, 122–3, 181. *See also* totalitarianism

diplomatic service (including consul, ambassador, attaché) 28, 36, 39, 77–9, 116
Donoso, José 36, 37, 111, 113, 115

Edwards, Jorge 79, 80
Eltit, Daniela 181
English, James 4, 6, 20, 28, 72, 77, 93, 94, 105, 179–80
    capital intraconversion 4, 72, 177
    prize game (see prizes as a game)
Esquivel, Laura 98, 144

Falco, Federico 68
Feire, Espido 15, 67
Feria. See book fair
festival film 166
film festival 8, 166
Fondo Nacional para la Cultura (FONCA) grants Mexico 98, 157, 159, 165, 175
Foucault, Michel
    discourse 72
Franco, Francisco/Franco regime 3, 20, 51–6, 63, 82, 121, 122
Freixas, Laura 127, 152
Fuentes, Carlos 16, 39, 42, 79, 86, 87, 90, 112, 113, 116, 119, 120, 123, 131, 135
    La muerte de Artemio Cruz 120
    La región más transparente 123
    Terra nostra 42

Gallegos, Rómulo 41–2. See also Index of prizes for the Premio Rómulo Gallegos
Gallimard. See publishers
García Bergua, Ana 150
García Márquez, Gabriel 8, 16, 17, 42, 74, 77–82, 85, 86, 89, 112, 122, 180
Garro, Elena 107, 147, 149–51
Gelman, Juan 83–5
gender 3, 7, 11, 15, 20, 83, 96, 126, 135, 138, 139, 161
    authors as representatives of their 68, 76
    inequality 152

and literary history 120
and literary prestige 2, 90, 91, 107, 112, 125, 127, 138, 143, 146, 152, 153
    in literature 167–8, 172
Glantz, Margo 126, 129, 132, 139, 141, 146, 148, 151
globalization 2, 3, 5, 51, 56, 63, 169, 178
Goytisolo, Luis 116
Guerrero, Gustavo 40

Hay Festival. See book fair
Hecker, Liliana 141
Hernández, Juan 161
Herralde, Jorge 59, 98
histories of literature 26, 27
Huerta, David 132
Huggan, Graham 21
    cultural representatives 14, 73 (see also author as representative)
    postcolonial exotic 74, 89
humour (in literature) 94–7, 100, 102, 105, 107, 110

identity politics 2, 3, 15, 22, 23, 142–4, 153, 155, 161
indigenous languages 15, 159
    Guaraní 38
    literature in (see separate entry)
    Maya 159, 165
    Mazatec 162, 163
    Tzotzil 160
    Zapotec 159, 161, 162, 164, 170–1
indigenous literature. See literature in indigenous languages
Instituto Nacional de Bellas Artes (INBA) (Mexico)
    prizes organised by 135–6, 142, 157–8, 173, 175
internationalism 2, 3, 22, 54, 63, 69, 74
interpretive strategies 138, 139
Iparraguirre, Sylvia 141, 151
Isaza Calderón, Baltazar 29–33
Iwasaki, Fernando 23, 93–9, 109

*España, aparta de mí estos
    premios* 23, 94–6, 99, 100,
    102–5, 138
Un milagro informal 99

judge/juror/jury (of a prize) 22, 25,
    28–30, 32–4, 37, 39, 41, 42,
    45–8, 58–9, 62, 67, 78, 100,
    109–11, 116, 124, 126, 127,
    131, 138, 148–50, 152, 156,
    157, 162, 166, 173–5, 179
    as portrayed in fiction 94, 101,
        102, 104–7
    women as 139–43, 148

King Juan Carlos I of Spain 77, 83

Landeo, Pablo 156
Lara, Jesús 155
Leñero, Vicente 113, 114, 118
literary festival. *See* Book Fair
literary fiction 58, 65, 98, 166
literary field 2, 4–7, 9–13, 15, 20, 23,
    42, 43, 46, 51, 69, 75, 84, 93,
    94, 98, 100, 102, 103, 109, 112,
    125–7, 137, 143, 145, 152, 155,
    161, 163, 175, 177, 181
literatura light/light literature 98
literature in indigenous
    languages 3, 7, 11, 15, 24,
        155–75
    and bildungsroman (female) 169
    domestic abuse and gender
        in 167–9, 172
    education and bilingualism
        in 170–1
    environment in 168
    isolationism in 171–2
    legends and traditional beliefs
        in 167, 169–70
    migration in 168
    narcotrafficking in 168
    narrative voice in 167
Lobo, Tatiana 150
López y Fuentes, Gregorio 31, 170
Losada, Gonzalo 53
Loynaz, Dulce María 90, 131

Maduro, Nicolás 43
Mairena, Ana (pseudonym of Asunción
    Izquierdo Albiñana) 24,
    111–14, 124
    Los extraordinarios 117–20
marginalization 17, 42, 72, 91
    of literature in indigenous
        languages 155, 175
    of women authors 24, 125, 143,
        152, 161
Marsé, Juan 59, 111
Martín, Luisgé 68
Mastretta, Ángeles 18, 98, 131, 141, 144
Matute, Ana María 90
McOndo movement 58
media conglomerates
    Bertelsmann 61
    Grupo Feltrinelli 59
    Grupo Planeta 57–9
    Grupo Santillana 60
    PRISA 15, 61
Mejias, Ulises A. 6, 181
Menchú, Rigoberta 158
Mercado, Tununa 126, 146, 148
Meruane, Lina 126, 148
middle brow fiction. *See literary fiction*
Miró, Ricardo 28
Mistral, Gabriela 73, 74, 77, 78, 80,
    81, 89, 128
Molina Cruz, Mario 165, 166
    *Xtille Zikw Belé, Ihén bene
    nhálhje ke Yu'Bza'o/ Pancho
    Culebro y los naguales de Tierra
    Azul* 165, 166, 168, 170–2
Montemayor, Carlos 159, 163
Montero, Rosa 141
Montoya, Pablo 45
multimedia literature 181
Muñiz Huberman, Angelina 151
Mutis, Álvaro 132

national identity 28, 31, 43
nationalism 2, 103
national literature 7, 30–2
nation-building 2, 5, 13, 18, 22, 23,
    25, 27–30, 32, 33, 37–9, 41, 43,
    46, 48, 51, 175, 178

neoliberal 2, 22, 24, 46, 69, 70, 177–80
Neruda, Pablo 74, 78–81, 86–7
network 1–3, 6–12, 17, 18, 22–4, 43, 46, 52, 64, 65, 69, 70, 94, 95, 100, 108, 112, 125, 128, 129, 145, 148, 149, 153, 155, 158, 173–5, 177–82
Nielsen, Gustavo 59
Nobel, Alfred 73, 87
Nobel Committee 13, 78, 79
    Espmark, Kjell 21, 79, 80, 88
    Gierow, Karl Ragnar 81
    Gyllensten, Lars 77, 82, 89
    Österling, Anders 79, 81, 88
    Wästberg, Per 82

Onetti, Juan Carlos 60, 83
Oroz, Rodolfo 36
Orozco, Olga 129, 132

Pacheco, José Emilio 83, 90
Padilla, Heriberto 39, 116
Padilla Affair 39, 116, 117, 120
Parra, Nicanor 77
Paz, Marcela 35
Paz, Octavio 74, 78, 80, 84, 85, 87, 88, 90, 131, 132
Piglia, Ricardo 59, 63–4
Piñeiro, Claudia 126, 141, 148, 152
Pinochet, Augusto 2, 19, 25, 34–7, 73
Pitol, Sergio 79, 86, 90, 132
politics
    definition of 4
Poniatowska, Elena 83, 86, 89–90, 131, 137, 141, 180
postcolonial 21, 52, 64, 74, 76, 123
prestige
    definition of 3–4
prizes
    acceptance speech 3, 13, 14, 17, 19, 21, 23, 27, 38, 40, 46–8, 67, 71–7, 79–89, 91, 93, 125, 150, 161
    and anthologies of winning texts 19, 20, 161
    (award) ceremony 14, 40, 45, 46, 60, 65, 66, 68, 72, 74, 75, 77, 79–81, 84, 106, 108–9, 146, 149, 152, 160
    boycott or refusal of 11, 27, 28, 47–8, 179–80
    comparisons with Anglophone contexts 4, 20, 21, 28, 47, 56–7, 64, 93
    comparisons with Francophone contexts 4, 20, 21, 143, 145, 150, 166
    for criticism 135
    discourses surrounding 28, 94
    for essay 31, 32, 39, 59, 163, 179
    as a game 28, 48, 93–102, 105, 108–10
    and genre 7, 32, 95, 128, 135–6, 164, 172
    as gift/exchange 1, 27, 39, 48–9, 71–2, 77, 80, 105
    and the law 23, 29, 31–4, 37, 38, 43, 48–9, 159
    for lifetime achievement or complete works 128, 131, 132, 142, 146, 156
    and money 16, 27, 33, 42, 44, 45, 51, 57, 62, 70, 75, 90–1, 97, 100, 102, 103, 105, 125, 144–7, 149, 153, 157, 163, 178
    named after women 141–2
    national prizes 2, 3, 13–15, 17–21, 25–38, 43, 48, 69–70, 131–4, 142, 156, 170, 175, 178, 181
    as networked (*see* network)
    number of entries 1, 32, 51, 59, 61, 147
    as a pact 2, 3, 11, 12, 14, 17, 27, 37, 77, 155, 161
    for poetry 19, 31, 32, 39, 44, 130, 141, 163, 174, 179
    press coverage of 11, 23–5, 42, 44–8, 52, 62, 66–7, 125, 128, 143, 149–52, 156, 160–1
    public-private partnerships 2, 16, 24, 46, 69, 177–9

publisher-run/privately run 2, 3, 5, 11, 15, 16, 18–20, 49, 51–71, 73, 93, 127, 137, 149, 178
state-sponsored 2, 5, 9, 11, 13, 15, 20, 23, 25–49, 51, 52, 65, 69–71, 98, 133, 135–6, 142, 149, 155, 157, 177
for *testimonio* 39
for unpublished works 27, 28, 54, 67, 128, 135, 136, 138, 163
and use of pseudonyms 58–9, 68, 108, 128, 138
for women authors/women-only prizes 7, 18, 143–53
publishers
Alfaguara Editorial 46, 52, 59–63, 67, 99
Anagrama Editorial 10, 23, 59–60, 62, 68, 98
Cartonera 180
Curbstone Press 144, 145
Editorial Losada 51–3
Emecé Editores 51, 53, 58
Espasa-Calpe 52
Fondo de Cultura Económica (FCE) 144–6
Gallimard 40, 54, 116
Gianggiacomo Feltrinelli Editore 59
Grove Press 54
Indigo Coté-Femmes 145
Joaquín Mortiz 53, 58
Penguin Random House 61, 62, 67
Rowohlt-Verlag 54
Siglo XXI Editores 23, 52, 64–5, 179
Sudamericana 53
Tumbona Ediciones 181
Weidenfeld and Nicolson 54
Puga, María Luisa 90
Puig, Manuel 111

Quintana, Pilar 67, 68

Ramírez, Sergio 45, 63, 79, 80, 87, 131

Regino, Juan Gregorio 162, 164
Restrepo, Laura 149, 150
Revueltas, José 90, 135
Ríos Cruz, Esteban 173, 174
Rivera Garza, Cristina 149, 151–2, 182
Roa Bastos, Augusto 75, 80, 83, 85, 90, 123, 131
Rojas, Gonzalo 89
role of the author. *See* author
Rosa, Isaac 47
Rulfo, Juan 116

Sábato, Ernesto 83, 87
Sánchez-Andrade, Cristina 149, 150
Sánchez Prado, Ignacio 8, 12, 17, 19, 21, 58, 64, 69, 177, 181
strategic occidentalism 69
Sartre, Jean-Paul 73, 87
scandal/controversy 2, 13, 17, 19, 27–9, 34–8, 42, 47, 48, 76, 77, 79, 82, 84, 91, 147
Scarpa, Roque Esteban 35
Seix, Víctor 54
Seix Barral 20, 42, 52–4, 56, 57, 59, 63, 111–13, 115–17, 120
Biblioteca Formentor 111
self-publishing 181
Semprún, Jorge 116
Serrano, Marcela 94, 149–51
Sesé, Silvia 68
soft power 1
Sommer, Doris 15, 22, 26
spokesperson. *See* author
Sueiro, Daniel 111
Suez, Perla 48
Swedish Academy 21, 71, 74, 75, 79–82. *See also* Nobel Committee

Tatyisvai, Kalu 173
Tejera, Nivaria 24, 111–17, 119–24
Espero la noche para soñarte, Revolución 115, 122
Fuir la spirale 122
Le ravin 115
Sonámbulo del sol 120–4

Toledo Paz, Natalia 174
Torres, Ana Teresa 48
totalitarianism 2, 22, 34, 37, 49, 79, 81, 85. See also dictatorship
Traba, Marta 112
translation 56, 59, 142, 144–5, 151, 156, 163, 166, 174

UNESCO 79
  City of Literature 178
  Collection of Representative Works 54, 74
  World Book City 179
universal literature 12, 37, 62, 72, 76, 84, 86–91, 150. See also world literature
Usón, Clara 151–2

Valenzuela, Luisa 139
Vallejo, Fernando 47, 67, 132
value 2, 4, 7, 9, 10, 14, 20, 22, 34, 35, 47, 59, 68, 99, 100, 105–9, 182

Vargas Llosa, Mario 14, 16, 39–42, 74, 78, 82, 85, 88, 113, 116, 131
  'La literatura es fuego' 40
  Presidential campaign 78
Vázquez Montalbán, Manuel 20, 95
Vila-Matas, Enrique 46
Vitale, Ida 81, 83, 129, 131, 132
Volpi, Jorge 58, 95, 152

women-only prizes. See prizes for women authors
world literature 7–9, 12, 16, 17, 22, 23, 88, 89, 91, 181
World War II/Second World War 3, 54, 74, 76

YouTube 23, 52, 62, 67, 68, 182

Zambrano, María 86
Zañartu, Sandy 35
Zapatista uprising 158

www.ingramcontent.com/pod-product-compliance
Lightning Source LLC
Chambersburg PA
CBHW062224300426
44115CB00012BA/2215